S0-BZT-118

SECRET CODES

FOR CONSOLES AND HANDHELDS

EXCLUSIVE SCHOLASTIC EDITION

A NOTE TO PARENTS

This book is an exclusive Scholastic edition that has been edited to remove all Mature-rated codes, as well as games that include excessive violence, sexual content, and inappropriate codes for children.

This book includes only E, E+, and T-rated games.

In addition, this book provides a listing of the ESRB ratings for all games included inside.

EARLY CHILDHOOD

 Titles rated EC (Early Childhood) have content that may be suitable for ages 3 and older. Contains no material that parents would find inappropriate.

EVERYONE

 Titles rated E (Everyone) have content that may be suitable for ages 6 and older. Titles in this category may contain minimal cartoon, fantasy or mild violence and/or infrequent use of mild language.

EVERYONE 10+

 Titles rated E10+ (Everyone 10 and older) have content that may be suitable for ages 10 and older. Titles in this category may contain more cartoon, fantasy or mild violence, mild language, and/or minimal suggestive themes.

TEEN

 Titles rated T (Teen) have content that may be suitable for ages 13 and older. Titles in this category may contain violence, suggestive themes, crude humor, minimal blood and/or infrequent use of strong language.

MATURE

 Titles rated M (Mature) have content that may be suitable for persons ages 17 and older. Titles in this category may contain intense violence, blood and gore, sexual content, and/or strong language.

ADULTS ONLY

 Titles rated AO (Adults Only) have content that should only be played by persons 18 years and older. Titles in this category may include prolonged scenes of intense violence and/or graphic sexual content and nudity.

GAMECUBE™

EVERYONE

BRATZ: FOREVER DIAMONDZ

CARS

CURIOUS GEORGE

DONKEY KONGA

MADDEN NFL 07

MARIO GOLF: TOADSTOOL TOUR

MARIO POWER TENNIS

MARIO SUPERSTAR BASEBALL

PIKMIN 2

ROBOTS

SPONGEBOB SQUAREPANTS: CREATURE FROM THE KRUSTY KRAB

TAK: THE GREAT JUJU CHALLENGE

YU-GI-OH: FALSEBOUND KINGDOM

EVERYONE 10+

AVATAR: THE LAST AIRBENDER

CHICKEN LITTLE

ICE AGE 2: THE MELTDOWN

LEGO STAR WARS II: THE ORIGINAL TRILOGY

MONSTER HOUSE

NEED FOR SPEED CARBON

OVER THE HEDGE

SHREK SUPERSLAM

TEENAGE MUTANT NINJA TURTLES 3: MUTANT NIGHTMARE

TY THE TASMANIAN TIGER 3: NIGHT OF THE QUINKAN

TEEN

ALIEN HOMINID

THE INCREDIBLE HULK : ULTIMATE DESTRUCTION

PETER JACKSON'S KING KONG: THE OFFICIAL GAME OF THE MOVIE

THE SIMS 2: PETS

TONY HAWK'S AMERICAN WASTELAND

ULTIMATE SPIDER-MAN

X-MEN LEGENDS II: RISE OF APOCALYPSE

X-MEN: THE OFFICIAL GAME

GAMECUBE™

3

GAMECUBE™

Table of Contents

ALIEN HOMINID

ALL LEVELS, MINI-GAMES, AND HATS
Select Player 1 Setup or Player 2 Setup and change the name to ROYGBIV.

HATS FOR 2-PLAYER GAME
Go to the Options screen and rename your alien one of the following:

ABE	Top Hat	#11
APRIL	Blond Wig	#4
BEHEMOTH	Red Cap	#24
CLETUS	Hunting Hat	#3
DANDY	Flower Petal Hat	#13

GOODMAN	Black Curly Hair	#7
GRRL	Flowers	#10
PRINCESS	Tiara	#12
SUPERFLY	Afro	#6
TOMFULP	Brown Messy Hair	#2

AVATAR: THE LAST AIRBENDER

ALL TREASURE MAPS
Select Code Entry from Extras
and enter 37437.

1 HIT DISHONOR
Select Code Entry from Extras
and enter 54641.

DOUBLE DAMAGE
Select Code Entry from Extras
and enter 34743.

UNLIMITED COPPER
Select Code Entry from Extras and enter 23637.

UNLIMITED CHI
Select Code Entry from Extras and enter 24463.

UNLIMITED HEALTH
Select Code Entry from Extras and enter 94677.

NEVERENDING STEALTH
Select Code Entry from Extras
and enter 53467.

CHARACTER CONCEPT ART GALLERY
Select Code Entry from Extras
and enter 97831.

BRATZ: FOREVER DIAMONDZ

1000 BLINGZ
While in the Bratz Office, use the Cheat computer to enter SIZZLN.

2000 BLINGZ
While in the Bratz Office, use the Cheat computer to enter FLAUNT.

PET TREATS
While in the Bratz Office, use the Cheat computer to enter TREATZ.

GIFT SET A
While in the Bratz Office, use the Cheat computer to enter STYLIN.

GIFT SET B
While in the Bratz Office, use the Cheat computer to enter SKATIN.

GIFT SET C
While in the Bratz Office, use the Cheat computer to enter JEWELZ.

GIFT SET E
While in the Bratz Office, use the Cheat computer to enter DIMNDZ.

CARS

UNLOCK EVERYTHING
Select Cheat Codes from the Options and enter IF900HP.

ALL CHARACTERS
Select Cheat Codes from the Options and enter YAYCARS.

ALL CHARACTER SKINS
Select Cheat Codes from the Options and enter R4MONE.

ALL MINI-GAMES AND COURSES
Select Cheat Codes from the Options and enter MATTL66.

MATER'S COUNTDOWN CLEAN-UP MINI-GAME & MATER'S SPEEDY CIRCUIT
Select Cheat Codes from the Options and enter TRGTEXC.

FAST START
Select Cheat Codes from the Options and enter IMSPEED.

INFINITE BOOST
Select Cheat Codes from the Options and enter VROOOOM.

ART
Select Cheat Codes from the Options and enter CONC3PT.

VIDEOS
Select Cheat Codes from the Options and enter WATCHIT.

CHICKEN LITTLE

INVINCIBILITY
Select Cheat Codes from the Extras menu and enter
Baseball, Baseball, Baseball, Shirt.

BIG FEET
Select Cheat Codes from the Extras menu and enter Hat,
Glove, Glove, Hat.

BIG HAIR
Select Cheat Codes from the Extras menu and enter
Baseball, Bat, Bat, Baseball.

BIG HEAD
Select Cheat Codes from the Extras menu and enter Hat,
Helmet, Helmet, Hat.

PAPER PANTS
Select Cheat Codes from the Extras menu and enter Bat,
Bat, Hat, Hat.

SUNGLASSES
Select Cheat Codes from the Extras menu and enter
Glove, Glove, Helmet, Helmet.

UNDERWEAR
Select Cheat Codes from the Extras menu and enter Hat,
Hat, Shirt, Shirt.

CURIOUS GEORGE

CURIOUS GEORGE GOES APE
Pause the game, hold Z and press B, B, A, Y, B.

UNLIMITED BANANAS
Pause the game, hold Z and press A, X, X, Y, A.

ROLLERSKATES AND FEZ HAT
Pause the game, hold Z and press X, A, A, A, B.

UPSIDE DOWN GRAVITY MODE
Pause the game, hold Z and press Y, Y, B, A, A.

DONKEY KONGA

100M VINE CLIMB (1 OR 2 PLAYERS)
Collect 4800 coins to unlock this mini-game for purchase at DK Town.

BANANA JUGGLE (1 OR 2 PLAYERS)
Collect 5800 coins to unlock this mini-game for purchase at DK Town.

BASH K. ROOL (1 PLAYER)
Collect 5800 coins to unlock this mini-game for purchase at DK Town.

ICE AGE 2: THE MELTDOWN

ALL BONUSES
Pause the game and press Down, Left, Up, Down, Down,
Left, Right, Right.

LEVEL SELECT
Pause the game and press Up, Right, Right, Left, Right,
Right, Down, Down.

UNLIMITED PEBBLES
Pause the game and press Down, Down, Left, Up, Up,
Right, Up, Down.

INFINITE ENERGY
Pause the game and press Down, Left, Right, Down,
Down, Right, Left, Down.

INFINITE HEALTH
Pause the game and press Up, Right, Down, Up, Left,
Down, Right, Left.

THE INCREDIBLE HULK: ULTIMATE DESTRUCTION

You must collect a specific comic in the game to activate each code. After collecting the appropriate comic, you can enter the following codes. If you don't have the comic and enter the code, you receive a message "That code cannot be activated... yet". Enter the cheats at the Code Input screen.

UNLOCKED: CABS GALORE
Select Code Input from the Extras menu and enter CABBIES.

UNLOCKED: GORILLA INVASION
Select Code Input from the Extras menu and enter kingkng.

UNLOCKED: MASS TRANSIT
Select Code Input from the Extras menu and enter TRANSIT.

UNLOCKED: 5000 SMASH POINTS
Select Code Input from the Extras menu and enter SMASH5.

UNLOCKED: 10000 SMASH POINTS
Select Code Input from the Extras menu and enter SMASH10.

UNLOCKED: 15000 SMASH POINTS
Select Code Input from the Extras menu and enter SMASH15.

UNLOCKED: AMERICAN FLAG SHORTS
Select Code Input from the Extras menu and enter AMERICA.

UNLOCKED: CANADIAN FLAG SHORTS
Select Code Input from the Extras menu and enter OCANADA.

UNLOCKED: FRENCH FLAG SHORTS
Select Code Input from the Extras menu and enter Drapeau.

UNLOCKED: GERMAN FLAG SHORTS
Select Code Input from the Extras menu and enter DEUTSCH.

UNLOCKED: ITALIAN FLAG SHORTS
Select Code Input from the Extras menu and enter MUTANDA.

UNLOCKED: JAPANESE FLAG SHORTS
Select Code Input from the Extras menu and enter FURAGGU.

UNLOCKED: SPANISH FLAG SHORTS
Select Code Input from the Extras menu and enter BANDERA.

UNLOCKED: UK FLAG SHORTS
Select Code Input from the Extras menu and enter FSHNCHP.

UNLOCKED: COW MISSILES
Select Code Input from the Extras menu and enter CHZGUN.

UNLOCKED: DOUBLE HULK'S DAMAGE
Select Code Input from the Extras menu and enter DESTROY.

UNLOCKED: DOUBLE POWER COLLECTABLES
Select Code Input from the Extras menu and enter BRINGIT.

UNLOCKED: BLACK AND WHITE
Select Code Input from the Extras menu and enter RETRO.

UNLOCKED: SEPIA
Select Code Input from the Extras menu and enter HISTORY.

UNLOCKED: ABOMINATION
Select Code Input from the Extras menu and enter VILLAIN.

UNLOCKED: GRAY HULK
Select Code Input from the Extras menu and enter CLASSIC.

UNLOCKED: JOE FIXIT SKIN
Select Code Input from the Extras menu and enter SUITFIT.

UNLOCKED: WILD TRAFFIC
Select Code Input from the Extras menu and enter FROGGIE.

UNLOCKED: LOW GRAVITY
Select Code Input from the Extras menu and enter PILLOWS.

LEGO STAR WARS II: THE ORIGINAL TRILOGY

BEACH TROOPER
At Mos Eisley Canteena, select Enter Code and enter UCK868. You still need to select Characters and purchase this character for 20,000 studs.

BEN KENOBI (GHOST)
At Mos Eisley Canteena, select Enter Code and enter BEN917. You still need to select Characters and purchase this character for 1,100,000 studs.

BESPIN GUARD
At Mos Eisley Canteena, select Enter Code and enter VHY832. You still need to select Characters and purchase this character for 15,000 studs.

BIB FORTUNA
At Mos Eisley Canteena, select Enter Code and enter WTY721. You still need to select Characters and purchase this character for 16,000 studs.

BOBA FETT
At Mos Eisley Canteena, select Enter Code and enter HLP221. You still need to select Characters and purchase this character for 175,000 studs.

DEATH STAR TROOPER
At Mos Eisley Canteena, select Enter Code and enter BNC332. You still need to select Characters and purchase this character for 19,000 studs.

EWOK
At Mos Eisley Canteena, select Enter Code and enter TTT289. You still need to select Characters and purchase this character for 34,000 studs.

GAMORREAN GUARD
At Mos Eisley Canteena, select Enter Code and enter YZF999. You still need to select Characters and purchase this character for 40,000 studs.

GONK DROID
At Mos Eisley Canteena, select Enter Code and enter NFX582. You still need to select Characters and purchase this character for 1,550 studs.

GRAND MOFF TARKIN
At Mos Eisley Canteena, select Enter Code and enter SMG219. You still need to select Characters and purchase this character for 38,000 studs.

GREEDO
At Mos Eisley Canteena, select Enter Code and enter NAH118. You still need to select Characters and purchase this character for 60,000 studs.

HAN SOLO (HOOD)
At Mos Eisley Canteena, select Enter Code and enter YWM840. You still need to select Characters and purchase this character for 20,000 studs.

IG-88
At Mos Eisley Canteena, select Enter Code and enter NXL973. You still need to select Characters and purchase this character for 30,000 studs.

IMPERIAL GUARD

At Mos Eisley Canteena, select Enter Code and enter MMM111. You still need to select Characters and purchase this character for 45,000 studs.

IMPERIAL OFFICER

At Mos Eisley Canteena, select Enter Code and enter BBV889. You still need to select Characters and purchase this character for 28,000 studs.

IMPERIAL SHUTTLE PILOT

At Mos Eisley Canteena, select Enter Code and enter VAP664. You still need to select Characters and purchase this character for 29,000 studs.

IMPERIAL SPY

At Mos Eisley Canteena, select Enter Code and enter CVT125. You still need to select Characters and purchase this character for 13,500 studs.

JAWA

At Mos Eisley Canteena, select Enter Code and enter JAW499. You still need to select Characters and purchase this character for 24,000 studs.

LOBOT

At Mos Eisley Canteena, select Enter Code and enter UUB319. You still need to select Characters and purchase this character for 11,000 studs.

PALACE GUARD

At Mos Eisley Canteena, select Enter Code and enter SGE549. You still need to select Characters and purchase this character for 14,000 studs.

REBEL PILOT

At Mos Eisley Canteena, select Enter Code and enter CYG336. You still need to select Characters and purchase this character for 15,000 studs.

REBEL TROOPER (HOTH)

At Mos Eisley Canteena, select Enter Code and enter EKU849. You still need to select Characters and purchase this character for 16,000 studs.

SANDTROOPER

At Mos Eisley Canteena, select Enter Code and enter YDV451. You still need to select Characters and purchase this character for 14,000 studs.

SKIFF GUARD

At Mos Eisley Canteena, select Enter Code and enter GBU888. You still need to select Characters and purchase this character for 12,000 studs.

SNOWTROOPER

At Mos Eisley Canteena, select Enter Code and enter NYU989. You still need to select Characters and purchase this character for 16,000 studs.

STROMTROOPER

At Mos Eisley Canteena, select Enter Code and enter PTR345. You still need to select Characters and purchase this character for 10,000 studs.

THE EMPEROR

At Mos Eisley Canteena, select Enter Code and enter HHY382. You still need to select Characters and purchase this character for 275,000 studs.

TIE FIGHTER

At Mos Eisley Canteena, select Enter Code and enter HDY739. You still need to select Characters and purchase this character for 60,000 studs.

TIE FIGHTER PILOT

At Mos Eisley Canteena, select Enter Code and enter NNZ316. You still need to select Characters and purchase this character for 21,000 studs.

TIE INTERCEPTOR

At Mos Eisley Canteena, select Enter Code and enter QYA828. You still need to select Characters and purchase this character for 40,000 studs.

TUSKEN RAIDER

At Mos Eisley Canteena, select Enter Code and enter PEJ821. You still need to select Characters and purchase this character for 23,000 studs.

UGNAUGHT

At Mos Eisley Canteena, select Enter Code and enter UGN694. You still need to select Characters and purchase this character for 36,000 studs.

MADDEN NFL 07

MADDEN CARDS

Select Madden Cards from My Madden, then select Madden Codes and enter the following:

CARD	PASSWORD	CARD	PASSWORD
#199 Gold Lame Duck Cheat	5LAWOO	#245 1993 Bills Gold	DLA3I7
#200 Gold Mistake Free Cheat	XL7SP1	#246 1994 49ers Gold	DR7EST
#210 Gold QB on Target Cheat	WROAOR	#247 1996 Packers Gold	F8LUST
#220 Super Bowl XLI Gold	RLA9R7	#248 1998 Broncos Gold	FIES95
#221 Super Bowl XLII Gold	WRLUF8	#249 1999 Rams Gold	S9OUSW
#222 Super Bowl XLIII Gold	NIEV4A	#250 Bears Pump Up the Crowd	B1OUPH
#223 Super Bowl XLIV Gold	M5AB7L	#251 Bengals Cheerleader	DRL2SW
#224 Aloha Stadium Gold	YI8P8U	#252 Bills Cheerleader	1PLUYO
#225 1958 Colts Gold	B57QLU	#253 Broncos Cheerleader	3ROUJO
#226 1966 Packers Gold	1PL1FL	#254 Browns Pump Up the Crowd	T1UTOA
#227 1968 Jets Gold	MIE6WO	#255 Buccaneers Cheerleader	S9EWRI
#228 1970 Browns Gold	CL2TOE	#256 Cardinals Cheerleader	57IEPI
#229 1972 Dolphins Gold	NOEB7U	#257 Chargers Cheerleader	F7UHL8
#230 1974 Steelers Gold	YOOFLA	#258 Chiefs Cheerleader	PRI5SL
#231 1976 Raiders Gold	MOA11I	#259 Colts Cheerleader	1R5AMI
#232 1977 Broncos Gold	C8UM7U	#260 Cowboys Cheerleader	Z2ACHL
#233 1978 Dolphins Gold	VIU007	#261 Dolphins Cheerleader	C5AHLE
#234 1980 Raiders Gold	NLAPH3	#262 Eagles Cheerleader	PO7DRO
#235 1981 Chargers Gold	COAGI4	#263 Falcons Cheerleader	37USPO
#236 1982 Redskins Gold	WL8BRI	#264 49ers Cheerleader	KLOCRL
#237 1983 Raiders Gold	HOEW71	#265 Giants Pump Up the Crowd	C4USPI
#238 1984 Dolphins Gold	M1AM1E	#266 Jaguars Cheerleader	MIEH7E
#239 1985 Bears Gold	QOETO8	#267 Jets Pump Up the Crowd	COLUXI
#240 1986 Giants Gold	ZI8S2L	#268 Lions Pump Up the Crowd	3LABLU
#241 1988 49ers Gold	SP2A8H	#269 Packers Pump Up the Crowd	4HO7VO
#242 1990 Eagles Gold	2L4TRO	#270 Panthers Cheerleader	F2IASP
#243 1991 Lions Gold	J1ETRI	#282 All AFC Team Gold	PRO9PH
#244 1992 Cowboys Gold	W9UVI9	#283 All NFC Team Gold	RLATH7

MARIO GOLF: TOADSTOOL TOUR

At the Title screen, press Start + Z to access the Password screen. Enter the following to open up bonus tournaments:

TARGET BULLSEYE TOURNAMENT
Enter CEUFPXJ1.

HOLLYWOOD VIDEO TOURNAMENT
Enter BJGQBULZ.

CAMP HYRULE TOURNAMENT
Enter 0EKW5G7U.

BOWSER BADLANDS TOURNAMENT
Enter 9L3L9KHR.

BOWSER JR.'S JUMBO TOURNAMENT
Enter 2GPL67PN.

MARIO OPEN TOURNAMENT
Enter GGAA241H.

PEACH'S INVITATIONAL TOURNAMENT
Enter ELBUT3PX.

MARIO POWER TENNIS

EVENT MODE
At the Title screen, press Z + Start.

MARIO SUPERSTAR BASEBALL

STAR DASH MINI-GAME
Complete Star difficulty on all mini-games.

BABY LUIGI
Complete Challenge Mode with Yoshi.

DIXIE KONG
Complete Challenge Mode with Donkey Kong.

HAMMER BRO
Complete Challenge Mode with Bowser.

MONTY MOLE
Complete Challenge Mode with Mario.

PETEY PIRANHA
Complete Challenge Mode with Wario.

TOADETTE
Complete Challenge Mode with Peach.

KOOPA CASTLE STADIUM
Complete Challenge Mode.

MONSTER HOUSE

FULL HEALTH
During a game, hold L + R and press A, A, A, Y.

REFILL SECONDARY WEAPON AMMO
During a game, hold L + R and press Y, Y, A, A.

ALL TOY MONKEYS AND ART GALLERY
During a game, hold L + R and press Y, X, Y, X, B, B, B, A.

NEED FOR SPEED CARBON

INFINITE CREW CHARGE
At the Main menu, press Down, Up, Up, Right, Left, Left, X

INFINITE NITROUS
At the Main menu, press Left, Up, Left, Down, Left, Down, Right, X

INFINITE SPEEDBREAKER
At the Main menu, press Down, Right, Right, Left, Right, Up, Down, X

NEED FOR SPEED CARBON LOGO VINYLS
At the Main menu, press Right, Up, Down, Up, Down, Left, Right, X

NEED FOR SPEED CARBON SPECIAL LOGO VINYLS
At the Main menu, press Up, Up, Down, Down, Down, Down, Up, X

OVER THE HEDGE

COMPLETE LEVELS
Pause the game, hold L + R and press Y, X, Y, X, X, B.

ALL MINI-GAMES
Pause the game, hold L + R and press Y, X, Y, Y, B, B.

ALL MOVES
Pause the game, hold L + R and press Y, X, Y, B, B, X.

EXTRA DAMAGE
Pause the game, hold L + R and press Y, X, Y, X, Y, B.

MORE HP FROM FOOD
Pause the game, hold L + R and press Y, X, Y, X, B, Y.

ALWAYS POWER PROJECTILE
Pause the game, hold L + R and press Y, X, Y, X, B, X.

BONUS COMIC 14
Pause the game, hold L + R and press Y, X, B, B, X, Y.

BONUS COMIC 15
Pause the game, hold L + R and press Y, Y, B, X, B, X.

PETER JACKSON'S KING KONG: THE OFFICIAL GAME OF THE MOVIE

At the Main menu, hold L + R and press Down, X, Up, Y, Down, Down, Up, Up. Release L + R to access the Cheat option. The Cheat option is also available on the Pause menu.

GOD MODE
Select Cheat and enter 8wonder

ALL CHAPTERS
Select Cheat and enter KKst0ry.

AMMO 999
Select Cheat and enter KK 999 mun.

MACHINE GUN
Select Cheat and enter KKcapone.

REVOLVER
Select Cheat and enter KKtigun.

SNIPER RIFLE
Select Cheat and enter KKsn1per.

INFINITE SPEARS
Select Cheat and enter lance 1nf.

ONE-HIT KILLS
Select Cheat and enter GrosBras.

EXTRAS
Select Cheat and enter KKmuseum.

PIKMIN 2

TITLE SCREEN
At the Title screen, press the following for a variety of options:

Press R to make the Pikmin form NINTENDO.

Press L to go back to PIKMIN 2.

Press X to get a beetle.

Use the C-Stick to move it around.

Press L to dispose of the Beetle.

Press Y to get a Chappie.

Use the C-Stick to move it around.

Press Z to eat the Pikmin.

Press L to dispose of Chappie.

ROBOTS

BIG HEAD
Pause the game and press Up, Down, Down, Up, Right, Right, Left, Right.

INVINCIBLE
Pause the game and press Up, Right, Down, Up, Left, Down, Right, Left.

UNLIMITED SCRAP
Pause the game and press Down, Down, Left, Up, Up, Right, Up, Down.

SHREK SUPERSLAM

ALL CHARACTERS AND LEVELS
At the Title screen, press L, R, X, B.

ALL CHALLENGES
At the Title screen, press Y, Y, Y, X, X, X, Y, B, X, B, B, B, Up, Down, Left, Right, L, R.

ALL STORY MODE CHAPTERS
At the Title screen, press Y, B, R, X.

ALL MEDALS AND TROPHIES
At the Title screen, press R, L, Y, B.

SUPER SPEED MODIFIER
At the Title screen, press L, L, R, R, L, R, L, R, B, X, Y, Y.

PIZZA ONE
At the Title screen, press Up, Up, Y, Y, Right, Right, X, X, Down, Down, L, R, Left, Left, B, B, L, R.

PIZZA TWO
At the Title screen, press X, X, B, B, R, R, Left, Left, L, L.

PIZZA THREE
At the Title screen, press Down, Down, Right, X, Up, Y, Left, B, L, L.

SLAMMAGEDDON
At the Title screen, press Up, Up, Down, Down, Left, Right, Left, Right, Y, B, B, L, R.

THE SIMS 2: PETS

CHEAT GNOME
During a game, press L, L, R, A, A, Up.

ADVANCE 6 HOURS
After activating the Cheat Gnome, press Up, Left, Down, Right, R during a game. Select the Gnome to access the cheat.

GIVE SIM SIMOLEANS
After activating the Cheat Gnome, enter the Advance 6 Hours cheat. Access the Gnome and exit. Enter the cheat again. Now, "Give Sim Simoleans" should be available from the Gnome.

CAT AND DOG CODES
When creating a family, press X to Enter Unlock Code.

Enter the following for new fur patterns.

FUR PATTERN/CAT OR DOG	UNLOCK CODE
Bandit Mask Cats	EEGJ2YRQZZAIZ9QHA64
Bandit Mask Dogs	EEGJ2YRQZQARQ9QHA64
Black Dot Cats	EEGJ2YRQQ1IQ9QHA64
Black Dot Dogs	EEGJ2YRQZZ1IQ9QHA64
Black Smiley Cats	EEGJ2YRQQZ1RQ9QHA64
Black Smiley Dogs	EEGJ2YRQQARQ9QHA64
Blue Bones Cats	EEGJ2YRQZZARQ9QHA64
Blue Bones Dogs	EEGJ2YRZZ11Z9QHA64
Blue Camouflage Cats	EEGJ2YRZZQ1IQ9QHA64
Blue Camouflage Dogs	EEGJ2YRQZZZ1RQ9QHA64
Blue Cats	EEGJ2YRQZZAIQ9QHA64
Blue Dogs	EEGJ2YRQQQ1IZ9QHA64
Blue Star Cats	EEGJ2YRQQZ1IZ9QHA64
Blue Star Dogs	EEGJ2YRQZQ1IQ9QHA64
Deep Red Cats	EEGJ2YRQQQAIQ9QHA64
Deep Red Dogs	EEGJ2YRQZQ1IZ9QHA64
Goofy Cats	EEGJ2YRQZQ1IZ9QHA64
Goofy Dogs	EEGJ2YRZZZARQ9QHA64
Green Cats	EEGJ2YRQQQAIZ9QHA64
Green Dogs	EEGJ2YRQZQAIQ9QHA64
Green Flower Cats	EEGJ2YRQQZAIQ9QHA64
Green Flower Dogs	EEGJ2YRQQZZ1RQ9QHA64
Light Green Cats	EEGJ2YRZZQ1RQ9QHA64
Light Green Dogs	EEGJ2YRQQ01RQ9QHA64
Navy Hearts Cats	EEGJ2YRQZQZ1IQ9QHA64
Navy Hearts Dogs	EEGJ2YRQQZ11Q9QHA64
Neon Green Cats	EEGJ2YRZQQAIQ9QHA64
Neon Green Dogs	EEGJ2YRZQQAIQ9QHA64
Neon Yellow Cats	EEGJ2YRZZQARQ9QHA64
Neon Yellow Dogs	EEGJ2YRQQQZ9QHA64
Orange Diagonal Cats	EEGJ2YRQQZAIQ9QHA64
Orange Diagonal Dogs	EEGJ2YRZQZ1IZ9QHA64
Panda Cats	EEGJ2YRQZQAIZ9QHA64
Pink Cats	EEGJ2YRQZZ11Z9QHA64
Pink Dogs	EEGJ2YRZQZ1RQ9QHA64
Pink Vertical Strip Cats	EEGJ2YRQQQARQ9QHA64
Pink Vertical Strip Dogs	EEGJ2YRZZZZAIQ9QHA64
Purple Cats	EEGJ2YRQQQZAIQ9QHA64
Purple Dogs	EEGJ2YRQQZZAIQ9QHA64
Star Cats	EEGJ2YRZQZARQ9QHA64
Star Dogs	EEGJ2YRZQZAIZ9QHA64
White Paws Cats	EEGJ2YRQQQ1RQ9QHA64
White Paws Dogs	EEGJ2YRZQQ1IZ9QHA64
White Zebra Stripe Cats	EEGJ2YRZZZ11Z9QHA64
White Zebra Stripe Dogs	EEGJ2YRZZZ11Q9QHA64
Zebra Stripes Dogs	EEGJ2YRZZQAIZ9QHA64

SPONGEBOB SQUAREPANTS: CREATURE FROM THE KRUSTY KRAB

30,000 EXTRA Zs
Select Cheat Codes from the Extras menu and enter ROCFISH.

PUNK SPONGEBOB IN DIESEL DREAMING
Select Cheat Codes from the Extras menu and enter SPONGE. Select Activate Bonus Items to enable this bonus item.

HOT ROD SKIN IN DIESEL DREAMING
Select Cheat Codes from the Extras menu and enter HOTROD. Select Activate Bonus Items to enable this bonus item.

PATRICK TUX IN STARFISHMAN TO THE RESCUE
Select Cheat Codes from the Extras menu and enter PATRICK. Select Activate Bonus Items to enable this bonus item.

SPONGEBOB PLANKTON IN SUPER-SIZED PATTY
Select Cheat Codes from the Extras menu and enter PANTS. Select Activate Bonus Items to enable this bonus item.

PATRICK LASER COLOR IN ROCKET RODEO
Select Cheat Codes from the Extras menu and enter ROCKET. Select Activate Bonus Items to enable this bonus item.

PATRICK ROCKET SKIN COLOR IN ROCKET RODEO
Select Cheat Codes from the Extras menu and enter SPACE. Select Activate Bonus Items to enable this bonus item.

PLANKTON EYE LASER COLOR IN REVENGE OF THE GIANT PLANKTON MONSTER
Select Cheat Codes from the Extras menu and enter LASER. Select Activate Bonus Items to enable this bonus item.

HOVERCRAFT VEHICLE SKIN IN HYPNOTIC HIGHWAY—PLANKTON
Select Cheat Codes from the Extras menu and enter HOVER. Select Activate Bonus Items to enable this bonus item.

TAK: THE GREAT JUJU CHALLENGE

BONUS SOUND EFFECTS
In Juju's Potions, select Universal Card and enter the following numbers for Bugs, Crystals and Fruit: 20, 17, 5.

BONUS SOUND EFFECTS 2

In Juju's Potions, select Universal Card and enter the following numbers for Bugs, Crystals and Fruit: 50, 84, 92.

BONUS MUSIC TRACK 1

In Juju's Potions, select Universal Card and enter the following numbers for Bugs, Crystals and Fruit: 67, 8, 20.

BONUS MUSIC TRACK 2

In Juju's Potions, select Universal Card and enter the following numbers for Bugs, Crystals and Fruit: 6, 18, 3.

MAGIC PARTICLES

In Juju's Potions, select Universal Card and enter the following numbers for Bugs, Crystals and Fruit: 24, 40, 11.

MORE MAGIC PARTICLES

In Juju's Potions, select Universal Card and enter the following numbers for Bugs, Crystals and Fruit: 48, 57, 57.

VIEW JUJU CONCEPT ART

In Juju's Potions, select Universal Card and enter the following numbers for Bugs, Crystals and Fruit: Art 33, 22, 28.

VIEW VEHICLE ART

In Juju's Potions, select Universal Card and enter the following numbers for Bugs, Crystals and Fruit: 11, 55, 44.

VIEW WORLD ART

In Juju's Potions, select Universal Card and enter the following numbers for Bugs, Crystals and Fruit: 83, 49, 34.

TEENAGE MUTANT NINJA TURTLES 3: MUTANT NIGHTMARE

INVINCIBILITY

Select Passwords from the Options screen and enter MDLDSSLR.

HEALTH POWER-UPS BECOME SUSHI

Select Passwords from the Options screen and enter SLLMRSLD.

NO HEALTH POWER-UPS

Select Passwords from the Options screen and enter DMLDMRLD.

ONE-HIT DEFEATS TURTLE

Select Passwords from the Options screen and enter LDMSLRDD.

MAX OUGI

Select Passwords from the Options screen and enter RRDMLSDL.

UNLIMITED SHURIKEN

Select Passwords from the Options screen and enter LMDRRMSR.

NO SHURIKEN

Select Passwords from the Options screen and enter LLMSRDMS.

DONATELLO'S LEVEL 2 DINO ARMOR SCROLL

Select Passwords from the Options screen and enter MSSRDLMR.

DONATELLO'S LEVEL 3 DINO ARMOR SCROLL

Select Passwords from the Options screen and enter DLRLDMSR.

LEO'S LEVEL 2 DINO ARMOR SCROLL

Select Passwords from the Options screen and enter RLDMRMSD.

LEO'S LEVEL 3 DINO ARMOR SCROLL

Select Passwords from the Options screen and enter MLMSRRDS.

MICHELANGELO'S LEVEL 2 DINO ARMOR SCROLL

Select Passwords from the Options screen and enter SRDMMLRS.

MICHELANGELO'S LEVEL 3 DINO ARMOR SCROLL

Select Passwords from the Options screen and enter LSMRRDSL.

RAPHAEL'S LEVEL 2 DINO ARMOR SCROLL

Select Passwords from the Options screen and enter DRMDLLRS.

RAPHAEL'S LEVEL 3 DINO ARMOR SCROLL

Select Passwords from the Options screen and enter SMRDRSLD.

DOUBLE ENEMY ATTACK

Select Passwords from the Options screen and enter MSRLSMML.

DOUBLE ENEMY DEFENSE

Select Passwords from the Options screen and enter SLRMLSSM.

TONY HAWK'S AMERICAN WASTELAND

ALWAYS SPECIAL
Select Cheat Codes from the Options screen and enter uronfire. Pause the game and select Cheats from the Game Options to enable the cheat.

PERFECT RAIL
Select Cheat Codes from the Options screen and enter grindxpert. Pause the game and select Cheats from the Game Options to enable the cheat.

PERFECT SKITCH
Select Cheat Codes from the Options screen and enter h!tchar!de. Pause the game and select Cheats from the Game Options to enable the cheat.

PERFECT MANUAL
Select Cheat Codes from the Options screen and enter 2wheels!. Pause the game and select Cheats from the Game Options to enable the cheat.

MOON GRAVITY
Select Cheat Codes from the Options screen and enter 2them00n. Pause the game and select Cheats from the Game Options to enable the cheat.

MAT HOFFMAN
Select Cheat Codes from the Options screen and enter the_condor.

JASON ELLIS
Select Cheat Codes from the Options screen and enter sirius-dj.

TY THE TASMANIAN TIGER 3: NIGHT OF THE QUINKAN

100,000 OPALS
During a game, press Start, Start, Y, Start, Start, Y, X, A, X, A.

ALL CHASSIS
During a game, press Start, Start, Y, Start, Start, Y, X, B, X, B.

ULTIMATE SPIDER-MAN

ALL CHARACTERS
Pause the game and select Controller Setup from the Options. Press Right, Down, Right, Down, Left, Up, Left, Right.

ALL COVERS
Pause the game and select Controller Setup from the Options. Press Left, Left, Right, Left, Up, Left, Left, Down.

ALL CONCEPT ART
Pause the game and select Controller Setup from the Options. Press Down, Down, Down, Up, Down, Up, Left, Left.

ALL LANDMARKS
Pause the game and select Controller Setup from the Options. Press Up, Right, Down, Left, Down, Up, Right, Left.

X-MEN LEGENDS II: RISE OF APOCALYPSE

ALL CHARACTERS
At the Team Management screen, press Right, Left, Left, Right, Up, Up, Up, Start.

ALL SKINS
At the Team Management screen, press Down, Up, Left, Right, Up, Up, Start.

ALL SKILLS
At the Team Management screen, press Left, Right, Left, Right, Down, Up, Start.

LEVEL 99
At the Team Management screen, press Up, Down, Up, Down, Left, Up, Left, Right, Start.

GOD MODE
Pause the game and press Down, Up, Down, Up, Right, Down, Right, Left, Start.

MOVE FASTER
Pause the game and press Up, Up, Up, Down, Up, Down, Start.

UNLIMITED XTREME TOKENS
Pause the game and press Left, Down, Right, Down, Up, Up, Down, Up, Start.

TOUCH OF DEATH
During a game, press Left, Left, Right, Left, Right, Up, Start.

100,000 TECH-BITS
At Forge or Beast's store, press Up, Up, Up, Down, Right, Right, Start.

ALL DANGER ROOM COURSES
At the Danger Room Course menu, press Right, Right, Left, Left, Up, Down, Up, Down, Start.

ALL COMICS

Select Review from the Main menu and press Right, Left, Left, Right, Up, Up, Right, Start.

ALL CUTSCENES

Select Review from the Main menu and press Left, Right, Right, Left, Down, Down, Left, Start.

ALL CONCEPTS

Select Review from the Main menu and press Left, Right, Left, Right, Up, Up, Down, Start.

ALL SCREENS

Select Review from the Main menu and press Right, Left, Right, Left, Up, Up, Down, Start.

X-MEN: THE OFFICIAL GAME

DANGER ROOM ICEMAN

At the Cerebro Files menu, press Right, Right, Left, Left, Down, Up, Down, Up, Start.

DANGER ROOM NIGHTCRAWLER

At the Cerebro Files menu, press Up, Up, Down, Down, Left, Right, Left, Right, Start.

DANGER ROOM WOLVERINE

At the Cerebro Files menu, press Down, Down, Up, Up, Right, Left, Right, Left, Start.

YU-GI-OH: FALSEBOUND KINGDOM

GOLD COINS

On an empty piece of land and during a mission, press Up, Up, Down, Down, Left, Right, Left, Right, B, A.

GAME BOY® ADVANCE

EVERYONE

ANIMAL SNAP:
RESCUE THEM 2 BY 2

BANJO PILOT

BARBIE AS THE PRINCESS
AND THE PAUPER

BARBIE IN THE
12 DANCING PRINCESSES

BIONICLE: TALES OF THE TOHUNGA

CARS

CURIOUS GEORGE

DK: KING OF SWING

DONKEY KONG COUNTRY 2:
DIDDY KONG'S QUEST

DRAKE AND JOSH

FINAL FANTASY I & II:
DAWN OF SOULS

JUSTICE LEAGUE HEROES:
THE FLASH

JUSTICE LEAGUE:
INJUSTICE FOR ALL

LEGO BIONICLE:
MAZE OF SHADOWS

MONSTER FORCE

PIRATES OF THE CARIBBEAN:
DEAD MAN'S CHEST

PRINCESS NATASHA:
STUDENT SECRET AGENT

RATATOUILLE

SECRET AGENT BARBIE:
ROYAL JEWELS MISSION

SHAMAN KING: LEGACY OF THE SPIRITS,
SOARING HAWK

SHAMAN KING: LEGACY OF THE SPIRITS,
SPRINTING WOLF

SUPER COLLAPSE 2

THAT'S SO RAVEN 2:
SUPERNATURAL STYLE

TONY HAWK'S UNDERGROUND 2

TRON 2.0: KILLER APP

ULTIMATE ARCADE GAMES

UNFABULOUS

YOSHI TOPSY-TURVY

YU-GI-OH! 7 TRIALS TO GLORY: WORLD
CHAMPIONSHIP TOURNAMENT 2005

YU-GI-OH! ULTIMATE MASTERS: WORLD
CHAMPIONSHIP TOURNAMENT 2006

E 10+

DRAGON BALL GT: TRANSFORMATION

TEEN

CASTLEVANIA: ARIA OF SORROW

CT SPECIAL FORCES 3: NAVY OPS

RIVER CITY RANSOM EX

STREET FIGHTER ALPHA 3

GAME BOY® ADVANCE

Table of Contents

ANIMAL SNAP: RESCUE THEM 2 BY 2

BLOCK BLASTER MINI-GAME

At the Main menu, hold L and press Up, Down, Left, Right, Right, Left, Down, Up.

 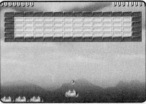

BANJO PILOT

GRUNTY

Defeat Grunty in the Broomstick battle race. Then, you can purchase Grunty from Cheato.

HUMBA WUMBA

Defeat Humba Wumba in the Jiggu battle race. Then, you can purchase Humba Wumba from Cheato.

JOLLY

Defeat Jolly in the Pumpkin battle race. Then, you can purchase Jolly from Cheato.

KLUNGO

Defeat Klungo in the Skull battle race. Then, you can purchase Klungo from Cheato.

BARBIE AS THE PRINCESS AND THE PAUPER

PASSWORDS

LEVEL	PASSWORD
1-2	Preminger, Wolfie, Erika, Serafina
1-3	Wolfie, Preminger, Serafina, Preminger
1-4	Preminger, Wolfie, Serfania, Wolfie
Boss 1	Serafina, Woflia. Erika, Preminger
2-1	Princess Anneliese, Preminger, Wolfie, Erika
2-2	Preminger, Princess Anneliese, Wolfie, Erika
2-3	Preminger, Serafina, Preminger, Erika
2-4	Serafina, Erika, Preminger, Wolfie
Boss 2	Preminger, Erika, Serafina, Wolfie
3-1	Wolfie, Preminger, Wolfie, Erika
3-2	Serafina, Preminger, Erika, Serafina
3-3	Erika, Wolfie, Serafina, Princess Anneliese
3-4	Erika, Serafina, Erika, Preminger
Boss 3	Preminger, Serafina, Princess Anneliese, Serafina
4-1	Wolfie, Serafina, Preminger, Serafina
4-2	Preminger, Serafina, Princess Anneliese, Preminger
4-3	Wolfie, Serafina, Erika, Serafina
Boss 4	Erika, Serafina, Princess Anneliese, Wolfie
Final Boss	Erika, Princess Anneliese, Princess Anneliese, Man
Arcade Level	Princess Anneliese, Serafina, Erika, Wolfie

BARBIE IN THE 12 DANCING PRINCESSES

EASY PASSWORDS

LEVEL	PASSWORD
2-a	Cat, Cat, Slippers, Prince
2-b	Cat, Old Lady, Bird, Monkey
3-a	Old Lady, Slippers, Slippers, Slippers
3-b	Blonde Girl, Blonde Girl, Monkey, Blonde Girl
4-a	Old Lady, Brunette Girl, Cat, Brunette Girl
4-b	Monkey, Prince, Blonde Girl, Bird
5-a	Old Lady, Bird, Slippers, Monkey
5-b	Brunette Girl, Bird, Blonde Girl, Old Lady
6-a	Prince, Monkey, Blonde, Old Lady
6-b	Brunette Girl, Cat, Old Lady, Slippers
7-a	Blonde Girl, Brunette Girl, Prince, Old Lady
7-b	Monkey, Cat, Blonde Girl, Old Lady
8	Blonde Girl, Blonde Girl, Prince, Brunette Girl

BIONICLE: TALES OF THE TOHUNGA

EVERYTHING BUT THE MINI-GAMES
Enter B9RBRN as a name.

GALI MINI-GAME
Enter 9MA268 as a name.

KOPAKA MINI-GAME
Enter V33673 as a name.

LEWA MINI-GAME
Enter 3LT154 as a name.

ONUA MINI-GAME
Enter 8MR472 as a name.

POHATU MINI-GAME
Enter 5MG834 as a name.

TAHU MINI-GAME
Enter 4CR487 as a name.

CARS

ALL LEVELS AND 90 BOLTS
At the Title screen, press Up, Up, Down, Down, Left, Right, Left, Right, B, A.

ALL CARS
At the Title screen, press Right, Down, Right, B.

ALL CAR COLORS
At the Title screen, press Up, Up, Left, Right, Right, Left, Down, Down.

RADIATOR CAP SECRET CIRCUIT
At the Title screen, press Left, Left, Right, Right, B, B, A.

ALL SCREENSHOTS AT THE DRIVE-IN
At the Title screen, press Left, Down, Right, A.

CASTLEVANIA: ARIA OF SORROW

NO ITEMS
Start a new game with the name NOUSE to use no items in the game.

NO SOULS
Start a new game with the name NOSOUL to use no souls in the game.

CT SPECIAL FORCES 3: NAVY OPS

LEVEL 1-2
Enter 5073 as a password.

LEVEL 2-1
Enter 1427 as a password.

LEVEL 2-2
Enter 2438 as a password.

LEVEL 2-3
Enter 7961 as a password.

LEVEL 2-4
Enter 8721 as a password.

LEVEL 3-1
Enter 5986 as a password.

LEVEL 3-2
Enter 2157 as a password.

LEVEL 3-3
Enter 4796 as a password.

LEVEL 3-4
Enter 3496 as a password.

LEVEL 3-5
Enter 1592 as a password.

LEVEL 3-6
Enter 4168 as a password.

LEVEL 3-7
Enter 1364 as a password.

LEVEL 4-1
Enter 7596 as a password.

LEVEL 4-2
Enter 9108 as a password.

LEVEL 4-3
Enter 6124 as a password.

LEVEL 4-4
Enter 7234 as a password.

LEVEL 4-5
Enter 6820 as a password.

LEVEL 5-1
Enter 2394 as a password.

LEVEL 5-2
Enter 4256 as a password.

LEVEL 5-3
Enter 0842 as a password.

CURIOUS GEORGE

PASSWORDS

LEVEL	PASSWORD
2	TNTDBHNQ
3	TNTDBHBQ
6	PSTDHHSS
8	TNSDBHAG

DK: KING OF SWING

ATTACK BATTLE 3
At the Title screen, press Up + L + A + B to bring up a password screen. Enter 65942922.

CLIMBING RACE 5
At the Title screen, press Up + L + A + B to bring up a password screen. Enter 55860327.

OBSTACLE RACE 4
At the Title screen, press Up + L + A + B to bring up a password screen. Enter 35805225.

UNLOCK TIME ATTACK
Complete the game as DK.

UNLOCK DIDDY MODE
Collect 24 medals as DK.

UNLOCK BUBBLES
Complete Diddy Mode with 24 Medals.

UNLOCK KREMLING
Collect 6 gold medals in Jungle Jam.

UNLOCK KING K. ROOL
Collect 12 gold medals in Jungle Jam.

DONKEY KONG COUNTRY 2: DIDDY KONG'S QUEST

ALL LEVELS
Select Cheats from the Options and enter freedom.

START WITH 15 LIVES
Select Cheats from the Options and enter helpme.

START WITH 55 LIVES
Select Cheats from the Options and enter weakling.

START WITH 10 BANANA COINS
Select Cheats from the Options and enter richman.

START WITH 50 BANANA COINS
Select Cheats from the Options and enter wellrich.

NO DK OR HALF WAY BARRELS
Select Cheats from the Options and enter rockard.

MUSIC PLAYER
Select Cheats from the Options and enter onetime.

CREDITS
Select Cheats from the Options and enter kredits.

DRAGON BALL GT: TRANSFORMATION

REFILL ENERGY
During a game, press Down, Up, Right, Right, Right, Left, Right, Left, B.

REFILL HEALTH
During a game, press Down, Up, Left, Left, Up, Right, Down, B.

PICCOLO
At the Main menu, press Left, Right, Left Right, Up, Up, Down, B.

SUPER BABY VEGETA
At the Main menu, press Left, Right, Left Right, Down, Down, Up, B.

SUPER SAIYAN 4 GOKU
At the Main menu, press Left, Right, Left Right, Down, Down, Down, B.

SUPER SAIYAN KID GOKU
At the Main menu, press Left, Right, Left Right, Up, Up, Up, B.

SUPER SAIYAN VEGETA
At the Main menu, press Left, Right, Left Right, Up, Down, Down, B.

DRAKE AND JOSH

PASSWORDS

LEVEL	PASSWORD
1-1	6731
1-2	6165
1-3	7475
1-4	8636
2-1	7716
2-2	5725
3-1	3576
3-2	8285
4-1	7546
4-2	7621
4-3	2875
5-1	5147
6-1	5285
6-2	8273
Cafeteria Panic Mini-game	7576
Soda Pop Blues Mini-game	5688
Stage Fright Mini-game	2548

FINAL FANTASY I & II: DAWN OF SOULS

FF I TILE GAME
During a game of Final Fantasy I and after you get the ship, hold A and press B about 55 times.

FF II CONCENTRATION GAME
Once you obtain the Snowcraft, hold B and press A about 20 times.

JUSTICE LEAGUE HEROES: THE FLASH

ALL HEROES
At the Title screen, hold B and press Up, Down, Left, Right, Right, Left, Down, Up, Select.

ALL POWERS
At the Title screen, hold B and press Down, Down, Down, Down, Left, Right, Up, Down, Select.

LIVES
At the Title screen, hold B and press Up, Down, Up, Up, Down, Down, Up, Down, Select.

BIG FLASH
At the Title screen, hold B and press Left, Up, Right, Down, Left, Up, Right, Down, Select.

SMALL FLASH
At the Title screen, hold B and press Down, Down, Down, Left, Up, Up, Up, Right, Select.

BIG BAD GUYS
At the Title screen, hold B and press Up, Up, Down, Down, Left, Right, Left, Right, Select.

SMALL BAD GUYS
At the Title screen, hold B and press Down, Down, Up, Up, Right, Left, Right, Left, Select.

JUSTICE LEAGUE: INJUSTICE FOR ALL

CAN'T BE HIT
Pause the game, press Select and unpause.

LEGO BIONICLE: MAZE OF SHADOWS

HUAI SNOWBALL SLING MINI-GAME
Start a new game and enter V33673 as the character's name. Once in the game, pause, save and quit to find the mini-game.

IGNALU LAVA SURFING MINI-GAME
Start a new game and enter 4CR487 as the character's name. Once in the game, pause, save and quit to find the mini-game.

KEWA BIRD RIDING MINI-GAME
Start a new game and enter 3LT154 as the character's name. Once in the game, pause, save and quit to find the mini-game.

KOLI FOOTBALL MINI-GAME
Start a new game and enter 5MG834 as the character's name. Once in the game, pause, save and quit to find the mini-game.

NGALAWA BOAT RACE MINI-GAME
Start a new game and enter 9MA268 as the character's name. Once in the game, pause, save and quit to find the mini-game.

USSAL CRAB DIG MINI-GAME
Start a new game and enter 8MR472 as the character's name. Once in the game, pause, save and quit to find the mini-game.

MONSTER FORCE

RESTART LEVEL
Pause the game, hold L + R and press A.

FINISH LEVEL
During a game, hold L + R + A and press Up.

PLAY AS MINA OR DREW
At the Character Select screen, hold L + R + B and press Right.

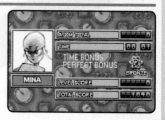

PIRATES OF THE CARIBBEAN: DEAD MAN'S CHEST

1,000 GOLD
Pause the game, press Select and then press A, L, Select, R, Right, Right.

INVINCIBILITY
Pause the game, press Select and then press R, L, Up, Up, Left, Right.

RESTORE HEALTH
Pause the game, press Select and then press Select, R, A, L, Left, Right.

ALL SHIP UPGRADES
Pause the game, press Select and then press Right, Left, Left, Down, Up, Select.

BEST JACK UPGRADES
Pause the game, press Select and then press Right, L, Down, A, Left, Select.

RESTORE GROG/FOOD
Pause the game, press Select and then press A, Select, Left, Down, Right, Up.

UNLOCK RUMORS
Pause the game, press Select and then press A, L, Select, A, Right, Up.

MAGIC WIND
Pause the game, press Select and then press Up, R, Down, Left, Left, Right.

PRINCESS NATASHA: STUDENT SECRET AGENT

ALL GADGETS
Select Codes from the Extras menu and enter OLEGSGIZMO.

EXTRA LEVELS
Select Codes from the Extras menu and enter SMASHROBOT.

INFINITE LIVES
Select Codes from the Extras menu and enter CRUSHLUBEK.

RATATOUILLE

INVINCIBILITY
Enter X4V!3RJ as a password.

ALL CHAPTERS
Enter H3L!X3! as a password. Press L or R at the Chapter Select screen.

ALL MINI-GAMES
Enter JV4ND1Z as a password.

ALL BONUS PICTURES
Enter 3R1CQRR as a password.

RIVER CITY RANSOM EX

Select the status menu and change your name to the following:

MAX STATS
DAMAX

$999999.99
PLAYA

CUSTOM CHAR
XTRA0

CUSTOM SELF
XTRA1

CUSTOM MOVE
XTRA2

CLEAR SAVE
ERAZE

TECHNIQUES 1
FUZZY. This group includes Mach Punch, Dragon Kick, Acro Circus, Grand Slam, Javelin Man, Slick Trick, Nitro Port, Twin Kick, Deadly Shot, Top Spin, Helicopter, Torpedo.

TECHNIQUES 2
WUZZY. This group includes Slap Happy, Pulper, Headbutt, Kickstand, Big Bang, Wheel Throw, Glide Chop, Head Bomb, Chain Chump, Jet Kick, Shuriken, Flip Throw.

TECHNIQUES 3
WAZZA. This group includes Boomerang, Charge It, Bat Fang, Flying Kick, Speed Drop, Bomb Blow, Killer Kick, Bike Kick, Slam Punk, Dragon Knee, God Fist, Hyperguard.

TECHNIQUES 4
BEAR*. This group includes PhoenixWing, Inlines, Springlines, Rocketeers, Air Merc's Narcishoes, Magic Pants, Pandora Box, Skaterz, Custom Fit.

SECRET AGENT BARBIE: ROYAL JEWELS MISSION

ALL SECRETS
Enter TTTTTS as a password.

ENGLAND—THE ROYAL TOWER
Enter BBBBCG as a password.

ENGLAND—STREET CHASE
Enter DBBFCM as a password.

CHINA—CITY STREETS
Enter FBBFFQ as a password.

CHINA—SECRET HIDEOUT
Enter GBBPFH as a password.

CHINA—GOLDEN CITY
Enter HBBPKN as a password.

CHINA—THE PALACE
Enter JCBPKQ as a password.

ITALY—OPERA HOUSE
Enter KCBTKC as a password.

ITALY—CANAL CHASE
Enter LCGTKJ as a password.

ITALY—FASHION DISTRICT
Enter MCHTKL as a password.

ITALY—SCUBA SEARCH
Enter NCHTTC as a password.

MEXICO—SUNNY CITY
Enter PCRTTN as a password.

SHAMAN KING: LEGACY OF THE SPIRITS, SOARING HAWK

SPIRIT OF FIRE
At the Title screen, press Right, Right, L, Left + R, Down, R, Right, B.

SHAMAN KING: LEGACY OF THE SPIRITS, SPRINTING WOLF

SPIRIT OF FIRE
At the Title screen, press Right, Right, L, Left + R, Down, R, Right, B.

STREET FIGHTER ALPHA 3

ALL FIGHTERS
At the Title screen, press Left, Right, Down, Right, L, L, A, L, L, B, R, A, Up.

ALL MODES
At the Title screen, press A, Up, A, L, R, Right, L, Right, A, Down, Right. Now press L, Right, A, R, Up,L, Right, B, A, Up, Right, Down, Right.

PLAY AS SUPER BISON
At the Character Select screen, hold Start and select Bison.

PLAY AS SHIN AKUMA
At the Character Select screen, hold Start and select Akuma.

ALTERNATE COSTUMES
At the Character Select screen, press L or R.

FINAL BATTLE
At the Speed Select option, hold A + B.

SUPER COLLAPSE 2

PUZZLE MODE PASSWORDS

PUZZLE	PASSWORD	PUZZLE	PASSWORD
2	G6CLG	8	TCLV5
3	69MR3	9	G5DYR
4	F6DHM	10	GDXSV
5	2XNSX	11	FVH4M
6	RQCJD	12	7TD4K
7	DL4NX	13	F6GS4

THAT'S SO RAVEN 2: SUPERNATURAL STYLE

COSTUME MODE
At the Title screen, press Left, Right, Up, Down, B, B, B, Up, Down.

UNLIMITED ENERGY MODE
At the Title screen, press B, B, L, R, Up, Down, Up, Left, Right.

TONY HAWK'S UNDERGROUND 2

TENNIS SHOOTER MINIGAME
Once you unlock Bam's character on the map, talk to him. Knock down the rollerbladers, then go back. He'll give you the Tennis Shooter mini-game. Once you've completed three levels, save your game to access Tennis Shooter at any time from the Main menu.

TRON 2.0: KILLER APP

ALL MINIGAMES
At the Title screen, press Left, Left, Left, Left, Up, Right, Down, Down, Select.

ULTIMATE ARCADE GAMES

ALL GAMES
At the Main menu, press L (x4), R, L, R, Left, Up, Right, Down, Left, Up, Right, Down, R, L, R, L, Select.

ALL CHALLENGES
At the Main menu, press L (x4), R, L, L, R, R, Up (x3), Down, Down, Left, Up, Right, Down, Select.

UNFABULOUS

PASSWORDS
Select Continue and enter the following:

PASSWORD	EFFECT
End of Game	Zach, Brandywine, Addie, Addie
Credits	Geena, Ben, Addie, Ben
Mini Game	Ben, Zach, Ben, Addie

YOSHI TOPSY-TURVY

CHALLENGE MODE AND CHALLENGE 1
Defeat Bowser for the second time in Story Mode.

CHALLENGES 2, 3, 4
Complete the Egg Gallery in Story Mode.

FINAL CHALLENGE
Earn all Golds in Story Mode.

YU-GI-OH! 7 TRIALS TO GLORY: WORLD CHAMPIONSHIP TOURNAMENT 2005

PURPLE TITLE SCREEN
Completing the game changes the Title screen from blue to purple. To switch it back, press Up, Up, Down, Down, Left, Right, Left, Right, B, A at the Title screen.

CREDITS
Defeat the game, then press Up, Up, Down, Down, Left, Right, Left, Right, B, A.

CARD PASSWORDS
At the password machine, press R and enter a password.
Refer to the Card List for YU-GI-OH! GX TAG FORCE for PSP. All cards are not available in World Championship Tournament 2005.

YU-GI-OH! ULTIMATE MASTERS: WORLD CHAMPIONSHIP TOURNAMENT 2006

CARD PASSWORDS
Enter the 8-digit codes at the Password screen to unlock that card for purchase.
Refer to the Card List for YU-GI-OH! GX TAG FORCE for PSP. All cards may not be available in World Championship Tournament 2006.

NINTENDO DS™

EVERYONE

ADVANCE WARS: DUAL STRIKE

ANIMANIACS: LIGHTS, CAMERA, ACTION!

ASPHALT URBAN GT

ATV: QUAD FRENZY

BIG MUTHA TRUCKERS

BRAIN AGE: TRAIN YOUR BRAIN IN MINUTES A DAY

BUBBLE BOBBLE REVOLUTION

BUST-A-MOVE DS

CARS

CARTOON NETWORK RACING

THE CHRONICLES OF NARNIA: THE LION, THE WITCH AND THE WARDROBE

DRAGON QUEST HEROES: ROCKET SLIME

DRAWN TO LIFE

FEEL THE MAGIC: XY/XX

FINAL FANTASY FABLES: CHOCOBO TALES

KIRBY: CANVAS CURSE

LEGO STAR WARS II: THE ORIGINAL TRILOGY

MADDEN NFL 2005

METROID PRIME PINBALL

NEED FOR SPEED CARBON: OWN THE CITY

NEW SUPER MARIO BROS.

NINTENDOGS

PAC-PIX

PRINCESS NATASHA

PUYO POP FEVER

RACE DRIVER: CREATE & RACE

RIDGE RACER DS

SIMCITY DS

THE SIMS 2

SPECTROBES

SPIDER-MAN 2

STAR TREK: TACTICAL ASSAULT

STAR WARS EPISODE III: REVENGE OF THE SITH

TEENAGE MUTANT NINJA TURTLES 3: MUTANT NIGHTMARE

TIGER WOODS PGA TOUR

TOM CLANCY'S SPLINTER CELL CHAOS THEORY

TONY HAWK'S DOWNHILL JAM

TRAUMA CENTER: UNDER THE KNIFE

THE URBZ: SIMS IN THE CITY

WORLD CHAMPIONSHIP POKER

YU-GI-OH! NIGHTMARE TROUBADOUR

YU-GI-OH! WORLD CHAMPIONSHIP TOURNAMENT 2007

ZOO KEEPER

ZOO TYCOON DS

EVERYONE 10+

CODE LYOKO

JAM SESSIONS

LUNAR KNIGHTS

TEEN

ALEX RIDER: STORMBREAKER

CASTLEVANIA: DAWN OF SORROW

CASTLEVANIA: PORTRAIT OF RUIN

JUICED 2: HOT IMPORT NIGHTS

THE NEW YORK TIMES CROSSWORDS

PIRATES OF THE CARIBBEAN: DEAD MAN'S CHEST

Table of Contents

ADVANCE WARS: DUAL STRIKE

ADVANCE WARS MAP
Select Map from the Design Room menu and immediately press and hold L + R. You will get a map that spells out Advance Wars.

By having old versions of advance wars inserted in your DS at the same time as Dual Strike, you can unlock new buyables at the the Battle Maps Shop!

ADVANCE WARPAPER

Insert Advance Wars in the GBA slot of your Nintendo DS. Start Advance Wars: Dual Strike. Select Battle Maps and purchase Advance Warpaper. Select Display from the Design Room and choose Classic 1.

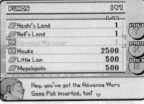

HACHI'S LAND

Insert Advance Wars in the GBA slot of your Nintendo DS. Start Advance Wars: Dual Strike. Select Battle Maps and purchase Hachi's Land for 1.

NELL'S LAND

Insert Advance Wars in the GBA slot of your Nintendo DS. Start Advance Wars: Dual Strike. Select Battle Maps and purchase Nell's Land for 1.

ADVANCE WARPAPER 2

Insert Advance Wars 2: Black Hole Rising in the GBA slot of your Nintendo DS. Start Advance Wars: Dual Strike. Select Battle Maps and purchase Advance Warpaper 2. Select Display from the Design Room and choose Classic 2.

LASH'S LAND

Insert Advance Wars 2: Black Hole Rising in the GBA slot of your Nintendo DS. Start Advance Wars: Dual Strike. Select Battle Maps and purchase Lash's Land for 1.

STRUM'S LAND

Insert Advance Wars 2: Black Hole Rising in the GBA slot of your Nintendo DS. Start Advance Wars: Dual Strike. Select Battle Maps and purchase Strum's Land for 1.

ALEX RIDER: STORMBREAKER

10,000 SPY POINTS
Select Password from the Main menu and enter 5204025.

EVERYTHING HALF PRICE AT SHOP
Select Password from the Main menu and enter 4298359.

BLACK BELT AVAILABLE FOR PURCHASE
Select Password from the Main menu and enter JESSICA PARKER.

DISK 6 AVAILABLE AFTER COMPLETING GAME
Select Password from the Main menu and enter 6943059.

FUGU AVAILABLE FOR PURCHASE
Select Password from the Main menu and enter RENATO CELANI.

M16 BADGE AVAILABLE FOR PURCHASE
Select Password from the Main menu and enter VICTORIA PARR.

SUNGLASSES AVAILABLE FOR PURCHASE
Select Password from the Main menu and enter SARYL HIRSCH.

HARD LEVEL
Select Password from the Main menu and enter 9785711.

GALLERY
Select Password from the Main menu and enter 9603717.

OUTFIT CHANGE
Select Password from the Main menu and enter 6894098.

ANIMANIACS: LIGHTS, CAMERA, ACTION!

SKIP LEVEL
Pause the game and press L, L, R, R, Down, Down.

DISABLE TIME
Pause the game and press L, R, Left, Left, Up, Up.

KINGSIZE PICKUPS
Pause the game and press Right, Right, Right, Left, Left, Left, R, L.

PASSWORDS

LEVEL	PASSWORD	LEVEL	PASSWORD
1	Wakko, Wakko, Wakko, Wakko, Wakko	9	Dot, Dot, Yakko, Pinky, Wakko
2	Dot, Yakko, Brain, Wakko, Pinky	10	Brain, Dot, Brain, Yakko, Wakko
3	Yakko, Dot, Wakko, Wakko, Brain	11	Akko, Yakko, Pinky, Dot, Dot
4	Pinky, Yakko, Yakko, Dot, Brain	12	Pinky, Pinky, Brain, Dot, Wakko
5	Pinky, Pinky, Yakko, Wakko, Wakko	13	Yakko, Wakko, Pinky, Wakko, Brain
6	Brain, Dot, Brain, Pinky, Yakko	14	Pinky, Wakko, Brain, Wakko, Yakko
7	Brain, Pinky, Wakko, Pinky, Brain	15	Dot, Pinky, Wakko, Wakko, Yakko
8	Brain Pinky, Pinky, Wakko, Wakko		

ASPHALT URBAN GT

MONEY FOR NOTHING
Buy the Chevrolet 2005 Corvette C6 for $45,000. Then, go to your garage and sell it for $45,500.

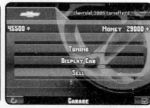

ATV: QUAD FRENZY

FLY MODE
At the Title screen, press A + Y + X.

BIG MUTHA TRUCKERS

EVIL BOB TRUCK
At the Title screen, press X, L, R, R, A, B, Y, Y, R.

BRAIN AGE: TRAIN YOUR BRAIN IN MINUTES A DAY

BRAIN AGE CHECK SELECTION MENU
At the Daily Training Menu, hold Select while choosing Brain Age Check.

TOP 3 LISTS
At the Daily Training Menu, hold Select while choosing Graph.

BUBBLE BOBBLE REVOLUTION

BONUS LEVELS IN CLASSIC MODE
At the Classic mode Title screen, press L, R, L, R, L, R, Right, Select. Touch the door at Level 20.

POWER UP! MODE IN CLASSIC VERSION
At the Classic mode Title screen, press Select, R, L, Left, Right, R, Select, Right.

SUPER BUBBLE BOBBLE IN CLASSIC VERSION
You must first defeat the boss with two players. At the Classic mode Title screen, press Left, R, Left, Select, Left, L, Left, Select.

BUST-A-MOVE DS

DARK WORLD
First you must complete the game. At the Title screen, press A Left Right A.

SOUND TEST
At the Main menu, press Select, A, B, Left, Right, A, Select, Right.

CARS

SECRET MUSIC TRACK FOR RAMONES STYLE
At the Title screen, press Up, Down, Up, Down, A, B, X, Y.

EVERYTHING EXCEPT HIDDEN MUSIC
At the Title screen press Up, Up, Down, Down, Left, Right, Left, Right, B, A, B.

CARTOON NETWORK RACING

The following codes will disable the ability to save:

UNLOCK EVERYTHING
Select Nickname from the Options and enter GIMMIE.

ENABLES ALL HAZARDS AND PICKUPS IN TIME TRIAL
Select Nickname from the Options and enter AAARGH.

ROCKETS TURN NON-INVULNERABLE OPPONENTS INTO STONE
Select Nickname from the Options and enter STONEME.

UNLIMITED DUMB ROCKETS
Select Nickname from the Options and enter ROCKETMAN.

UNLIMITED SUPERPOWER ENERGY
Select Nickname from the Options and enter SPINACH.

TOP-DOWN VIEW
Select Nickname from the Options and enter IMACOPTER.

CASTLEVANIA: DAWN OF SORROW

POTION
Complete Boss Rush Mode.

RPG
Complete Boss Rush Mode in less than 5 minutes.

DEATH'S ROBE
Complete Boss Rush Mode in less than 6 minutes.

TERROR BEAR
Complete Boss Rush Mode in less than 7 minutes.

NUNCHAKUS
Complete Boss Rush Mode in less than 8 minutes.

CASTLEVANIA: PORTRAIT OF RUIN

JAPANESE VOICEOVERS
At the Main menu, hold L and press A.

THE CHRONICLES OF NARNIA: THE LION, THE WITCH AND THE WARDROBE

RESTORE HEALTH
At the Main menu, press Left, Right, Up, Down, A (x4).

INVINCIBILITY
At the Main menu, press A, Y, X, B, Up, Up, Down, Down.

ARMOR
At the Main menu, press A, X, Y, B, Up, Up, Up, Down.

EXTRA MONEY
At the Main menu, press Up, X, Up, X, Down, B, Down, B.

ALL BLESSINGS.
At the Main menu, press Left, Up, A, B, Right, Down, X, Y.

MAXIMUM ATTRIBUTES
At the Main menu, press Left, B, Up, Y, Down, X, Right, A.

MAX SKILLS
At the Main menu, press A, Left, Right, B, Down, Up, X, X.

STRONGER ATTACKS
At the Main menu, press A, Up, B, Down, X, X, Y, Y.

CODE LYOKO

CODELYOKO.COM SECRET FILES
Enter the following as Secret Codes on the My Secret Album page of www.codelyoko.com:

SECRET FILE	CODE
Dark Enemies Wallpaper	9L8Q
Desert Sketch	6G7T
Fight Video	4M9P
FMV Ending	5R5K
Forest Sketch	8C3X
Ice Sketch	2F6U
Mountain Sketch	7E5V
Overbike	3Q4L

SECRET FILE	CODE
Overboard	8P3M
Overwing	8N2N
Scorpion Video	9H8S
Scorpion Wallpaper	3D4W
Sector 5 Sketch	5J9R
Ulrich	9A9Z
Yumi	4B2Y

DRAGON QUEST HEROES: ROCKET SLIME

KNIGHTRO TANK IN MULTIPLAYER
While in the church, press Y, L, L, Y, R, R, Y, Up, Down, Select.

THE NEMESIS TANK IN MULTIPLAYER
While in the church, press Y, R, R, up, L, L, Y, Down, Down, Down, Y, Select.

DRAWN TO LIFE

ALIEN TEMPLATES
Enter draw mode, hold L and press X, Y, B, A, A.

ANIMAL TEMPLATES
Enter draw mode, hold L and press B, B, A, A, X.

ROBOT TEMPLATES
Enter draw mode, hold L and press Y, X, Y, X, A.

SPORTS TEMPLATES
Enter draw mode, hold L and press Y, A, B, A, X.

FEEL THE MAGIC: XY/XX

RECORD YOUR VOICE ON THE TITLE SCREEN
While at the Title screen, hold Down + Y to record whatever you want into the microphone. It will now play back whatever you recorded at random intervals while the title music plays. However, if you wish to play it back immediately, press Down + X. Down-Left + X will play it back slowly, while Down-Right + X will speed it up.

HARD MODE
Defeat the game on Normal difficulty.

HARDER MODE
Defeat the game on Hard difficulty.

FINAL FANTASY FABLES: CHOCOBO TALES

OMEGA – WAVE CANNON CARD
Select Send from the Main menu and then choose Download Pop-Up Card. Press L, L, Up, B, B, Left.

JAM SESSIONS

BONUS SONGS
At the Free Play menu, press Up, Up, Down, Down, Left, Right, Left, Right. This unlocks I'm Gonna Miss Her by Brad Paisley, Needles and Pins by Tom Petty, and Wild Thing by Jimi Hendrix.

JUICED 2: HOT IMPORT NIGHTS

$5000
At the Cheat menu, enter HSAC.

ALL CARS
At the Cheat menu, enter SRAC.

ALL RACES
At the Cheat menu, enter EDOM.

ALL TRACKS
At the Cheat menu, enter KART.

KIRBY: CANVAS CURSE

JUMP GAME
Defeat the game with all five characters. Select the game file to get Jump Game next to the options on the Main menu.

LEGO STAR WARS II: THE ORIGINAL TRILOGY

10 STUDS
At the Mos Eisley cantina, enter 4PR28U.

OBI WAN GHOST
At the Mos Eisley cantina, enter BEN917.

LUNAR KNIGHTS

SOUND DATA (BOKTAI)
With Boktai in the GBA slot, purchase this from the General Store in Acuna.

SOUND DATA (BOKTAI 2)
With Boktai 2 in the GBA slot, purchase this from the General Store in Acuna.

MADDEN NFL 2005

THREE DOWNS FOR OPPONENT
Touch the spot in the middle of the Main menu and enter SHORTTIME.

FIVE DOWNS
Touch the spot in the middle of the Main menu and enter LONGTIME.

HARDER HITS
Touch the spot in the middle of the Main menu and enter SMASHMOUTH.

MORE FUMBLES
Touch the spot in the middle of the Main menu and enter SUPERSLICK.

MORE INTERCEPTIONS
Touch the spot in the middle of the Main menu and enter BADPASS.

MORE SACKS
Touch the spot in the middle of the Main menu and enter SAD SACK.

METROID PRIME PINBALL

PHAZON MINES
Complete Omega Pirate in Multi Mission mode.

PHENDRANA DRIFTS
Complete Thardus in Multi Mission mode.

NEED FOR SPEED CARBON: OWN THE CITY

INFINITE NITROUS
At the Main menu, press Up, Up, Down, Left, A, B, B, A.

NEW SUPER MARIO BROS.

PLAY AS LUIGI IN SINGLE PLAYER
At the Select a File screen, hold L + R while selecting a saved game.

SECRET CHALLENGE MODE
On the map, pause the game and press L, R, L, R, X, X, Y, Y.

THE NEW YORK TIMES CROSSWORDS

BLACK & WHITE
At the Main menu, press Up, Up, Down, Down, B, B, Y, Y.

NINTENDOGS

FEED DOG LIGHT BULB
When the light bulb appears above your dog, grab it and drag it to his/her mouth.

PAC-PIX

BUTTERFLY HIDDEN GESTURE
Select Sketchbook from the Gallery. Draw a figure eight. The drawing should fly upwards.

CHERRIES HIDDEN GESTURE
Select Sketchbook from the Gallery. Draw a pair of cherries starting with one of the circles.

POGO STICK HIDDEN GESTURE
Select Sketchbook from the Gallery. Draw a P and it will bounce off the screen.

RAIN CLOUD HIDDEN GESTURE

Select Sketchbook from the Gallery. Draw a cloud and it will turn blue and rain will fall from the drawing.

SNAKE HIDDEN GESTURE

Select Sketchbook from the Gallery. Draw a squiggly line. It will turn green and slither away.

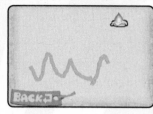

TREBLE CLEF HIDDEN GESTURE

Select Sketchbook from the Gallery. Draw a treble clef.

SHOOT ARROWS AT PAC-MAN

After you have earned the Arrow gesture in Chapter 4, select Sketchbook from the Gallery. Draw an arrow facing Pac-man.

PIRATES OF THE CARIBBEAN: DEAD MAN'S CHEST

10 GOLD

During a game, press Right, X, X, Right, Left.

INVINCIBILITY

During a game, press Up, Down, Left, Right (x5), Left, Right, Up, Down, Left, Right, Up (x5), Left.

UNLIMITED POWER

During a game, press Up, Up, Down, Down, Left, Right, Left, Right, L, R.

RESTORE HEALTH

During a game, press Y, Y, Select, Left, Right, Left, Right, Left.

RESTORE SAVVY

During a game, press X, X, Select, Up, Down, Up, Down, Up.

GHOST FORM MODE

During a game, press Y, X, Y, X, Y, X.

SEASICKNESS MODE

During a game, press X, X, Y, X, X, Y.

SILLY WEAPONS

During a game, press Y, Y, X, Y (x3).

AXE

During a game, press Left, L, L, Down, Down, Left, Up, Up, Down, Down.

BLUNDERBUSS

During a game, press Down, L, L, Down (x3).

CHICKEN

During a game, press Right, L, L, Up, Down, Down.

EXECUTIONER AXE

During a game, press Right, L, L, Up, Down, Up, Right, Right, Left(x2).

PIG

During a game, press Right, R, R, Down, Up, Up.

PISTOL

During a game, press Down, L, L, Down, Down, Right.

RIFLE
During a game, press Left, L, L, Up (x3).

FAST MUSIC
During a game, press Y, Select, Y (x4).

SLOW MUSIC
During a game, press Y, Select, X (x4).

DISABLE CHEATS
During a game, press X (x6).

PRINCESS NATASHA

ALL GADGETS
Select Codes from the Extras menu and enter OLEGSGIZMO.

EXTRA LEVELS
Select Codes from the Extras menu and enter SMASHROBOT.

INFINITE LIVES
Select Codes from the Extras menu and enter CRUSHLUBEK.

PUYO POP FEVER

ALL CHARACTERS AND CUTSCENES
Select Gallery from the Options. Highlight cutscene viewer, hold X and press Up, Down, Left, Right.

RACE DRIVER: CREATE & RACE

ALL CHALLENGES
Select Cheat Codes from Extras and enter 942785.

ALL CHAMPIONSHIPS
Select Cheat Codes from Extras and enter 761492.

ALL REWARDS
Select Cheat Codes from Extras and enter 112337.

FREE DRIVE
Select Cheat Codes from Extras and enter 171923.

NO DAMAGE
Select Cheat Codes from Extras and enter 505303.

EASY STEERING
Select Cheat Codes from Extras and enter 611334.

MINIATURE CARS
Select Cheat Codes from Extras and enter 374288.

MM VIEW
Select Cheat Codes from Extras and enter 467348.

RIDGE RACER DS

00-AGENT CAR
Finish more than ten races in multi-player.

CADDY CAR
Finish more than ten races in multi-player.

GALAGA '88 CAR
Finish more than ten races in multi-player.

MARIO RACING CAR
Finish more than ten races in multi-player.

POOKA CAR
Finish more than ten races in multi-player.

RED SHIRT RAGE CAR
Finish more than ten races in multi-player.

SHY GUY CAR
Finish more than ten races in multi-player.

GALAGA PAC JAM SONG
Unlock the Pooka car.

MUSHROOM KINGDOM II SONG
Unlock the DK Team Racing car.

SIMCITY DS

LANDMARK BUILDINGS
Select Landmark Collection from the Museum menu. Choose Password and enter the following:

BUILDING	PASSWORD	BUILDING	PASSWORD
Anglican Cathedral (UK)	kipling	National Museum (Taiwan)	yuantlee
Arc de Triomphe (France)	gaugin	Neuschwanstein Castle (Germany)	beethoven
Atomic Dome (Japan)	kawabata	Notre Dame (France)	hugo
Big Ben (UK)	orwell	Palace of Fine Arts (USA)	bunche
Bowser Castle (Nintendo)	hanafuda	Palacio Real (Spain)	cervantes
Brandenburg Gate (Germany)	gropius	Paris Opera (France)	daumier
Coit Tower	kerouac	Parthenon (Greece)	callas
Conciergerie (France)	rodin	Pharos of Alexandria (Egypt)	zewail
Daibutsu (Japan)	mishima	Rama IX Royal Park (Thailand)	phu
Edo Castle (Japan)	shonagon	Reichstag (Germany)	goethe
Eiffel Tower (France)	camus	Sagrada Familia (Spain)	dali
Gateway Arch (USA)	twain	Shuri Castle (Japan)	basho
Grand Central Station (USA)	f.scott	Smithsonian Castle (USA)	pauling
Great Pyramids (Egypt)	mahfouz	Sphinx (Egypt)	haykal
Hagia Sofia (Turkey)	ataturk	St Paul's Cathedral (UK)	defoe
Helsinki Cathedral (Finland)	kivi	St. Basil's Cathedral (Russia)	tolstoy
Himeji Castle (Japan)	hokusai	St. Stephen's Cathedral (Austria)	mozart
Holstentor (Germany)	durer	Statue of Liberty (USA)	pollack
Independence Hall (USA)	mlkingjr	Stockholm Palace (Sweden)	bergman
Jefferson Memorial (USA)	thompson	Taj Mahal (India)	tagore
Kokkai (Japan)	soseki	Tower of London (UK)	maugham
LA Landmark (USA)	hemingway	Trafalgar Square (UK)	joyce
Lincoln Memorial (USA)	melville	United Nations (UN)	amnesty
Liver Building (UK)	dickens	United States Capitol (USA)	poe
Melbourne Cricket Ground (Australia)	damemelba	Washington Monument	capote
Metropolitan Cath. (UK)	austen	Westminster Abbey (UK)	greene
Moai (Chile)	allende	White House (USA)	Steinbeck
Mt. Fuji (Japan)	hiroshige		

THE SIMS 2

MONGOO MONKEY FOR THE CASINO
Start the game with Sims 2 in the GBA slot of your Nintendo DS.

SPECTROBES

CARD INPUT SYSTEM
When the Upsilon Cube is unearthed and shown to Aldous, the Card Input System feature becomes available. This will allow you to input data from Spectrobe Cards. These give you new Spectrobes and Custom Parts. If you get your hands on a Spectrobe Card and the system is unlocked, investigate the card input system in the spaceship's lower deck. Follow the instructions on the upper screen to match the four corner points of the card to the corners of the touch screen. Touch the screen through the seven holes in the card in the order indicated on the card. If the code you input is correct, you receive Spectrobes, custom Parts, minerals or Cubes.

You can input the same card a maximum of four times. This means that you can only obtain four of the same Spectrobes from a single card. You can only input cards once. And some cards cannot be input until you have reached a certain point in the game.

The following table gives you a seven character code which refers to the spots you touch in order. The first four characters have you touching the four corners and the final three are spots among the 12 in the middle. To get Cyclone Geo, Hammer Geo, Ice Geo, Plasma Geo, or Thunder Geo, you must first beat the game.

EFFECT	CODE
Aobasat Apex	BACD HEP
Cyclone Geo	CDAB LGM
Danaphant Tuska	ABDC ELI
Danilob	DABC GLO
Emerald Mineral	BACD FKN
Grilden Biblad	ABDC FIH
Grildragos Drafly	CDAB MHK
Gristar	BACD GJN
Hammer Geo	ABDC ELH
Harumitey Lazos	DABC ILM
Ice Geo	CDAB HEK
Inataflare Auger	ABDC IGH
Inkalade	ABDC GLP
Iota Cube	ABDC OHE
Komainu	CDAB HMJ
Kugaster Sonara	DABC LOE
Mossax Jetspa (Custom Color 1)	BACD JML
Naglub	ABDC EJM
Plasma Geo	BACD KLE
Rho Cube	BACD PNI
Ruby Mineral	CDAB FKO
Samukabu	ABDC OIL

EFFECT	CODE
Samurite Voltar	BACD LHM
Sapphire Mineral	ABDC FJO
Segulos Propos	CDAB KIH
Seguslice	CDAB GKP
Shakor Bristle	DABC MLK
Sigma Cube	CDAB PML
Tau Cube	DABC LIF
Thunder Geo	DABC MEL
Vilagrisp (Custom Part)	DABC EIN
Vilakroma	BACD NLM
Vilakroma (Custom Color 1)	CDAB LJI
Vilakroma (Custom Color 2)	DABC EGP
Windora	ABDC MGP
Windora (Custom Color 1)	DABC EHG
Windora (Custom Color 2)	CDAB JPM
Windora Ortex	BACD IPG
Windora Ortex (Custom Color 1)	ABDC MPH
Windora Ortex (Custom Color 2)	DABC MGH
Windora Sordina	CDAB PEO
Windora Sordina (Custom Color 1)	BACD MOH
Windora Sordina (Custom Color 2)	ABDC LEN
Wing Geo (must beat game	DABC MNP

SPIDER-MAN 2

ALL SPECIAL MOVES
Load the game with Spider-Man: Mysterio's Menace for Game Boy Advance in the Nintendo DS.

STAR TREK: TACTICAL ASSAULT

KLINGON CAMPAIGN
At the Main menu, press Up, Down, Left, Right, Select, Start, X.

UNLOCK MISSIONS
At the Main menu, press Up, Down, Left, Right, Select, Start, Start.

EXTRA CREW UPGRADES
At the Main menu, press Up, Down, Left, Right, Select, Start, Select.

ALL SHIPS IN SKIRMISH AND MULTIPLAYER
At the Main menu, press Up, Down, Left, Right, Select, Start, Y.

ANY SHIP IN MISSIONS
At the Main menu, press Up, Down, Left, Right, Select, Start, B.

STAR WARS EPISODE III: REVENGE OF THE SITH

MASTER DIFFICULTY
Defeat the game.

ANAKIN'S STARFIGHTER
Beat the Anakin bot in multiplayer.

DARTH VADER'S TIE FIGHTER
Defeat the Darth Vader bot in multiplayer.

GENERAL GREVIOUS'S STARFIGHTER
Defeat the General Grevious bot in multiplayer.

MILLENIUM FALCON
Defeat the Solo bot in multiplayer.

SLAVE I
Defeat the Fett bot in multiplayer.

X-WING
Defeat the Luke bot in multiplayer.

TEENAGE MUTANT NINJA TURTLES 3: MUTANT NIGHTMARE

CRYSTALS ARE EASTER EGGS
Select Input Password from the Options and enter SRDSLLMS.

CRYSTALS ARE JACK-O-LANTERNS
Select Input Password from the Options and enter DRSSMRLD.

CRYSTALS ARE SANTAS
Select Input Password from the Options and enter LLDMSRMD.

LIFE ICONS ARE PIZZA
Select Input Password from the Options and enter DDRMLRDS.

COWABUNGA
At the Title screen, press U, U, D, D, L, R, L, R, B, A.

TIGER WOODS PGA TOUR 2005

EMERALD DRAGON
Earn $1,000,000.

GREEK ISLES
Earn $1,500,000.

PARADISE COVER
Earn $2,000,000.

EA SPORTS FAVORITES
Earn $5,000,000

MEAN8TEEN
Earn $10,000,000.

FANTASY SPECIALS
Earn $15,000,000.

LEGEND COMPILATION 1
Defeat Hogan in Legend Tour.

LEGEND COMPILATION 2
Defeat Gary Player in Legend Tour.

LEGEND COMPILATION 3
Defeat Ballesteros in Legend Tour.

LEGEND COMPILATION 4
Defeat Palmer in Legend Tour.

LEGEND COMPILATION 5
Defeat Nicklaus in Legend Tour.

THE HUSTLER'S DREAM 18
Defeat The Hustler in Legend Tour.

TIGER'S DREAM 18
Defeat Tiger Woods in Legend Tour.

TOM CLANCY'S SPLINTER CELL CHAOS THEORY

UNLIMITED AMMO/GADGETS
Defeat the game.

CHARACTER SKINS
Defeat the game.

TONY HAWK'S DOWNHILL JAM

ALWAYS SNOWSKATE
Select Buy Stuff from the Skateshop. Choose Enter Code and enter SNOWSK8T.

MIRRORED MAPS
Select Buy Stuff from the Skateshop. Choose Enter Code and enter MIRRORBALL.

ABOMINABLE SNOWMAN OUTFIT
Select Buy Stuff from the Skateshop. Choose Enter Code and enter BIGSNOWMAN.

ZOMBIE SKATER OUTFIT
Select Buy Stuff from the Skateshop. Choose Enter Code and enter ZOMBIEALIVE.

TRAUMA CENTER: UNDER THE KNIFE

X1: KYRIAKI MISSION
Defeat the game. Find the X Missions under Challenge Mode.

X2: DEFTERA MISSION
Defeat X1 : Kyriaki Mission. Find the X Missions under Challenge Mode.

X3: TRITI MISSION
Defeat X2 : Deftera Mission. Find the X Missions under Challenge Mode.

X4: TETARTI MISSION
Defeat X3 : Triti Mission. Find the X Missions under Challenge Mode.

X5: PEMPTI MISSION
Defeat X4 : Tetarti Mission. Find the X Missions under Challenge Mode.

X6: PARAKEVI MISSION
Defeat X5 : Pempti Mission. Find the X Missions under Challenge Mode.

X7: SAVATO MISSION
Defeat X6 : Parakevi Mission. Find the X Missions under Challenge Mode.

THE URBZ: SIMS IN THE CITY

CLUB XIZZLE
Once you gain access to Club Xizzle, enter with the password "bucket."

WORLD CHAMPIONSHIP POKER

UNLOCK CASINOS

At the Title screen, press Y, X, Y, B, L, R. Then press the following direction:

DIRECTION	CASINO
Left	Amazon
Right	Nebula
Down	Renaissance

YU-GI-OH! NIGHTMARE TROUBADOUR

CREDITS

Unlock the Password Machine by defeating the Expert Cup. Enter the Duel Shop and select the Slot maching. Enter 00000375.

SOUND TEST

Unlock the Password Machine by defeating the Expert Cup. Enter the Duel Shop and select the Slot maching. Enter 57300000.

YU-GI-OH! WORLD CHAMPIONSHIP 2007

CARD PASSWORDS

Select Password from the Shop and enter one of the Card Passwords. You must already have that card or have it in a pack list for the password to work. Refer to the Card List for YU-GI-OH! GX TAG FORCE for PSP. All cards may not be available in World Championship 2007.

ZOO KEEPER

GEKIMUZU DIFFICULTY

Earn a high score in all 4 modes.

Here are the high scores needed for each mode:

MODE	SCORE
Zoo keeper	200000
Tokoton 100	800000
Quest mode	10000
Time attack	600000

ZOO TYCOON DS

UNLOCK EVERYTHING

At the Main menu, press Up, Up, Down, Down, Left, Right, Left, Right, Up, Up, Down , Down, Left, Right, Left, Right.

Nintendo Wii™

EVERYONE

MADDEN NFL 07

MYSIMS

SPONGEBOB SQUAREPANTS: CREATURE
FROM THE KRUSTY KRAB

SSX BLUR

TIGER WOODS PGA TOUR 07

TIGER WOODS PGA TOUR 08

WII SPORTS

EVERYONE 10+

AVATAR: THE LAST AIRBENDER

DISNEY'S CHICKEN LITTLE: ACE IN ACTION

THE GRIM ADVENTURES OF BILLY &
MANDY

ICE AGE 2: THE MELTDOWN

NEED FOR SPEED CARBON

RAMPAGE: TOTAL DESTRUCTION

SHREK THE THIRD

SPIDER-MAN: FRIEND OR FOE

SURF'S UP

TMNT

TONY HAWK'S DOWNHILL JAM

TEEN

GUITAR HERO III: LEGENDS OF ROCK

MARVEL ULTIMATE ALLIANCE

PRINCE OF PERSIA RIVAL SWORDS

THE SIMS 2: CASTAWAY

TONY HAWK'S PROVING GROUND

TRANSFORMERS: THE GAME

Table of Contents

Nintendo Wii™ Virtual Console Games

EVERYONE

ADVENTURES OF LOLO
ADVENTURES OF LOLO 2
ALTERED BEAST
BOMBERMAN '93
CHEW MAN FU
COMIX ZONE
DR. ROBOTNIK'S MEAN BEAN MACHINE
DUNGEON EXPLORER
ECCO THE DOLPHIN
F-ZERO X

GOLDEN AXE
GRADIUS
GRADIUS III
ICE HOCKEY
MILITARY MADNESS
RISTAR
SOLOMON'S KEY
SONIC THE HEDGEHOG
WARIO'S WOODS

Table of Contents

Wii™

AVATAR: THE LAST AIRBENDER

UNLIMITED HEALTH
Select Code Entry from Extras and enter 94677.

UNLIMITED CHI
Select Code Entry from Extras and enter 24463.

UNLIMITED COPPER
Select Code Entry from Extras and enter 23637.

NEVERENDING STEALTH
Select Code Entry from Extras and enter 53467.

1 HIT DISHONOR
Select Code Entry from Extras and enter 54641.

DOUBLE DAMAGE
Select Code Entry from Extras and enter 34743.

ALL TREASURE MAPS
Select Code Entry from Extras and enter 37437.

THE CHARACTER CONCEPT ART GALLERY
Select Code Entry from Extras and enter 97831.

DISNEY'S CHICKEN LITTLE: ACE IN ACTION

ALL LEVELS
Select the Cheats option and enter Right, Up, Left, Right, Up.

ALL WEAPONS
Select the Cheats option and enter Right, Down, Right, Left.

UNLIMITED SHIELD
Select the Cheats option and enter Right, Down, Right, Down, Right.

THE GRIM ADVENTURES OF BILLY & MANDY

CONCEPT ART
At the Main menu, hold 1 and press Up, Up, Down, Down, Left, Right, Left, Right.

GUITAR HERO III: LEGENDS OF ROCK

To enter the following cheats, strum the guitar and hold the buttons listed. For example, if it says Yellow + Orange, hold Yellow and Orange as you strum. Air Guitar, Precision Mode and Performance Mode can be toggled on and off from the Cheats menu. You can also change between five different levels of Hyperspeed at this menu.

ALL SONGS
Select Cheats from the Options. Choose Enter Cheat and enter Yellow + Orange, Red + Blue, Red + Orange, Green + Blue, Red + Yellow, Yellow + Orange, Red + Yellow, Red + Blue, Green + Yellow, Green + Yellow, Yellow + Blue, Yellow + Blue, Yellow + Orange, Yellow + Orange, Yellow + Blue, Yellow, Red, Red + Yellow, Red, Yellow, Orange.

AIR GUITAR
Select Cheats from the Options. Choose Enter Cheat and enter Blue + Yellow, Green + Yellow, Green + Yellow, Red + Blue, Red + Blue, Red + Yellow, Red + Yellow, Blue + Yellow, Green + Yellow, Green + Yellow, Red + Blue, Red + Blue, Red + Yellow, Red + Yellow, Green + Yellow, Green + Yellow, Red + Yellow, Red + Yellow.

PRECISION MODE
Select Cheats from the Options. Choose Enter Cheat and enter Green + Red, Green + Red, Green + Red, Red + Yellow, Red + Yellow, Red + Blue, Red + Blue, Yellow + Blue, Yellow + Orange, Yellow + Orange, Green + Red, Green + Red, Green + Red, Red + Yellow, Red + Yellow, Red + Blue, Red + Blue, Yellow + Blue, Yellow + Orange, Yellow + Orange.

HYPERSPEED
Select Cheats from the Options. Choose Enter Cheat and enter Orange, Blue, Orange, Yellow, Orange, Blue, Orange, Yellow.

PERFORMANCE MODE
Select Cheats from the Options. Choose Enter Cheat and enter Red + Yellow, Red + Blue, Red + Orange, Red + Blue, Red + Yellow, Green + Blue, Red + Yellow, Red + Blue.

ICE AGE 2: THE MELTDOWN

INFINITE PEBBLES
Pause the game and press Down, Down, Left, Up, Up, Right, Up, Down.

INFINITE ENERGY
Pause the game and press Down, Left, Right, Down, Down, Right, Left, Down.

INFINITE HEALTH
Pause the game and press Up, Right, Down, Up, Left, Down, Right, Left.

MADDEN NFL 07

MADDEN CARDS

Select Madden Cards from My Madden. Then select Madden Codes and enter the following:

CARD	PASSWORD	CARD	PASSWORD
#199 Gold Lame Duck Cheat	5LAWOO	#241 1988 49ers Gold	SP2A8H
#200 Gold Mistake Free Cheat	XL7SP1	#242 1990 Eagles Gold	2L4TRO
#210 Gold QB on Target Cheat	WROAOR	#243 1991 Lions Gold	J1ETRI
#220 Super Bowl XLI Gold	RLA9R7	#244 1992 Cowboys Gold	W9UVI9
#221 Super Bowl XLII Gold	WRLUF8	#245 1993 Bills Gold	DLA3I7
#222 Super Bowl XLIII Gold	NIEV4A	#246 1994 49ers Gold	DR7EST
#223 Super Bowl XLIV Gold	M5AB7L	#247 1996 Packers Gold	F8LUST
#224 Aloha Stadium Gold	YI8P8U	#248 1998 Broncos Gold	FIES95
#225 1958 Colts Gold	B57QLU	#249 1999 Rams Gold	S9OUSW
#226 1966 Packers Gold	1PL1FL	#250 Bears Pump Up the Crowd	B1OUPH
#227 1968 Jets Gold	MIE6WO	#251 Bengals Cheerleader	DRL2SW
#228 1970 Browns Gold	CL2TOE	#252 Bills Cheerleader	1PLUYO
#229 1972 Dolphins Gold	NOEB7U	#253 Broncos Cheerleader	3ROUJO
#230 1974 Steelers Gold	YOOFLA	#254 Browns Pump Up the Crowd	T1UTOA
#231 1976 Raiders Gold	MOA11I	#255 Buccaneers Cheerleader	S9EWRI
#232 1977 Broncos Gold	C8UM7U	#256 Cardinals Cheerleader	57IEPI
#233 1978 Dolphins Gold	VIU007	#257 Chargers Cheerleader	F7UHL8
#234 1980 Raiders Gold	NLAPH3	#258 Chiefs Cheerleader	PRI5SL
#235 1981 Chargers Gold	COAGI4	#259 Colts Cheerleader	1R5AMI
#236 1982 Redskins Gold	WL8BRI	#260 Cowboys Cheerleader	Z2ACHL
#237 1983 Raiders Gold	HOEW71	#261 Dolphins Cheerleader	C5AHLE
#238 1984 Dolphins Gold	M1AM1E	#262 Eagles Cheerleader	PO7DRO
#239 1985 Bears Gold	QOETO8	#263 Falcons Cheerleader	37USPO
		#264 49ers Cheerleader	KLOCRL
		#265 Giants Pump Up the Crowd	C4USPI
		#266 Jaguars Cheerleader	MIEH7E
		#267 Jets Pump Up the Crowd	COLUXI
		#268 Lions Pump Up the Crowd	3LABLU
		#269 Packers Pump Up the Crowd	4HO7VO
		#270 Panthers Cheerleader	F2IASP
		#282 All AFC Team Gold	PRO9PH
		#283 All NFC Team Gold	RLATH7

#240 1986 Giants Gold	ZI8S2L

Wii™

MARVEL ULTIMATE ALLIANCE

UNLOCK ALL SKINS
At the Team menu, press Up, Down, Left, Right, Left, Right, Plus.

UNLOCKS ALL HERO POWERS
At the Team menu, press Left, Right, Up, Down, Up, Down, Plus.

ALL HEROES TO LEVEL 99
At the Team menu, press Up, Left, Up, Left, Down, Right, Down, Right, Plus.

UNLOCK ALL HEROES
At the Team menu, press Up, Up, Down, Down, Left, Left, Left, Plus.

UNLOCK DAREDEVIL
At the Team menu, press Left, Left, Right, Right, Up, Down, Up, Down, Plus.

UNLOCK SILVER SURFER
At the Team menu, press Down, Left, Left, Up, Right, Up, Down, Left, Plus.

GOD MODE
During gameplay, press Up, Down, Up, Down, Up, Left, Down, Right, Plus.

TOUCH OF DEATH
During gameplay, press Left, Right, Down, Down, Right, Left, Plus.

SUPER SPEED
During gameplay, press Up, Left, Up, Right, Down, Right, Plus.

FILL MOMENTUM
During gameplay, press Left, Right, Right, Left, Up, Down, Down, Up, Plus.

UNLOCK ALL COMICS
At the Review menu, press Left, Right, Right, Left, Up, Up, Right, Plus.

UNLOCK ALL CONCEPT ART
At the Review menu, press Down, Down, Down, Right, Right, Left, Down, Plus.

UNLOCK ALL CINEMATICS
At the Review menu, press Up, Left, Left, Up, Right, Right, Up, Plus.

UNLOCK ALL LOAD SCREENS
At the Review menu, press Up, Down, Right, Left, Up, Up Down, Plus.

UNLOCK ALL COURSES
At the Comic Missions menu, press Up, Right, Left, Down, Up, Right, Left, Down, Plus.

MYSIMS

PASSWORD SCREEN
Press the Minus button to bring up the pause screen. Then enter the following with the Wii Remote: 2, 1, Down, Up, Down, Up, Left, Left, Right, Right. Now you can enter the following passwords:

Outfits

Camouflage pants	N10ng5g
Diamond vest	Tglg0ca
Genie outfit	Gvsb3k1
Kimono dress	I3hkdvs
White jacket	R705aan

Furniture

Bunk bed	F3nevr0
Hourglass couch	Ghtymba
Modern couch	T7srhca
Racecar bed	Ahvmrva
Rickshaw bed	Itha7da

NEED FOR SPEED CARBON

CASTROL CASH
At the Main menu, press Down, Up, Left, Down, Right, Up, Button 1, B. This gives you 10,000 extra cash.

INFINITE CREW CHARGE
At the Main menu, press Down, Up, Up, Right, Left, Left, Right, Button 1.

INFINITE NITROUS
At the Main menu, press Left, Up, Left, Down, Left, Down, Right, Button 1.

INFINITE SPEEDBREAKER
At the Main menu, press Down, Right, Right, Left, Right, Up, Down, Button 1.

NEED FOR SPEED CARBON LOGO VINYLS
At the Main menu, press Right, Up, Down, Up, Down, Left, Right, Button 1.

NEED FOR SPEED CARBON SPECIAL LOGO VINYLS
At the Main menu, press Up, Up, Down, Down, Down, Down, Up, Button 1.

PRINCE OF PERSIA RIVAL SWORDS

BABY TOY WEAPON
Pause the game and enter the following code. Use the D-pad for the directions.
Left, Left, Right, Right, Z, Nunchuck down, Nunchuck down, Z, Up, Down

CHAINSAW
Pause the game and enter the following code. Use the D-pad for the directions.
Up, Up, Down, Down, Left, Right, Left, Right, Z, Nunchuck down, Z, Nunchuck down

SWORDFISH
Pause the game and enter the following code. Use the D-pad for the directions.
Up, Down, Up, Down, Left, Right, Left, Right, Z, Nunchuck down, Z, Nunchuck down

TELEPHONE SWORD
Pause the game and enter the following code. Use the D-pad for the directions.
Right, Left, Right, Left, Down, Down, Up, Up, Z, Nunchuck Down, Z, Z, Nunchuck Down, Nunchuck Down

RAMPAGE: TOTAL DESTRUCTION

ALL MONSTERS
At the Main menu, press Minus + Plus to access the Cheat menu and enter 141421.

INVULNERABLE TO ATTACKS
At the Main menu, press Minus + Plus to access the Cheat menu and enter 986960.

ALL SPECIAL ABILITIES
At the Main menu, press Minus + Plus to access the Cheat menu and enter 011235.

ALL LEVELS
At the Main menu, press Minus + Plus to access the Cheat menu and enter 271828.

CPU VS CPU DEMO
At the Main menu, press Minus + Plus to access the cheat menu and enter 082864.

FAST CPU VS CPU DEMO
At the Main menu, press Minus + Plus to access the cheat menu and enter 874098.

ONE HIT DESTROYS BUILDINGS
At the Main menu, press Minus + Plus to access the Cheat menu and enter 071767.

OPENING MOVIE
At the Main menu, press Minus + Plus to access the Cheat menu and enter 667300.

ENDING MOVIE
At the Main menu, press Minus + Plus to access the Cheat menu and enter 667301.

CREDITS
At the Main menu, press Minus + Plus to access the Cheat menu and enter 667302.

VERSION INFORMATION
At the Main menu, press Minus + Plus to access the Cheat menu and enter 314159.

CLEAR CHEATS
At the Main menu, press Minus + Plus to access the Cheat menu and enter 000000.

SHREK THE THIRD

10,000 GOLD COINS
At the gift shop, press Up, Up, Down, Up, Right, Left.

THE SIMS 2: CASTAWAY

CHEAT GNOME
During a game, press B, Z, Up, Down, B. You can now use this Gnome to get the following:

MAX ALL MOTIVES
During a game, press Minus, Plus, Z, Z, A.

MAX CURRENT INVENTORY
During a game, press Left, Right, Left, Right, A.

MAX RELATIONSHIPS
During a game, press Z, Plus, A, B, 2.

ALL RESOURCES
During a game, press A, A, Down, Down, A.

ALL CRAFTING PLANS
During a game, press Plus, Plus, Minus, Minus, Z.

ADD 1 TO SKILL
During a game, press 2, Up, Right, Z, Right.

SPIDER-MAN: FRIEND OR FOE

NEW GREEN GOBLIN AS A SIDEKICK
While standing in the Helicarrier between levels, press Left, Down, Right, Right, Down, Left.

SANDMAN AS A SIDEKICK
While standing in the Helicarrier between levels, press Right, Right, Right, Up, Down, Left.

VENOM AS A SIDEKICK
While standing in the Helicarrier between levels, press Left, Left, Right, Up, Down, Down.

5000 TECH TOKENS
While standing in the Helicarrier between levels, press Up, Up, Down, Down, Left, Right.

SPONGEBOB SQUAREPANTS: CREATURE FROM THE KRUSTY KRAB

30,000 EXTRA Z'S
Select Cheat Codes from the Extras menu and enter ROCFISH.

PUNK SPONGEBOB IN DIESEL DREAMING
Select Cheat Codes from the Extras menu and enter SPONGE. Select Activate Bonus Items to enable this bonus item.

HOT ROD SKIN IN DIESEL DREAMING
Select Cheat Codes from the Extras menu and enter HOTROD. Select Activate Bonus Items to enable this bonus item.

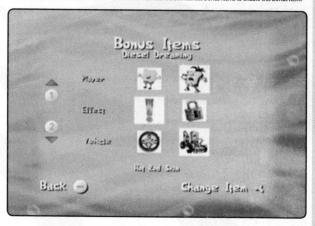

PATRICK TUX IN STARFISHMAN TO THE RESCUE
Select Cheat Codes from the Extras menu and enter PATRICK. Select Activate Bonus Items to enable this bonus item.

SPONGEBOB PLANKTON IN SUPER-SIZED PATTY
Select Cheat Codes from the Extras menu and enter PANTS. Select Activate Bonus Items to enable this bonus item.

PATRICK LASER COLOR IN ROCKET RODEO
Select Cheat Codes from the Extras menu and enter ROCKET. Select Activate Bonus Items to enable this bonus item.

PATRICK ROCKET SKIN COLOR IN ROCKET RODEO
Select Cheat Codes from the Extras menu and enter SPACE. Select Activate Bonus Items to enable this bonus item.

PLANKTON ASTRONAUT SUIT IN REVENGE OF THE GIANT PLANKTON MONSTER
Select Cheat Codes from the Extras menu and enter ROBOT. Select Activate Bonus Items to enable this bonus item.

PLANKTON EYE LASER COLOR IN REVENGE OF THE GIANT PLANKTON MONSTER
Select Cheat Codes from the Extras menu and enter LASER. Select Activate Bonus Items to enable this bonus item.

PIRATE PATRICK IN ROOFTOP RUMBLE
Select Cheat Codes from the Extras menu and enter PIRATE. Select Activate Bonus Items to enable this bonus item.

HOVERCRAFT VEHICLE SKIN IN HYPNOTIC HIGHWAY—PLANKTON
Select Cheat Codes from the Extras menu and enter HOVER. Select Activate Bonus Items to enable this bonus item.

SSX BLUR

ALL CHARACTERS
Select Cheats from the Options menu and enter NoHolds.

ENTIRE MOUNTAIN UNLOCKED
Select Cheats from the Options menu and enter MasterKey.

ALL OUTFITS
Select Cheats from the Options menu and enter ClothShop.

YETI OUTFIT
Select Cheats from the Options menu and enter WildFur.

Wii™

ALL CHAMPIONSHIP LOCATIONS

Select Cheat Codes from the Extras menu and enter FREEVISIT.

ALL LEAF SLIDE STAGES

Select Cheat Codes from the Extras menu and enter GOINGDOWN.

ALL MULTIPLAYER LEVELS

Select Cheat Codes from the Extras menu and enter MULTIPASS.

ALL BOARDS

Select Cheat Codes from the Extras menu and enter MYPRECIOUS.

ASTRAL BOARD

Select Cheat Codes from the Extras menu and enter ASTRAL.

MONSOON BOARD

Select Cheat Codes from the Extras menu and enter MONSOON.

TINE SHOCKWAVE BOARD

Select Cheat Codes from the Extras menu and enter TINYSHOCKWAVE.

ALL CHARACTER CUSTOMIZATIONS

Select Cheat Codes from the Extras menu and enter TOPFASHION.

PLAY AS ARNOLD

Select Cheat Codes from the Extras menu and enter TINYBUTSTRONG.

PLAY AS ELLIOT

Select Cheat Codes from the Extras menu and enter SURPRISEGUEST.

PLAY AS GEEK

Select Cheat Codes from the Extras menu and enter SLOWANDSTEADY.

PLAY AS TANK EVANS

Select Cheat Codes from the Extras menu and enter IMTHEBEST.

PLAY AS TATSUHI KOBAYASHI

Select Cheat Codes from the Extras menu and enter KOBAYASHI.

PLAY AS ZEKE TOPANGA

Select Cheat Codes from the Extras menu and enter THELEGEND.

ALL VIDEOS AND SPEN GALLERY

Select Cheat Codes from the Extras menu and enter WATCHMOVIE.

ART GALLERY

Select Cheat Codes from the Extras menu and enter NICEPLACE.

TIGER WOODS PGA TOUR 07

ALL CHARACTERS
Select Password from the Options menu and enter gameface.

UNLOCK ADIDAS ITEMS
Select Password from the Options menu and enter three stripes.

UNLOCK BRIDGESTONE ITEMS
Select Password from the Options menu and enter shojiro.

UNLOCK COBRA ITEMS
Select Password from the Options menu and enter snakeking.

UNLOCK EA SPORTS ITEMS
Select Password from the Options menu and enter inthegame.

UNLOCK GRAFALLOY ITEMS
Select Password from the Options menu and enter just shafts.

UNLOCK MACGREGOR ITEMS
Select Password from the Options menu and enter mactec.

UNLOCK MIZUNO ITEMS
Select Password from the Options menu and enter rihachinrzo.

UNLOCK NIKE ITEMS
Select Password from the Options menu and enter justdoit.

UNLOCK OAKLEY ITEMS
Select Password from the Options menu and enter jannard.

UNLOCK PGA TOUR ITEMS
Select Password from the Options menu and enter lightning.

UNLOCK PING ITEMS
Select Password from the Options menu and enter solheim.

UNLOCK PRECEPT ITEMS
Select Password from the Options menu and enter guys are good.

UNLOCK TAYLORMADE ITEMS
Select Password from the Options menu and enter mradams.

TIGER WOODS PGA TOUR 08

ALL CLUBS
Select Passwords from the Options and enter PROSHOP.

ALL GOLFERS
Select Passwords from the Options and enter GAMEFACE.

BRIDGESTONE ITEMS
Select Passwords from the Options and enter NOTJUSTTIRES.

BUICK ITEMS
Select Passwords from the Options and enter THREESTRIPES.

CLEVELAND GOLF ITEMS
Select Passwords from the Options and enter CLEVELAND.

COBRA ITEMS
Select Passwords from the Options and enter SNAKEKING.

EA ITEMS
Select Passwords from the Options and enter INTHEGAME.

GRAFALLOY ITEMS
Select Passwords from the Options and enter JUSTSHAFTS.

MIZUNO ITEMS
Select Passwords from the Options and enter RIHACHINRIZO.

NIKE ITEMS
Select Passwords from the Options and enter JUSTDOIT.

PRECEPT ITEMS
Select Passwords from the Options and enter GUYSAREGOOD.

TMNT

CHALLENGE MAP 2
At the Main menu, hold Z and press A, A, A, 1, A.

DON'S BIG HEAD GOODIE
At the Main menu, hold Z and press 1, A, C, 2.

TONY HAWK'S DOWNHILL JAM

BOARDS

BOARD	COMPLETE EVENT
Street Issue	Street Issue Slalom (Tier 1)
Solar	Tourist Trap (Tier 1)
Chaos	Vista Point Race (Random)
Kuni	Hong Kong Race (Tier 2)
Red Rascal	San Francisco Elimination (Tier 3)
Cruiser	Grind Time (Tier 4)
Illuminate	Machu Pichu Top to Bottom Tricks (Tier 4)
Dark Sign	He-Man Club/Girl Power (Tier 5)
Spooky	Clearance Sale (Tier 6)
Black Icer	Precision Shopping Slalom (Tier 7)
Ripper	Del Centro Slalom (Tier 7)
Dispersion	Machu Picchu Top to Bottom Race (Tier 7)
Makonga	Mall Rats (Tier 8)
Goddess of Speed	The Hills Are Alive Tricks (Tier 9)
Dragon	Swiss Elimination (Tier 9)

OUTFITS

CHARACTER	OUTFIT	COMPLETE EVENT
Gunnar	High-G Armor	Gunnar's Threads (Tier 1)
Kyla	Shooting Star	Cuzco Challenge Race (Tier 2)
Tony	Business Camouflage	Mountain High Race (Random)
Budd	The Bohemian	Catacombs Slalom (Tier 2)
Tiffany	Baby Blue	Tourist Spot Slalom (Tier 2)
Ammon	Money Suit	Edinburgh Full Tricks (Tier 3)
Jynx	Black Tuesday	Road to Cuzco Race (Tier 3)
Jynx	Graveyard Casual	Cable Car Tricks (Random)
Crash	Bombs Away	Fallen Empire Race (Tier 4)
MacKenzie	Spitfire Squadron	Edinburgh Full Race (Tier 4)
Gunnar	Street Creds	Favela Rush (Tier 4)
Crash	Brace for Impact	Out of the Woods Race (Tier 5)
Kyla	Touchdown	Clear the Streets (Tier 5)
Tony	Mariachi Loco	Out of the Woods Tricks (Random)
MacKenzie	Killer Bee	High Street Slalom (Tier 6)
Ammon	Tommy T	Seaside Village Race (Tier 6)
Budd	Power of Chi	Rome Elimination (Tier 6)
Crash	Space Monkey	Lift Off (Tier 7)
Jynx	Funeral Fun	Del Centro Race (Tier 7)
Budd	Toys for Bob	Waterfront Race (Random)
MacKenzie	Street Combat	Parking Lot Shuffle (Tier 7)
Gunnar	Black Knight	Park It Anywhere (Tier 7)
Tiffany	Nero Style	Rome Burning (Tier 7)
Tiffany	Military Chic	Shopping Spree (Tier 8)
Ammon	Tan Suit	Saturday Matinee (Tier 9)
Tony	Downhill Jam	Hills Are Alive Race (Tier 9)
Kyla	Alpine Red	San Francisco Full Slalom (Tier 9)

SKATERS

SKATER	COMPLETE EVENT
Kevin Staab	Kevin's Challenge (Random)
MacKenzie	MacKenzie's Challenge (Tier 2)
Crash	Crash Test (Tier 3)
Armando Gnutbagh	Unknown Skater (Tier 10)

CHEAT CODES

Select Cheat Codes from the Options menu and enter the following cheats. Select Toggle Cheats to enable/disable them.

FREE BOOST
Enter OOTBAGHFOREVER.

ALWAYS SPECIAL
Enter POINTHOGGER.

UNLOCK MANUALS
Enter IMISSMANUALS.

PERFECT RAIL
Enter LIKETILTINGAPLATE.

PERFECT MANUAL
Enter TIGHTROPEWALKER.

PERFECT STATS
Enter IAMBOB.

EXTREME CAR CRASHES
Enter WATCHFORDOORS.

FIRST-PERSON SKATER
Enter FIRSTPERSONJAM.

SHADOW SKATER
Enter CHIMNEYSWEEP.

DEMON SKATER
Enter EVILCHIMNEYSWEEP.

MINI SKATER
Enter DOWNTHERABBITHOLE.

GIGANTO-SKATER
Enter IWANNABETALLTALL.

INVISIBLE BOARD
Enter LOOKMANOBOARD.

INVISIBLE SKATER
Enter NOWYOUSEEME.

PICASSO SKATER
Enter FOURLIGHTS.

CHIPMUNK VOICES
Enter HELLOHELIUM.

DISPLAY COORDINATES
Enter DISPLAYCOORDINATES.

LARGE BIRDS
Enter BIRDBIRDBIRDBIRD.

REALLY LARGE BIRDS
Enter BIRDBIRDBIRDBIRDBIRD.

TINY PEOPLE
Enter SHRINKTHEPEOPLE.

*There is no need to toggle on
the following cheats. They take
effect after entering them.*

ALL EVENTS
Enter ADVENTURESOFKWANG.

ALL SKATERS
Enter IMINTERFACING.

ALL BOARDS/OUTFITS
Enter RAIDTHEWOODSHED.

ALL MOVIES
Enter FREEBOZZLER.

TONY HAWK'S PROVING GROUND

Select Cheat Codes from the Options and enter the following cheats. Some codes need to be enabled by selecting Cheats from the Options during a game.

UNLOCK	CHEAT
Unlocks Bosco	MOREMILK
Unlocks Cam	NOTACAMERA
Unlocks Cooper	THECOOP
Unlocks Eddie X	SKETCHY
Unlocks El Patinador	PILEDRIVER
Unlocks Eric	FLYAWAY
Unlocks Judy Nails	LOVEROCKNROLL
Unlocks Mad Dog	RABBIES
Unlocks MCA	INTERGALACTIC
Unlocks Mel	NOTADUDE
Unlocks Rube	LOOKSSMELLY
Unlocks Spence	DAPPER

UNLOCK	CHEAT
Unlocks Shayne	MOVERS
Unlocks TV Producer	SHAKER
Unlock FDR	THEPREZPARK
Unlock Lansdowne	THELOCALPARK
Unlock Air & Space Museum	THEINDOORPARK
Unlocks all Fun Items	OVERTHETOP
Unlock all Game Movies	WATCHTHIS
Unlock all Rigger Pieces	IMGONNABUILD
All specials unlocked and in player's special list	LOTSOFTRICKS
Full Stats	BEEFEDUP
Give player +50 skill points	NEEDSHELP

The following cheats lock you out of the Leaderboards:

Unlocks Perfect Manual	STILLAINTFALLIN
Unlocks Perfect Rail	AINTFALLIN
Unlocks Unlimited Focus	MYOPIC

You cannot use the Video Editor with the following cheats:

Invisible Man	THEMISSING
Mini Skater	TINYTATER

TRANSFORMERS: THE GAME

INFINITE HEALTH
At the Main menu, press Left, Left, Up, Left, Right, Down, Right.

INFINITE AMMO
At the Main menu, press Up, Down, Left, Right, Up, Up, Down.

NO MILITARY OR POLICE
At the Main menu, press Right, Left, Right, Left, Right, Left, Right.

ALL MISSIONS
At the Main menu, press Down, Up, Left, Right, Right, Right, Up, Down.

BONUS CYBERTRON MISSIONS
At the Main menu, press Right, Up, Up, Down, Right, Left, Left.

GENERATION 1 SKIN: JAZZ
At the Main menu, press Left, Up, Down, Down, Left, Up, Right.

GENERATION 1 SKIN: MEGATRON
At the Main menu, press Down, Left, Left, Down, Right, Right, Up.

GENERATION 1 SKIN: OPTIMUS PRIME
At the Main menu, press Down, Right, Left, Up, Down, Down, Left.

GENERATION 1 SKIN: ROBOVISION OPTIMUS PRIME
At the Main menu, press Down, Down, Up, Up, Right, Right, Right.

GENERATION 1 SKIN: STARSCREAM
At the Main menu, press Right, Down, Left, Left, Down, Up, Up.

WII SPORTS

BOWLING BALL COLOR

After selecting your Mii, hold the following direction on the D-pad and press A at the warning screen:

DIRECTION	COLOR
Up	Blue
Right	Gold
Down	Green
Left	Red

NO HUD IN GOLF

Hold 2 as you select a course to disable the power meter, map, and wind speed meter.

BLUE TENNIS COURT

After selecting your Mii, hold 2 and press A at the warning screen.

Nintendo Wii™: Virtual Console

For the Virtual Console games, a Classic Controller may be needed to enter some codes.

ADVENTURES OF LOLO

PASSWORDS

LEVEL	PASSWORD	LEVEL	PASSWORD
1-2	BCBT	6-2	CQZG
1-3	BDBR	6-3	CRZD
1-4	BGBQ	6-4	CTZC
1-5	BHBP	6-5	CVZB
2-1	BJBM	7-1	CYYZ
2-2	BKBL	7-2	CZYY
2-3	BLBK	7-3	DBYV
2-4	BMBJ	7-4	DCYT
2-5	BPBH	7-5	DDYR
3-1	BQBG	8-1	DGYQ
3-2	BRBD	8-2	DHYP
3-3	BTBC	8-3	DJYM
3-4	BVBB	8-4	DKYL
3-5	BYZZ	8-5	DLYK
4-1	BZZY	9-1	DMYJ
4-2	CBZV	9-2	DPYH
4-3	CCZT	9-3	DQYG
4-4	CDZR	9-4	DRYD
4-5	CGZQ	9-5	DTYC
5-1	CHZP	10-1	DVYB
5-2	CJZM	10-2	DYYZ
5-3	CKZL	10-3	DZYV
5-4	CLZK	10-4	GBVV
5-5	CMZJ	10-5	GCVT
6-1	CPZH		

ADVENTURES OF LOLO 2

MORE DIFFICULTIES
Enter PROA, PROB, PROC, or PROD as a password.

PASSWORDS

LEVEL	PASSWORD	LEVEL	PASSWORD
1-1	PPHP	6-1	HZKC
1-2	PHPK	6-2	HYKL
1-3	PQPD	6-3	HMKB
1-4	PVPT	6-4	HJKR
1-5	PRPJ	6-5	HTKV
2-5	PCPZ	7-1	HDKQ
2-5	PLPY	7-2	HKKH
2-5	PBPM	7-3	QPKP
2-5	PGPG	7-4	QHDK
2-5	PZPC	7-5	QDDD
3-1	PYPL	8-1	QVDT
3-2	PMPB	8-2	QRDJ
3-3	PJPR	8-3	QBDM
3-4	PTPV	8-4	QLDY
3-5	PDPQ	8-5	QCDZ
4-1	PKPH	9-1	QGDG
4-2	HPPP	9-2	QZDC
4-3	HHKK	9-3	QYDL
4-4	HQKD	9-4	QMDB
4-5	HVKT	9-5	QJDR
5-1	HRKJ	10-1	QTDV
5-2	HBKM	10-2	QDDQ
5-3	HLKY	10-3	QKDH
5-4	HCKZ	10-4	VPDP
5-5	HGKG	10-5	VHTK

ALTERED BEAST

LEVEL SELECT
At the Title screen, press B + Start.

BEAST SELECT
At the Title screen, hold A + B + C + Down/Left and press Start.

SOUND TEST
At the Title screen, hold A + C + Up/Right and press Start.

BOMBERMAN '93

PASSWORDS

LEVEL	PASSWORD	LEVEL	PASSWORD
A-1	CBCCBBDB	D-5	JHGFKJKC
A-2	DDCDBBGB	D-6	KKHFKJLC
A-3	FFDDBBJB	D-7	KLHFKJMC
A-4	GHFDBCLB	D-8	LMHFKJNC
A-5	GJFDBCMB	E-1	NFHFTJQC
A-6	HKFDBCNB	E-2	PGJFTJSC
A-7	HLFDBCPB	E-3	PHJFTJTC
A-8	JNFDBCQB	E-4	GFHFTDBD
B-1	GCDDCCKB	E-5	GGHFTDCD
B-2	HFFFCCMB	E-6	HHHFTDDD
B-3	JGFFCCNB	E-7	JKHGTDGD
B-4	JHFFCCPB	E-8	KLJGTDJD
B-5	KKGFCCRB	F-1	KCJGTJGD
B-6	LLGFCCSB	F-2	LDKGTJJD
B-7	LMGFCCTB	F-3	LFKGTJKD
B-8	CKFFCHBC	F-4	MHLGTJLD
C-1	LFGFFCQB	F-5	MJLGTHLD
C-2	LGGFFCRB	F-6	MKLGTJND
C-3	MHGFFCSB	F-7	NLLGTJPD
C-4	DFGFFHBC	F-8	QNMHTJSD
C-5	DGGFFHCC	G-1	JBLHTXBF
C-6	FHGFFJFC	G-2	KCMHTXDF
C-7	GKGFFJGC	G-3	KDMHTXFF
C-8	GLGFFJHC	G-4	LGNHTXHF
D-1	GBGFKJFC	G-5	MHNHTXJF
D-2	HDGFKJGC	G-6	MJNHTXKF
D-3	HFGFKJHC	G-7	NLPHTXLF
D-4	JGGFKJJC	G-8	NMPHTXMF

CHEW MAN FU

GAME COMPLETE PASSWORDS
Select Password and enter 573300 or 441300.

COMIX ZONE

STAGE SELECT
At the Jukebox menu, press C on the following numbers:
14, 15, 18, 5, 13, 1, 3, 18, 15, 6
A voice says "Oh Yeah" when entered correctly. Then, press C on 1 through 6 to warp to that stage.

INVINCIBLE
At the Jukebox menu, press C on the following numbers:
3, 12, 17, 2, 2, 10, 2, 7, 7, 11
A voice says "Oh Yeah" when entered correctly.

CREDITS
At the Options menu press A + B + C.

DR. ROBOTNIK'S MEAN BEAN MACHINE

EASY PASSWORDS

STAGE	PASSWORD
02: Frankly	Red Bean, Red Bean, Red Bean, Has Bean
03: Humpty	Clear Bean, Purple Bean, Clear Bean, Green Bean
04: Coconuts	Red Bean, Clear Bean, Has Bean, Yellow Bean
05: Davy Sprocket	Clear Bean, Blue Bean, Blue Bean, Purple Bean
06: Skweel	Clear Bean, Red Bean, Clear Bean, Purple Bean
07: Dynamight	Purple Bean, Yellow Bean, Red Bean, Blue Bean
08: Grounder	Yellow Bean, Purple Bean, Has Bean, Blue Bean
09: Spike	Yellow Bean, Purple Bean, Has Bean, Blue Bean
10: Sir Ffuzy-Logik	Red Bean, Yellow Bean, Clear Bean, Has Bean
11: Dragon Breath	Green Bean, Purple Bean, Blue Bean, Clear Bean
12: Scratch	Red Bean, Has Bean, Has Bean, Yellow Bean
13: Dr. Robotnik	Yellow Bean, Has Bean, Blue Bean, Blue Bean

NORMAL PASSWORDS

STAGE	PASSWORD
02: Frankly	Has Bean, Clear Bean, Yellow Bean, Yellow Bean
03: Humpty	Blue Bean, Clear Bean, Red Bean, Yellow Bean
04: Coconuts	Yellow Bean, Blue Bean, Clear Bean, Purple Bean
05: Davy Sprocket	Has Bean, Green Bean, Blue Bean, Yellow Bean
06: Skweel	Green Bean, Purple Bean, Purple Bean, Yellow Bean
07: Dynamight	Purple Bean, Blue Bean, Green Bean, Has Bean
08: Grounder	Green Bean, Has Bean, Clear Bean, Yellow Bean
09: Spike	Blue Bean, Purple Bean, Has Bean, Has Bean
10: Sir Ffuzy-Logik	Has Bean, Red Bean, Yellow Bean, Clear Bean
11: Dragon Breath	Clear Bean, Red Bean, Red Bean, Blue Bean
12: Scratch	Green Bean, Green Bean, Clear Bean, Yellow Bean
13: Dr. Robotnik	Purple Bean, Yellow Bean, Has Bean, Clear Bean

HARD PASSWORDS

STAGE	PASSWORD
02: Frankly	Clear Bean, Green Bean, Yellow Bean, Yellow Bean
03: Humpty	Yellow Bean, Purple Bean, Clear Bean, Purple Bean
04: Coconuts	Blue Bean, Green Bean, Clear Bean, Blue Bean
05: Davy Sprocket	Red Bean, Purple Bean, Green Bean, Green Bean
06: Skweel	Yellow Bean, Yellow Bean, Clear Bean, Green Bean
07: Dynamight	Purple Bean, Clear Bean, Blue Bean, Blue Bean
08: Grounder	Clear Bean, Yellow Bean, Has Bean, Yellow Bean
09: Spike	Purple Bean, Blue Bean, Blue Bean, Green Bean
10: Sir Ffuzy-Logik	Clear Bean, Green Bean, Red Bean, Yellow Bean
11: Dragon Breath	Blue Bean, Yellow Bean, Yellow Bean, Has Bean
12: Scratch	Green Bean, Clear Bean, Clear Bean, Blue Bean
13: Dr. Robotnik	Has Bean, Clear Bean, Purple Bean, Has Bean

HARDEST PASSWORDS

STAGE	PASSWORD
02: Frankly	Blue Bean, Blue Bean, Green Bean, Yellow Bean
03: Humpty	Green Bean, Yellow Bean, Green Bean, Clear Bean
04: Coconuts	Purple Bean, Purple Bean, RedBean, Has Bean
05: Davy Sprocket	Green Bean, Red Bean, Purple Bean, Blue Bean
06: Skweel	Purple Bean, Clear Bean, Green Bean, Yellow Bean
07: Dynamight	Blue Bean, Purple Bean, Green Bean, Has Bean
08: Grounder	Clear Bean, Purple Bean, Yellow Bean, Has Bean
09: Spike	Purple Bean, Green Bean, Has Bean, Clear Bean
10: Sir Ffuzy-Logik	Green Bean, Blue Bean, Yellow Bean, Has Bean
11: Dragon Breath	Green Bean, Purple Bean, Has Bean, Red Bean
12: Scratch	Red Bean, Green Bean, Has Bean, Blue Bean
13: Dr. Robotnik	Red Bean, Red Bean, Clear Bean, Yellow Bean

DUNGEON EXPLORER

PLAY AS PRINCESS AKI
Enter JBBNJ HDCOG as a password.

PLAY AS THE HERMIT
Enter IMGAJ MDPAI as a password.

HOMING WEAPON
Enter HOMIN GAAAA as a password.

CHANGE NAMES
Enter CHECK NAMEA as a password.

INVINCIBILITY
Enter DEBDE DEBDA as a password, then press Plus + 2.

JUMP TO ANY LOCATION
After enabling the Invincibility code, enter one of the 15 bushes in front of Axis castle to jump to the following locations:

LOCATION	BUSH (STARTING FROM LEFT)
Natas	1
Balamous Tower	2
Rotterroad	3
Mistose Dungeon	4
Ratonix Dungeon	5
Reraport Maze	6
Rally Maze	7
Bullbeast	8
Melba Village	9
After Gutworm	10
Nostalgia Dungeon	11
Water Castle	12
Road to Cherry Tower	13
Stonefield	14
Karma Castle	15

ECCO THE DOLPHIN

DEBUG MENU
Pause the game with Ecco facing the screen and press Right, B, C, B, C, Down, C, Up.

INFINITE AIR
Enter LIFEFISH as a password.

PASSWORDS

LEVEL	PASSWORD
The Undercaves	WEFIDNMP
The Vents	BQDPXJDS
The Lagoon	JNSBRIKY
Ridge Water	NTSBZTKB
Open Ocean	YWGTTJNI
Ice Zone	HZIFZBMF
Hard Water	LRFJRQLI
Cold Water	UYNFRQLC
Island Zone	LYTIOQLZ
Deep Water	MNOPOQLR
The Marble	RJNTQQLZ
The Library	RTGXQQLE
Deep City	DDXPQQLJ
City of Forever	MSDBRQLA
Jurassic Beach	IYCBUNLB
Pteranodon Pond	DMXEUNLI
Origin Beach	EGRIUNLB
Trilobite Circle	IELMUNLB
Dark Water	RKEQUNLN
City of Forever 2	HPQIGPLA
The Tube	JUMFKMLB
The Machine	GXUBKMLF
The Last Fight	TSONLMLU

F-ZERO X

ALL TRACKS, VEHICLES, AND DIFFICULTIES
At the Mode Select screen, press Up on the D-pad, L, R, Up on the Right control stick, X, Y, ZR, Plus.

GOLDEN AXE

LEVEL SELECT
At the Character Select screen, in Arcade mode, hold Down/Left and press B + Start.

START WITH 9 CONTINUES
At the Character Select screen, in Arcade mode, hold Down/Left and then hold A + C. Release the buttons and select a character.

GRADIUS

MAX OUT WEAPONS
Pause the game and press Up, Up, Down, Down, Left, Right, Left, Right, B, A.

GRADIUS III

FULL POWER-UP
Pause the game and press Up, Up, Down, Down, L, R, L, R, B, A.

SUICIDE
Pause the game and press Up, Up, Down, Down, Left, Right, Left, Right, B, A.

ICE HOCKEY

NO GOALIES
At the Title screen, hold A + B on controllers 1 and 2. Then, press start on controller 1.

MILITARY MADNESS

PASSWORDS

LEVEL	PASSWORD
01	REVOLT
02	ICARUS
03	CYRANO
04	RAMSEY
05	NEWTON
06	SENECA
07	SABINE
08	ARATUS
09	GALIOS
10	DARWIN
11	PASCAL
12	HALLEY
13	BORMAN
14	APOLLO
15	KAISER
16	NECTOR
17	MILTON
18	IRAGAN
19	LIPTUS
20	INAKKA
21	TETROS
22	ARBINE
23	RECTOS
24	YEANTA
25	MONOGA
26	ATTAYA
27	DESHTA
28	NEKOSE
29	ERATIN
30	SOLCIS
31	SAGINE
32	WINNER

SOUND TEST
Enter ONGAKU as a password.

RISTAR

Select Passwords from the Options menu and enter the following:

LEVEL SELECT
ILOVEU

BOSS RUSH MODE
MUSEUM

TIME ATTACK MODE
DOFEEL

TOUGHER DIFFICULTY
SUPER

ONCHI MUSIC
MAGURO. Activate this from the Sound Test.

CLEARS PASSWORD
XXXXXX

GAME COPYRIGHT INFO
AGES

SOLOMON'S KEY

CONTINUE GAME
At the Game Deviation Value screen, hold Up + A + B.

SONIC THE HEDGEHOG

LEVEL SELECT
At the Title screen, press Up, Down, Left, Right. A sound of a ring being collected plays if the code is entered correctly. Hold A and press Start to access the Level Select.

CONTROL MODE
At the Title screen, press Up, C, Down, C, Left, C, Right, C. Then, hold A and press Start.

DEBUG MODE
After entering the Control Mode, hold A and press Start. Press A to change Sonic into another sprite. Press B to change back to Sonic. Press C to place that sprite. Pause the game and press A to restart. Hold B for slow motion and press C to advance a frame.

CHANGE DEMO
During the demo, hold C and Sonic will start making mistakes.

WARIO'S WOODS

HARD BATTLES
Highlight VS. Computer Mode, hold Left and press Start.

PLAYSTATION® 2

EVERYONE

4X4 EVO 2

ALIEN HOMINID

AVATAR: THE LAST AIRBENDER

BRATZ: FOREVER DIAMONDZ

BRATZ: THE MOVIE

CARS

CHICKEN LITTLE

EA SPORTS ARENA FOOTBALL

ICE AGE 2: THE MELTDOWN

IN THE GROOVE

LEGO STAR WARS II: THE ORIGINAL TRILOGY

MADDEN NFL 07

MAJOR LEAGUE BASEBALL 2K7

MLB 07: THE SHOW

MVP 07 NCAA BASEBALL

NASCAR 07

NASCAR 08

NBA 07

NBA 2K7

NBA 2K8

NBA LIVE 07

NCAA FOOTBALL 07

NCAA FOOTBALL 08

NEED FOR SPEED CARBON

NHL 08

OUTRUN 2006: COAST 2 COAST

OVER THE HEDGE

RATATOUILLE

SLY 3: HONOR AMONG THIEVES

SPLASHDOWN: RIDES GONE WILD

STRAWBERRY SHORTCAKE: THE SWEET DREAMS GAME

TAK: THE GREAT JUJU CHALLENGE

TEENAGE MUTANT NINJA TURTLES 3: MUTANT NIGHTMARE

TIGER WOODS PGA TOUR 07

TIGER WOODS PGA TOUR 08

TIM BURTON'S THE NIGHTMARE BEFORE CHRISTMAS: OOGIE'S REVENGE

TOKYO XTREME RACER DRIFT 2

TY THE TASMANIAN TIGER 3: NIGHT OF THE QUINKAN

EVERYONE 10+

AVATAR: THE LAST AIRBENDER—THE BURNING EARTH

BRAVE: THE SEARCH FOR SPIRIT DANCER

CAPCOM CLASSICS COLLECTION VOL. 2

CRASH OF THE TITANS

THE GRIM ADVENTURES OF BILLY & MANDY

THE LEGEND OF SPYRO: A NEW BEGINNING

SHREK THE THIRD

SPIDER-MAN: FRIEND OR FOE

STAR TREK: ENCOUNTERS

TEST DRIVE UNLIMITED

THRILLVILLE

THRILLVILLE: OFF THE RAILS

TIM BURTON'S THE NIGHTMARE BEFORE CHRISTMAS: OOGIE'S REVENGE

TMNT

TONY HAWK'S DOWNHILL JAM

PLAYSTATION® 2

TEEN

TEEN — CONTENT RATED BY ESRB

DOG'S LIFE
ERAGON
FLATOUT 2
FROM RUSSIA WITH LOVE
GUITAR HERO
GUITAR HERO II
GUITAR HERO III: LEGENDS OF ROCK
GUITAR HERO ENCORE: ROCKS THE 80S
.HACK//G.U. VOL. 1//REBIRTH
JUICED
JUICED 2: HOT IMPORT NIGHTS
L.A. RUSH
MARVEL ULTIMATE ALLIANCE
NARUTO: ULTIMATE NINJA 2
ONE PIECE: GRAND BATTLE
PUMP IT UP: EXCEED

STAR TREK: ENCOUNTERS
STAR WARS: BATTLEFRONT II
STREET FIGHTER ALPHA ANTHOLOGY
STUNTMAN IGNITION
SUPERMAN RETURNS
TAITO LEGENDS
THE DA VINCI CODE
THE SIMS 2: CASTAWAY
THE SIMS 2: PETS
TONY HAWK'S PROJECT 8
TONY HAWK'S PROVING GROUND
TRANSFORMERS: THE GAME
ULTIMATE SPIDER-MAN
VICTORIOUS BOXERS 2: FIGHTING SPIRIT
X-MEN: THE OFFICIAL GAME

Table of Contents

4X4 EVO 2

ALL TRUCKS
At the Title screen, press **L1**, **L2**, **R1**, **R2**, **L1**, **R1**.

$25,000
Pause the game and press **L2**, ⏺, **R1**, ⏺, **R1**, **L1**, ⏺, **L2**, ⏺, **R2**, ⏺, **R1**.

FASTER SPEED
Pause the game and press **L1**, **L2**, **R1**, **R2**, ⏺, ⏺.

NORMAL SPEED
Pause the game and press **L1**, **L2**, **R1**, **R2**, ⏺, ⏺.

SLOW SPEED
Pause the game and press **L1**, **L2**, **R1**, **R2**, ⏺, ⏺.

SLOWER SPEED
Pause the game and press **L1**, **L2**, **R1**, **R2**, ⏺, ⏺.

ALIEN HOMINID

ALL LEVELS, MINI-GAMES, & HATS

Select Player 1 Setup or Player 2 Setup and change the name to ROYGBIV.

HATS FOR 2-PLAYER GAME

Go to the Options and rename your alien one of the following:

Abe	cletus	grrl
april	dandy	princess
behemoth	Goodman	superfly

AVATAR: THE LAST AIRBENDER

ALL TREASURE MAPS
Select Code Entry from Extras and enter 37437.

1 HIT DISHONOR
Select Code Entry from Extras and enter 54641.

DOUBLE DAMAGE
Select Code Entry from Extras and enter 34743.

UNLIMITED COPPER
Select Code Entry from Extras and enter 23637.

UNLIMITED CHI
Select Code Entry from Extras and enter 24463.

UNLIMITED HEALTH
Select Code Entry from Extras and enter 94677.

NEVERENDING STEALTH
Select Code Entry from Extras and enter 53467.

CHARACTER CONCEPT ART GALLERY
Select Code Entry from Extras and enter 97831.

AVATAR: THE LAST AIRBENDER – THE BURNING EARTH

1 HIT DISHONOR
At the Main menu, press **L1** and select Code Entry. Enter 28260.

ALL BONUS GAME
At the Main menu, press **L1** and select Code Entry. Enter 99801.

ALL GALLERY ITEMS
At the Main menu, press **L1** and select Code Entry. Enter 85061.

DOUBLE DAMAGE
At the Main menu, press **L1** and select Code Entry. Enter 90210.

INFINITE HEALTH
At the Main menu, press **L1** and select Code Entry. Enter 65049.

MAX LEVEL
At the Main menu, press **L1** and select Code Entry. Enter 89121.

UNLIMITED SPECIAL ATTACKS
At the Main menu, press **L1** and select Code Entry. Enter 66206.

BRATZ: FOREVER DIAMONDZ

1000 BLINGZ
While in the Bratz Office, use the Cheat computer to enter SIZZLN.

2000 BLINGZ
While in the Bratz Office, use the Cheat computer to enter FLAUNT.

PET TREATS
While in the Bratz Office, use the Cheat computer to enter TREATZ.

GIFT SET A
While in the Bratz Office, use the Cheat computer to enter STYLIN.

GIFT SET B
While in the Bratz Office, use the Cheat computer to enter SKATIN.

GIFT SET C
While in the Bratz Office, use the Cheat computer to enter JEWELZ.

GIFT SET E
While in the Bratz Office, use the Cheat computer to enter DIMNDZ.

BRATZ: THE MOVIE

FEELIN' PRETTY CLOTHING LINE
In the Bratz office at the laptop computer, enter PRETTY.

HIGH SCHOOL CLOTHING LINE
In the Bratz office at the laptop computer, enter SCHOOL.

PASSION 4 FASHION CLOTHING LINE
In the Bratz office at the laptop computer, enter ANGELZ.

SWEETZ CLOTHING LINE
In the Bratz office at the laptop computer, enter SWEETZ.

BRAVE: THE SEARCH FOR SPIRIT DANCER

The following codes will disable saving.

INFINITE ARROWS
At the Main menu, press Down, Left, Up, Right, **R2**, **L2**, **R2**, **L2**.

INFINITE HEALTH
At the Main menu, press Up, Down, Up, Down, **L1**, **L2**, **R2**, **R1**.

INFINITE SPIRIT ENERGY
At the Main menu, press Left, Right, Left, Right, **R2**, **R2**, **L1**, **R2**.

LEVEL UNLOCK
At the Main menu, press Down, Down. Up, Down, R2, L2, Up, Down.

TOTEM UNLOCK
At the Main menu, press Up, Up, Down. ●, L1, Left, R1, Right.

ALTERNATE TOTEM UNLOCK
At the Main menu, press Up, Up, Down, ●, L1, Left, R1, Right.

CAPCOM CLASSICS COLLECTION VOL. 2

UNLOCK EVERYTHING
At the Title screen, press Left, Right, Up, Down, L1, R1, L1, R1. This code unlocks Cheats, Tips, Art, and Sound Tests.

CARS

UNLOCK EVERYTHING
Select Cheat Codes from the Options and enter IF900HP.

ALL CHARACTERS
Select Cheat Codes from the Options and enter YAYCARS.

ALL CHARACTER SKINS
Select Cheat Codes from the Options and enter R4MONE.

ALL MINI-GAMES AND COURSES
Select Cheat Codes from the Options and enter MATTL66.

MATER'S COUNTDOWN CLEAN-UP MINI-GAME AND MATER'S SPEEDY CIRCUIT
Select Cheat Codes from the Options and enter TRGTEXC.

FAST START
Select Cheat Codes from the Options and enter IMSPEED.

INFINITE BOOST
Select Cheat Codes from the Options and
enter VROOOOM.

ART
Select Cheat Codes from the Options and
enter CONC3PT.

VIDEOS
Select Cheat Codes from the Options and
enter WATCHIT.

CHICKEN LITTLE

INVINCIBILITY
Select Cheat Codes from the Extras menu and enter Baseball, Baseball, Baseball, Shirt.

BIG FEET
Select Cheat Codes from the Extras menu and enter Hat, Glove, Glove, Hat.

BIG HAIR
Select Cheat Codes from the Extras menu and enter Baseball, Bat, Bat, Baseball.

BIG HEAD
Select Cheat Codes from the Extras menu and enter Hat, Helmet, Helmet, Hat.

PAPER PANTS
Select Cheat Codes from the Extras menu and enter Bat, Bat, Hat, Hat.

SUNGLASSES
Select Cheat Codes from the Extras menu and enter Glove, Glove, Helmet, Helmet.

UNDERWEAR
Select Cheat Codes from the Extras menu and enter Hat, Hat, Shirt, Shirt.

CRASH OF THE TITANS

BIG HEAD CRASH
Pause the game, hold **R1**, and press ●, ●, ▲, ✖. Re-enter the code to disable.

SHADOW CRASH
Pause the game, hold **R1**, and press ▲, ●, ▲, ●. Re-enter the code to disable.

THE DA VINCI CODE

GOD MODE
Select Codes from the Options and enter VITRUVIAN MAN.

EXTRA HEALTH
Select Codes from the Options and
enter SACRED FEMININE.

MISSION SELECT
Select Codes from the Options and
enter CLOS LUCE 1519.

ONE-HIT FIST KILL
Select Codes from the Options and
enter PHILLIPS EXETER.

ONE-HIT WEAPON KILL
Select Codes from the Options and enter ROYAL HOLLOWAY.

ALL VISUAL DATABASE
Select Codes from the Options and enter APOCRYPHA.

ALL VISUAL DATABASE AND CONCEPT ART
Select Codes from the Options and enter ET IN ARCADIA EGO.

DOG'S LIFE

CHEAT MENU
During a game, press ● (Bark), ● (Bark), ● (Bark), hold ● (Growl), hold ● (Growl), hold ● (Growl), Left, Right, Down (Fart).

EA SPORTS ARENA FOOTBALL

BIG BALL
At the line of scrimmage, press **L1** + ●, Up, Up.

SMALL BALL
At the line of scrimmage, press **L1** + ●, Down, Down.

NORMAL SIZE BALL
At the line of scrimmage, press **L1** + ●, Up, Down.

MAX STATS IN QUICK PLAY
Load a profile with the name IronMen. This will maximize all players' stats in Quick Play.

ERAGON

FURY MODE
Pause the game, hold **L1** + **L2** + **R1** + **R2** and press ●, ●, ●, ●.

FLATOUT 2

ALL CARS AND 1,000,000 CREDITS
Select Enter Code from the Extras and enter GIEVEPIX.

1,000,000 CREDITS
Select Enter Code from the Extras and enter GIVECASH.

PIMPSTER CAR
Select Enter Code from the Extras and enter RUTTO.

FLATMOBILE CAR
Select Enter Code from the Extras and enter WOTKINS.

MOB CAR
Select Enter Code from the Extras and enter BIGTRUCK.

SCHOOL BUS
Select Enter Code from the Extras and enter GIEVCARPLZ.

ROCKET CAR
Select Enter Code from the Extras and enter KALJAKOPPA.

TRUCK
Select Enter Code from the Extras and enter ELPUEBLO.

FROM RUSSIA WITH LOVE

INFINITE HEALTH
During a game, press ✕, ✕, Up, ●, ▲, ✕, ✕.

INFINITE AMMO
During a game, press Up, Up, Down, Down, Left, ●, ●.

ASSAULT RIFLE
During a game, press ▲, ●, ●, ✕, ✕, Down, Down.

SOVIET HELICOPTER
During a game, press ▲, ●, ✕, ✕, Up, Down.

THE GRIM ADVENTURES OF BILLY & MANDY

CONCEPT ART
At the Main menu, hold ● and press Up, Up, Down, Down, Left, Right, Left, Right. Release ●.

GUITAR HERO

UNLOCK ALL
At the Main menu, press Yellow, Orange, Blue, Blue, Orange, Yellow, Yellow.

GUITAR HERO GUITAR CHEAT
At the Main menu, press Blue, Orange, Yellow, Blue, Blue.

CROWD METER CHEAT
At the Main menu, press Yellow, Blue, Orange, Orange, Blue, Blue, Yellow, Orange.

MONKEY HEAD CROWD CHEAT
At the Main menu, press Blue, Orange, Yellow, Yellow, Yellow, Blue, Orange.

SKULL HEAD CROWD CHEAT

At the Main menu, press Orange, Yellow, Blue, Blue, Orange, Yellow, Blue, Blue.

AIR GUITAR CHEAT

At the Main menu, press Orange, Orange, Blue, Yellow, Orange.

NO VENUE CHEAT

At the Main menu, press Blue, Yellow, Orange, Blue, Yellow, Orange.

GUITAR HERO II

AIR GUITAR

At the Main menu, press Yellow, Yellow, Blue, Orange, Yellow, Blue.

EYEBALL HEAD CROWD

At the Main menu, press Blue, Orange, Yellow, Orange, Yellow, Orange, Blue.

MONKEY HEAD CROWD

At the Main menu, press Orange, Blue, Yellow, Yellow, Orange, Blue, Yellow, Yellow.

FLAMING HEAD

At the Main menu, press Orange, Yellow, Orange, Orange, Yellow, Orange, Yellow, Yellow.

HORSE HEAD

At the Main menu, press Blue, Orange, Orange, Blue, Orange, Orange, Blue, Orange, Orange, Blue.

HYPER SPEED

At the Main menu, press Orange, Blue, Orange, Yellow, Orange, Blue, Orange, Yellow.

PERFORMANCE MODE

At the Main menu, press Yellow, Yellow, Blue, Yellow, Yellow, Yellow, Orange, Yellow, Yellow.

GUITAR HERO III: LEGENDS OF ROCK

To enter the following cheats, strum the guitar and hold the buttons indicated. For example, if it says Yellow + Orange, hold Yellow and Orange as you strum. Air Guitar, Precision Mode and Performance Mode can be toggled on and off from the Cheats menu. You can also change between five different levels of Hyperspeed at this menu.

ALL SONGS

Select Cheats from the Options. Choose Enter Cheat and enter Yellow + Orange, Red + Blue, Red + Orange, Green + Blue, Red + Yellow, Yellow + Orange, Red + Yellow, Red + Blue, Green + Yellow, Green + Yellow, Yellow + Blue, Yellow + Blue, Yellow + Orange, Yellow + Orange, Yellow + Blue, Yellow, Red, Red + Yellow, Red, Yellow, Orange.

AIR GUITAR

Select Cheats from the Options. Choose Enter Cheat and enter Blue + Yellow, Green + Yellow, Green + Yellow, Red + Blue, Red + Blue, Red + Yellow, Red + Yellow, Blue + Yellow, Green + Yellow, Green + Yellow, Red + Blue, Red + Blue, Red + Yellow, Red + Yellow, Green + Yellow, Green + Yellow, Red + Yellow, Red + Yellow.

PRECISION MODE

Select Cheats from the Options. Choose Enter Cheat and enter Green + Red, Green + Red, Green + Red, Red + Yellow, Red + Yellow, Red + Blue, Red + Blue, Yellow + Blue, Yellow + Orange, Yellow + Orange, Green + Red, Green + Red, Green + Red, Red + Yellow, Red + Yellow, Red + Blue, Red + Blue, Yellow + Blue, Yellow + Orange, Yellow + Orange.

HYPERSPEED

Select Cheats from the Options. Choose Enter Cheat and enter Orange, Blue, Orange, Yellow, Orange, Blue, Orange, Yellow.

PERFORMANCE MODE

Select Cheats from the Options. Choose Enter Cheat and enter Red + Yellow, Red + Blue, Red + Orange, Red + Blue, Red + Yellow, Green + Blue, Red + Yellow, Red + Blue.

GUITAR HERO ENCORE: ROCKS THE 80S

UNLOCK EVERYTHING

At the Main menu, press Blue, Orange, Yellow, Red, Orange, Yellow, Blue, Yellow, Red, Yellow, Blue, Yellow, Red, Yellow, Blue, Yellow.

HYPERSPEED

At the Main menu, press Yellow, Blue, Orange, Orange, Blue, Yellow, Yellow, Orange.

PERFORMANCE MODE

At the Main menu, press Blue, Blue, Orange, Yellow, Yellow, Blue, Orange, Blue.

AIR GUITAR

At the Main menu, press Yellow, Blue, Yellow, Orange, Blue, Blue.

EYEBALL HEAD CROWD

At the Main menu, press Yellow, Blue, Orange, Orange, Orange, Blue, Yellow.

MONKEY HEAD CROWD

At the Main menu, press Blue, Blue, Orange, Yellow, Blue, Blue, Orange, Yellow.

FLAME HEAD

At the Main menu, press Yellow, Orange, Yellow, Orange, Yellow, Orange, Blue, Orange.

HORSE HEAD

At the Main menu, press Blue, Orange, Orange, Orange, Yellow, Blue, Orange, Orange, Blue, Yellow.

.HACK//G.U. VOL. 1//REBIRTH

VOL.2 PREVIEW

On the desktop, hold R1 + R2 and press ●, ▲, ●, ▲. Release R1 and R2. Hold L1 + L2 and press Right, Up, Right, Up. Release L1 and L2 and press R3 + L3.

ICE AGE 2: THE MELTDOWN

INFINITE PEBBLES
Pause the game and press Down, Down, Left, Up, Up, Right, Up, Down.

INFINITE ENERGY
Pause the game and press Down, Left, Right, Down, Down, Right, Left, Down.

INFINITE HEALTH
Pause the game and press Up, Right, Down, Up, Left, Down, Right, Left.

IN THE GROOVE

ALL SONGS
At the Main menu, press Up, Right, Up, Right, Left, Down, Left, Down, Up, Right, Down, Left, Up, Left, Down, Right.

JUICED

ARCADE/CUSTOM MODE UNLOCKED
Select Cheats from the Extras menu and enter PINT.

JUICED 2: HOT IMPORT NIGHTS

ASCARI KZ1
Select Cheats and Codes from the DNA Lab menu and enter KNOX. Defeat the challenge to earn the car.

NISSAN SKYLINE R34 GT-R
Select Cheats and Codes from the DNA Lab menu and enter JWRS. Defeat the challenge to earn the car.

L.A. RUSH

$5,000
During a game, press Up, Down, Left, Right, ●, Left, R2, Up.

UNLIMITED N20

During a game, press Up, Down, Left, Right, ⬤, Up, Down, ⬤, Up.

ALL CARS IN GARAGE PIMPED

During a game, press Up, Down, Left, Right, ⬤, ⬤, R2, R1, Up, Down, Left, Right.

DISABLE POLICE

During a game, press Up, Down, Left, Right, R2, ⬤, Right, R1, Left.

FAST TRAFFIC

During a game, press Up, Down, Left, Right, ⬤, Right, ⬤, Left.

NO CATCH UP

Use C-VHARD as a profile name.

THE LEGEND OF SPYRO: A NEW BEGINNING

INFINITE HEALTH

Pause the game and press Up, Up, Down, Down, Left, Right, Left, Right, L1, L1, R1, R1.

LEGO STAR WARS II: THE ORIGINAL TRILOGY

BEACH TROOPER

At Mos Eisley Canteena, select Enter Code and enter UCK868. You still need to select Characters and purchase this character for 20,000 studs.

BEN KENOBI (GHOST)

At Mos Eisley Canteena, select Enter Code and enter BEN917. You still need to select Characters and purchase this character for 1,100,000 studs.

BESPIN GUARD

At Mos Eisley Canteena, select Enter Code and enter VHY832. You still need to select Characters and purchase this character for 15,000 studs.

BIB FORTUNA

At Mos Eisley Canteena, select Enter Code and enter WTY721. You still need to select Characters and purchase this character for 16,000 studs.

BOBA FETT

At Mos Eisley Canteena, select Enter Code and enter HLP221. You still need to select Characters and purchase this character for 175,000 studs.

DEATH STAR TROOPER

At Mos Eisley Canteena, select Enter Code and enter BNC332. You still need to select Characters and purchase this character for 19,000 studs.

EWOK

At Mos Eisley Canteena, select Enter Code and enter TTT289. You still need to select Characters and purchase this character for 34,000 studs.

GAMORREAN GUARD

At Mos Eisley Canteena, select Enter Code and enter YZF999. You still need to select Characters and purchase this character for 40,000 studs.

GONK DROID

At Mos Eisley Canteena, select Enter Code and enter NFX582. You still need to select Characters and purchase this character for 1,550 studs.

GRAND MOFF TARKIN

At Mos Eisley Canteena, select Enter Code and enter SMG219. You still need to select Characters and purchase this character for 38,000 studs.

GREEDO

At Mos Eisley Canteena, select Enter Code and enter NAH118. You still need to select Characters and purchase this character for 60,000 studs.

HAN SOLO (HOOD)

At Mos Eisley Canteena, select Enter Code and enter YWM840. You still need to select Characters and purchase this character for 20,000 studs.

IG-88

At Mos Eisley Canteena, select Enter Code and enter NXL973. You still need to select Characters and purchase this character for 30,000 studs.

IMPERIAL GUARD

At Mos Eisley Canteena, select Enter Code and enter MMM111. You still need to select Characters and purchase this character for 45,000 studs.

IMPERIAL OFFICER

At Mos Eisley Canteena, select Enter Code and enter BBV889. You still need to select Characters and purchase this character for 28,000 studs.

IMPERIAL SHUTTLE PILOT

At Mos Eisley Canteena, select Enter Code and enter VAP664. You still need to select Characters and purchase this character for 29,000 studs.

IMPERIAL SPY

At Mos Eisley Canteena, select Enter Code and enter CVT125. You still need to select Characters and purchase this character for 13,500 studs.

JAWA

At Mos Eisley Canteena, select Enter Code and enter JAW499. You still need to select Characters and purchase this character for 24,000 studs.

LOBOT

At Mos Eisley Canteena, select Enter Code and enter UUB319. You still need to select Characters and purchase this character for 11,000 studs.

PALACE GUARD

At Mos Eisley Canteena, select Enter Code and enter SGE549. You still need to select Characters and purchase this character for 14,000 studs.

REBEL PILOT

At Mos Eisley Canteena, select Enter Code and enter CYG336. You still need to select Characters and purchase this character for 15,000 studs.

REBEL TROOPER (HOTH)

At Mos Eisley Canteena, select Enter Code and enter EKU849. You still need to select Characters and purchase this character for 16,000 studs.

SANDTROOPER

At Mos Eisley Canteena, select Enter Code and enter YDV451. You still need to select Characters and purchase this character for 14,000 studs.

SKIFF GUARD

At Mos Eisley Canteena, select Enter Code and enter GBU888. You still need to select Characters and purchase this character for 12,000 studs.

SNOWTROOPER

At Mos Eisley Canteena, select Enter Code and enter NYU989. You still need to select Characters and purchase this character for 16,000 studs.

STROMTROOPER

At Mos Eisley Canteena, select Enter Code and enter PTR345. You still need to select Characters and purchase this character for 10,000 studs.

THE EMPEROR

At Mos Eisley Canteena, select Enter Code and enter HHY382. You still need to select Characters and purchase this character for 275,000 studs.

TIE FIGHTER

At Mos Eisley Canteena, select Enter Code and enter HDY739. You still need to select Characters and purchase this character for 60,000 studs.

TIE FIGHTER PILOT

At Mos Eisley Canteena, select Enter Code and enter NNZ316. You still need to select Characters and purchase this character for 21,000 studs.

TIE INTERCEPTOR

At Mos Eisley Canteena, select Enter Code and enter QYA828. You still need to select Characters and purchase this character for 40,000 studs.

TUSKEN RAIDER

At Mos Eisley Canteena, select Enter Code and enter PEJ821. You still need to select Characters and purchase this character for 23,000 studs.

UGNAUGHT

At Mos Eisley Canteena, select Enter Code and enter UGN694. You still need to select Characters and purchase this character for 36,000 studs.

MADDEN NFL 07

MADDEN CARDS

Select Madden Cards from My Madden, then select Madden Codes and enter the following:

CARD	PASSWORD	CARD	PASSWORD
#199 Gold Lame Duck Cheat	5LAWOO	#221 Super Bowl XLII Gold	WRLUF8
#200 Gold Mistake Free Cheat	XL7SP1	#222 Super Bowl XLIII Gold	NIEV4A
#210 Gold QB on Target Cheat	WROAOR	#223 Super Bowl XLIV Gold	M5AB7L
#220 Super Bowl XLI Gold	RLA9R7	#224 Aloha Stadium Gold	YI8P8U

CARD	PASSWORD	CARD	PASSWORD
#225 1958 Colts Gold	B57QLU	#249 1999 Rams Gold	S9OUSW
#226 1966 Packers Gold	1PL1FL	#250 Bears Pump Up the Crowd	B1OUPH
#227 1968 Jets Gold	MIE6WO	#251 Bengals Cheerleader	DRL2SW
#228 1970 Browns Gold	CL2TOE	#252 Bills Cheerleader	1PLUYO
#229 1972 Dolphins Gold	NOEB7U	#253 Broncos Cheerleader	3ROUJO
#230 1974 Steelers Gold	YOOFLA	#254 Browns Pump Up the Crowd	T1UTOA
#231 1976 Raiders Gold	MOA11I	#255 Buccaneers Cheerleader	S9EWRI
#232 1977 Broncos Gold	C8UM7U	#256 Cardinals Cheerleader	57IEPI
#233 1978 Dolphins Gold	VIUOO7	#257 Chargers Cheerleader	F7UHL8
#234 1980 Raiders Gold	NLAPH3	#258 Chiefs Cheerleader	PRI5SL
#235 1981 Chargers Gold	COAGI4	#259 Colts Cheerleader	1R5AMI
#236 1982 Redskins Gold	WL8BRI	#260 Cowboys Cheerleader	Z2ACHL
#237 1983 Raiders Gold	HOEW71	#261 Dolphins Cheerleader	C5AHLE
#238 1984 Dolphins Gold	M1AM1E	#262 Eagles Cheerleader	PO7DRO
#239 1985 Bears Gold	QOET08	#263 Falcons Cheerleader	37USPO
#240 1986 Giants Gold	ZI8S2L	#264 49ers Cheerleader	KLOCRL
#241 1988 49ers Gold	SP2A8H	#265 Giants Pump Up the Crowd	C4USPI
#242 1990 Eagles Gold	2L4TRO	#266 Jaguars Cheerleader	MIEH7E
#243 1991 Lions Gold	J1ETRI	#267 Jets Pump Up the Crowd	COLUXI
#244 1992 Cowboys Gold	W9UVI9	#268 Lions Pump Up the Crowd	3LABLU
#245 1993 Bills Gold	DLA3I7	#269 Packers Pump Up the Crowd	4HO7VO
#246 1994 49ers Gold	DR7EST	#270 Panthers Cheerleader	F2IASP
#247 1996 Packers Gold	F8LUST	#282 All AFC Team Gold	PRO9PH
#248 1998 Broncos Gold	FIES95	#283 All NFC Team Gold	RLATH7

MAJOR LEAGUE BASEBALL 2K7

MICKEY MANTLE ON THE FREE AGENTS LIST
Select Enter Cheat Code from the My 2K7 menu and enter themick.

MICKEY PINCH HITS
Select Enter Cheat Code from the My 2K7 menu and enter phmantle.

UNLOCK EVERYTHING
Select Enter Cheat Code from the My 2K7 menu and enter Derek Jeter. This does not unlock the Topps cheats.

MIGHTY MICK CHEAT
Select Enter Cheat Code from the My 2K7 menu and enter mightymick.

TRIPLE CROWN CHEAT
Select Enter Cheat Code from the My 2K7 menu and enter triplecrown.

BIG BLAST CHEAT
Select Enter Cheat Code from the My 2K7 menu and enter m4murder.

MARVEL ULTIMATE ALLIANCE

UNLOCK ALL SKINS
At the Team Menu, press Up, Down, Left, Right, Left, Right, Start.

UNLOCKS ALL HERO POWERS
At the Team Menu, press Left, Right, Up, Down, Up, Down, Start.

UNLOCK ALL HEROES
At the Team Menu, press Up, Up, Down, Down, Left, Left, Left, Start.

UNLOCK DAREDEVIL
At the Team Menu, press Left, Left, Right, Right, Up, Down, Up, Down, Start.

UNLOCK SILVER SURFER
At the Team Menu, press Down, Left, Left, Up, Right, Up, Down, Left, Start.

GOD MODE
During gameplay, press Up, Down, Up, Down, Up, Left, Down, Right, Start.

TOUCH OF DEATH
During gameplay, press Left, Right, Down, Down, Right, Left, Start.

SUPER SPEED
During gameplay, press Up, Left, Up, Right, Down, Right, Start.

FILL MOMENTUM
During gameplay, press Left, Right, Right, Left, Up, Down, Down, Up, Start.

UNLOCK ALL COMICS
At the Review menu, press Left, Right, Right, Left, Up, Up, Right, Start.

UNLOCK ALL CONCEPT ART
At the Review menu, press Down, Down, Down, Right, Right, Left, Down, Start.

UNLOCK ALL MOVIES
At the Review menu, press Up, Left, Left, Up, Right, Right, Up, Start.

UNLOCK ALL LOAD SCREENS
At the Review menu, press Up, Down, Right, Left, Up, Up Down, Start.

UNLOCK ALL COURSES
At the Comic Missions menu, press Up, Right, Left, Down, Up, Right, Left, Down, Start.

MLB 07: THE SHOW

CLASSIC STADIUMS
At the Main menu, press Down, Up, Right, Down, Up, Left, Down, Up.

GOLDEN/SLIVER ERA PLAYERS
At the Main menu, press Left, Up, Right, Down, Down, Left, Up, Down.

MVP 07 NCAA BASEBALL

ALL CHALLENGE ITEMS
In Dynasty Mode, create a player with the name David Hamel.

NARUTO: ULTIMATE NINJA 2

In Naruto's house, select Input Password. This is where you can enter an element, then three signs. Enter the following here:

1,000 RYO
Water, Hare, Monkey, Monkey
Water, Ram, Horse, Dog
Water, Horse, Horse, Horse
Water, Rat, Rooster, Boar
Water, Rat, Monkey, Rooster
Fire, Rat, Dragon, Dog

5,000 RYO
Water, Tiger, Dragon, Tiger
Water, Snake, Rooster, Horse

10,000 RYO
Fire, Tiger, Tiger, Rooster
Fire, Tiger, Dragon, Hare

NASCAR 07

$10,000,000
In Fight to the Top mode, enter your name as GiveMe More.

10,000,000 FANS
In Fight to the Top mode, enter your name as AllBow ToMe.

PRESTIGE LEVEL 10 WITH 2,000,000 POINTS
In Fight to the Top mode, enter your name as Outta MyWay.

100% TEAM PRESTIGE
In Fight to the Top mode, enter your name as MoMoney BlingBling.

ALL CHASE PLATES
In Fight to the Top mode, enter your name as ItsAll ForMe.

OLD SPICE TRACKS AND CARS.
In Fight to the Top mode, enter your name as KeepCool SmellGreat.

WALMART TRACK AND CARS
In Fight to the Top mode, enter your name as Walmart EveryDay.

NASCAR 08

ALL CHASE MODE CARS
Select Cheat Codes from the Options menu and enter checkered flag.

EA SPORTS CAR
Select Cheat Codes from the Options menu and enter ea sports car.

FANTASY DRIVERS
Select Cheat Codes from the Options menu and enter race the pack.

WALMART CAR AND TRACK
Select Cheat Codes from the Options menu and enter walmart everyday.

NBA 07

2006 CHARLOTTE BOBCATS ALTERNATE JERSEY
Select NBA.com from the Trophy Room. Press ● to bring up the Enter Code screen. Enter JKL846ETK5.

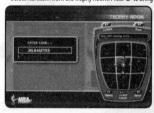

2006 NOK HORNETS ALTERNATE JERSEY
Select NBA.com from the Trophy Room. Press ● to bring up the Enter Code screen. Enter EL2E3T8H58.

2006 NEW JERSEY NETS ALTERNATE JERSEY
Select NBA.com from the Trophy Room. Press ● to bring up the Enter Code screen. Enter NB79D965D2.

2006 UTAH JAZZ ALTERNATE JERSEY
Select NBA.com from the Trophy Room. Press ● to bring up the Enter Code screen. Enter 228GG7585G.

2006 WASH WIZARDS ALTERNATE JERSEY
Select NBA.com from the Trophy Room. Press ● to bring up the Enter Code screen. Enter PL5285F37F.

2007 EASTERN ALL-STARS
Select NBA.com from the Trophy Room. Press ● to bring up the Enter Code screen. Enter 5F89RE3H8G.

2007 WESTERN ALL-STARS
Select NBA.com from the Trophy Room. Press ● to bring up the Enter Code screen. Enter 2H5E89EH8C.

NBA 2K7

ABA BALL
Select Codes from the Features menu and enter payrespect.

ALL-STAR BALL
Select Codes from the Features menu and enter ply8mia.

MAX DURABILITY
Select Codes from the Features menu and enter ironman.

UNLIMITED STAMINA

Select Codes from the Features menu and enter norest.

+10 DEFENSIVE AWARENESS

Select Codes from the Features menu and enter getstops.

+10 OFFENSIVE AWARENESS

Select Codes from the Features menu and enter inthezone.

2007 ALL-STAR UNIFORMS

Select Codes from the Features menu and enter syt6cii.

BOBCATS ALTERNATE

Select Codes from the Features menu and enter bcb8sta.

JAZZ ALTERNATE

Select Codes from the Features menu and enter zjb3lau.

NETS ALTERNATE

Select Codes from the Features menu and enter nrd4esj.

WIZARDS ALTERNATE

Select Codes from the Features menu and enter zw9idla.

ST. PATRICK'S DAY UNIFORMS

Select Codes from the Features menu and enter tpk7sgn.

VALENTINE'S DAY UNIFORMS

Select Codes from the Features menu and enter vdr5lya.

INTERNATIONAL ALL-STARS

Select Codes from the Features menu and enter tns9roi.

NBA 2K TEAM

Select Codes from the Features menu and enter bestsim.

SUPERSTARS

Select Codes from the Features menu and enter rta1spe

TOPPS 2K SPORTS ALL-STARS

Select Codes from the Features menu and enter topps2ksports.

NBA 2K8

ABA BALL

Select Codes from the Features menu and enter Payrespect.

NBA LIVE 07

ADIDAS ARTILLERY II BLACK & THE RBK ANSWER 9 VIDEO

Select NBA Codes from My NBA Live and enter 99B6356HAN.

ADIDAS ARTILLERY II

Select NBA Codes and enter NTGNFUE87H.

ADIDAS BTB LOW AND THE MESSAGE FROM ALLEN IVERSON VIDEO

Select NBA Codes and enter 7FB3KS9JQ0.

ADIDAS C-BILLUPS

Select NBA Codes and enter BV6877HB9N.

ADIDAS C-BILLUPS BLACK

Select NBA Codes and enter 85NVLDMWS5.

ADIDAS CAMPUS LT

Select NBA Codes and enter CLT2983NC8.

ADIDAS CRAZY 8
Select NBA Codes and enter CC98KKL814.

ADIDAS EQUIPMENT BBALL
Select NBA Codes and enter 22OIUJKMDR.

ADIDAS GARNETT BOUNCE
Select NBA Codes and enter HYIOUHCAAN.

ADIDAS GARNETT BOUNCE BLACK
Select NBA Codes and enter KDZ2MQL17W.

ADIDAS GIL-ZERO
Select NBA Codes and enter 23DN1PPOG4.

ADIDAS GIL-ZERO BLACK
Select NBA Codes and enter QQQ3JCUYQ7.

ADIDAS GIL-ZERO MID
Select NBA Codes and enter 1GSJC8JWRL.

ADIDAS GIL-ZERO MID BLACK
Select NBA Codes and enter 369V6RVU3G.

ADIDAS STEALTH
Select NBA Codes and enter FE454DFJCC.

ADIDAS T-MAC 6
Select NBA Codes and enter MCJK843NNC.

ADIDAS T-MAC 6 WHITE
Select NBA Codes and enter 84GF7EJG8V.

AIR JORDAN V
Select NBA Codes and enter PNBBX1EVT5.

AIR JORDAN V
Select NBA Codes and enter VIR13PC451.

AIR JORDAN V
Select NBA Codes and enter IB7G8NN91Z.

JORDAN MELO M3
Select NBA Codes and enter JUL38TC485.

CHARLOTTE BOBCATS 2006-2007 ALTERNATE JERSEY
Select NBA Codes and enter WEDX671H7S.

UTAH JAZZ 2006-2007 ALTERNATE JERSEY
Select NBA Codes and enter VCBI89FK83.

NEW JERSEY NETS 2006-2007 ALTERNATE JERSEY
Select NBA Codes and enter D4SAA98U5H.

WASHINGTON WIZARDS 2006-2007 ALTERNATE JERSEY
Select NBA Codes and enter QV93NLKXQC.

EASTERN ALL-STARS 2006-2007 ROAD JERSEY
Select NBA Codes and enter WOCNW4KL7L.

EASTERN ALL-STARS 2006-2007 HOME JERSEY
Select NBA Codes and enter 5654ND43N6.

WESTERN ALL-STARS 2006-2007 ROAD JERSEY
Select NBA Codes and enter XX93BVL20U.

WESTERN ALL-STARS 2006-2007 HOME JERSEY
Select NBA Codes and enter 993NSKL199.

NCAA FOOTBALL 07

#16 BAYLOR
Select Pennant Collection from My NCAA. Press Select and enter Sic Em.

#16 NIKE SPEED TD
Select Pennant Collection from My NCAA. Press Select and enter Light Speed.

#63 ILLINOIS
Select Pennant Collection from My NCAA. Press Select and enter Oskee Wow.

#160 TEXAS TECH
Select Pennant Collection from My NCAA. Press Select and enter Fight.

#200 FIRST AND FIFTEEN
Select Pennant Collection from My NCAA. Press Select and enter Thanks.

#201 BLINK
Select Pennant Collection from My NCAA. Press Select and enter For.

#202 BOING
Select Pennant Collection from My NCAA. Press Select and enter Registering.

#204 BUTTER FINGERS
Select Pennant Collection from My NCAA. Press Select and enter With EA.

#205 CROSSED THE LINE
Select Pennant Collection from My NCAA. Press Select and enter Tiburon.

#206 CUFFED
Select Pennant Collection from My NCAA. Press Select and enter EA Sports.

#207 EXTRA CREDIT
Select Pennant Collection from My NCAA. Press Select and enter Touchdown.

#208 HELIUM
Select Pennant Collection from My NCAA. Press Select and enter In The Zone.

#209 HURRICANE
Select Pennant Collection from My NCAA. Press Select and enter Turnover.

#210 INSTANT FREPLAY
Select Pennant Collection from My NCAA. Press Select and enter Impact.

#211 JUMBALAYA
Select Pennant Collection from My NCAA. Press Select and enter Heisman.

#212 MOLASSES
Select Pennant Collection from My NCAA. Press Select and enter Game Time.

#213 NIKE FREE
Select Pennant Collection from My NCAA. Press Select and enter Break Free.

#214 NIKE MAGNIGRIP
Select Pennant Collection from My NCAA. Press Select and enter Hand Picked.

#215 NIKE PRO
Select Pennant Collection from My NCAA. Press Select and enter No Sweat.

#219 QB DUD
Select Pennant Collection from My NCAA. Press Select and enter Elite 11.

#221 STEEL TOE
Select Pennant Collection from My NCAA. Press Select and enter Gridiron.

#222 STIFFED
Select Pennant Collection from My NCAA. Press Select and enter NCAA.

#223 SUPER DIVE
Select Pennant Collection from My NCAA. Press Select and enter Upset.

#224 TAKE YOUR TIME
Select Pennant Collection from My NCAA. Press Select and enter Football.

#225 THREAD & NEEDLE
Select Pennant Collection from My NCAA. Press Select and enter 06.

#226 TOUGH AS NAILS
Select Pennant Collection from My NCAA. Press Select and enter Offense.

#227 TRIP
Select Pennant Collection from My NCAA. Press Select and enter Defense.

#228 WHAT A HIT
Select Pennant Collection from My NCAA. Press Select and enter Blitz.

#229 KICKER HEX
Select Pennant Collection from My NCAA. Press Select and enter Sideline.

#273 2004 ALL-AMERICANS
Select Pennant Collection from My NCAA. Press Select and enter Fumble.

#274 ALL-ALABAMA
Select Pennant Collection from My NCAA. Press Select and enter Roll Tide.

#276 ALL-ARKANSAS
Select Pennant Collection from My NCAA. Press Select and enter Woopigsooie.

#277 ALL-AUBURN
Select Pennant Collection from My NCAA. Press Select and enter War Eagle.

#278 ALL-CLEMSON
Select Pennant Collection from My NCAA. Press Select and enter Death Valley.

#279 ALL-COLORADO
Select Pennant Collection from My NCAA. Press Select and enter Glory.

#280 ALL-FLORIDA
Select Pennant Collection from My NCAA. Press Select and enter Great To Be.

#281 ALL-FSU
Select Pennant Collection from My NCAA. Press Select and enter Uprising.

#282 ALL-GEORGIA
Select Pennant Collection from My NCAA. Press Select and enter Hunker Down.

#283 ALL-IOWA
Select Pennant Collection from My NCAA. Press Select and enter On Iowa.

#284 ALL-KANSAS STATE
Select Pennant Collection from My NCAA. Press Select and enter Victory.

#285 ALL-LSU
Select Pennant Collection from My NCAA. Press Select and enter Geaux Tigers.

#286 ALL-MIAMI
Select Pennant Collection from My NCAA. Press Select and enter Raising Cane.

#287 ALL-MICHIGAN
Select Pennant Collection from My NCAA. Press Select and enter Go Blue.

#288 ALL-MISSISSIPPI STATE
Select Pennant Collection from My NCAA. Press Select and enter Hail State.

#289 ALL-NEBRASKA
Select Pennant Collection from My NCAA. Press Select and enter Go Big Red.

#290 ALL-NORTH CAROLINA
Select Pennant Collection from My NCAA. Press Select and enter Rah Rah.

#291 ALL-NOTRE DAME
Select Pennant Collection from My NCAA. Press Select and enter Golden Domer.

#292 ALL-OHIO STATE
Select Pennant Collection from My NCAA. Press Select and enter Killer Nuts.

#293 ALL-OKLAHOMA
Select Pennant Collection from My NCAA. Press Select and enter Boomer.

#294 ALL-OKLAHOMA STATE
Select Pennant Collection from My NCAA. Press Select and enter Go Pokes.

#295 ALL-OREGON
Select Pennant Collection from My NCAA. Press Select and enter Quack Attack.

#296 ALL-PENN STATE
Select Pennant Collection from My NCAA. Press Select and enter We Are.

#297 ALL-PITTSBURGH
Select Pennant Collection from My NCAA. Press Select and enter Lets Go Pitt.

#298 ALL-PURDUE
Select Pennant Collection from My NCAA. Press Select and enter Boiler Up.

#299 ALL-SYRACUSE
Select Pennant Collection from My NCAA. Press Select and enter Orange Crush.

#300 ALL-TENNESSEE
Select Pennant Collection from My NCAA. Press Select and enter Big Orange.

#301 ALL-TEXAS
Select Pennant Collection from My NCAA. Press Select and enter Hook Em.

#302 ALL-TEXAS A&M
Select Pennant Collection from My NCAA. Press Select and enter Gig Em.

#303 ALL-UCLA
Select Pennant Collection from My NCAA. Press Select and enter MIGHTY.

#304 ALL-USC
Select Pennant Collection from My NCAA. Press Select and enter Fight On.

#305 ALL-VIRGINIA
Select Pennant Collection from My NCAA. Press Select and enter Wahoos.

#306 ALL-VIRGINIA TECH
Select Pennant Collection from My NCAA. Press Select and enter Tech Triumph.

#307 ALL-WASHINGTON
Select Pennant Collection from My NCAA. Press Select and enter Bow Down.

#308 ALL-WISCONSIN
Select Pennant Collection from My NCAA. Press Select and enter U Rah Rah.

#311 ARK MASCOT
Select Pennant Collection from My NCAA. Press Select and enter Bear Down.

#329 GT MASCOT
Select Pennant Collection from My NCAA. Press Select and enter RamblinWreck.

#333 ISU MASCOT
Select Pennant Collection from My NCAA. Press Select and enter Red And Gold.

#335 KU MASCOT
Select Pennant Collection from My NCAA. Press Select and enter Rock Chalk.

#341 MINN MASCOT
Select Pennant Collection from My NCAA. Press Select and enter Rah Rah Rah.

#344 MIZZOU MASCOT
Select Pennant Collection from My NCAA. Press Select and enter Mizzou Rah.

#346 MSU MASCOT
Select Pennant Collection from My NCAA. Press Select and enter Go Green.

#349 NCSU MASCOT
Select Pennant Collection from My NCAA. Press Select and enter Go Pack.

#352 NU MASCOT
Select Pennant Collection from My NCAA. Press Select and enter Go Cats.

#360 S CAR MASCOT
Select Pennant Collection from My NCAA. Press Select and enter Go Carolina.

#371 UK MASCOT
Select Pennant Collection from My NCAA. Press Select and enter On On UK.

#382 WAKE FOREST
Select Pennant Collection from My NCAA. Press Select and enter Go Deacs Go.

#385 WSU MASCOT
Select Pennant Collection from My NCAA. Press Select and enter All Hail.

#386 WVU MASCOT
Select Pennant Collection from My NCAA. Press Select and enter Hail WV.

NCAA FOOTBALL 08

PENNANT CODES
Go to My Shrine and select Pennants. Press Select and enter the following:

PENNANT	CODE	PENNANT	CODE
#200 1st & 15 Cheat	Thanks	#211 Jumbalaya Cheat	Heisman
#201 Blink Cheat	For	#212 Molasses Cheat	Game Time
#202 Boing Cheat	Registering	#213 Nike Free Cheat	Break Free
#204 Butter Fingers Cheat	With EA	#214 Nike Magnigrip Cheat	Hand Picked
#205 Crossed The Line Cheat	Tiburon	#215 Nike Pro Cheat	No Sweat
#206 Cuffed Cheat	EA Sports	#219 QB Dud Cheat	Elite 11
#207 Extra Credit Cheat	Touchdown	#221 Steel Toe Cheat	Gridiron
#208 Helium Cheat	In The Zone	#222 Stiffed Cheat	NCAA
#209 Hurricane Cheat	Turnover	#223 Super Dive Cheat	Upset
#210 Instant FrePlay Cheat	Impact	#226 Tough As Nail Cheat	Offense

PENNANT	CODE
#228 What A Hit Cheat	Blitz
#229 Kicker Hex Cheat	Sideline
#273 2004 All-American Team	Fumble
#274 All-Alabama Team	Roll Tide
#276 All-Arkansas Team	Woopigsooie
#277 All-Auburn Team	War Eagle
#278 All-Clemson Team	Death Valley
#279 All-Colorado Team	Glory
#281 All-FSU Team	Uprising
#282 All-Georgia Team	Hunker Down
#283 All-Iowa Team	On Iowa
#285 All-LSU Team	Geaux Tigers
#287 All-Michigan Team	Go Blue
#288 All-Mississippi State Team	Hail State
#289 All-Nebraska Team	Go Big Red
#291 All-Notre Dame Team	Golden Domer

PENNANT	CODE
#292 All-Ohio State Team	Killer Nuts
#293 All-Oklahoma Team	Boomer
#294 All-Oklahoma State Team	Go Pokes
#296 All-Penn State Team	We Are
#298 All-Purdue Team	Boiler Up
#300 All-Tennessee Team	Big Orange
#301 All-Texas Team	Hook Em
#302 All-Texas A&M Team	Gig Em
#303 All-UCLA Team	Mighty
#304 All-USC Team	Fight On
#305 All-Virginia Team	Wahoos
#307 All-Washington Team	Bow Down
#308 All-Wisconsin Team	U Rah Rah
#344 MSU Mascot Team	Mizzou Rah
#385 Wyo Mascot	All Hail
#386 Zips Mascot	Hail WV

NEED FOR SPEED CARBON

CASTROL CASH
At the Main menu, press Down, Up, Left, Down, Right, Up, ●, ●, ▲. This gives you 10,000 extra cash.

INFINITE CREW CHARGE
At the Main menu, press Down, Up, Up, Right, Left, Left, Right, ●.

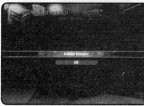

INFINITE NITROUS
At the Main menu, press Left, Up, Left, Down, Left, Down, Right, ●.

INFINITE SPEEDBREAKER
At the Main menu, press Down, Right, Right, Left, Right, Up, Down, ●.

NEED FOR SPEED CARBON LOGO VINYLS
At the Main menu, press Right, Up, Down, Up, Down, Left, Right, ●.

NEED FOR SPEED CARBON SPECIAL LOGO VINYLS
At the Main menu, press Up, Up, Down, Down, Down, Down, Up, ●.

NHL 08

ALL RBK EDGE JERSEYS
At the RBK Edge Code option, enter h3oyxpwksf8ibcgt.

ONE PIECE: GRAND BATTLE

CHOPPER'S 3RD COSTUME
At the Title screen, hold **L1** or **L2** and press Left, Right
✖, ⬤, ✖, △.

LUFFY'S 3RD COSTUME
At the Title screen, hold **L1** or **L2** and press Up, Up, ✖,
⬤, ✖, ✖.

ROBIN'S 3RD COSTUME
At the Title screen, hold **L1** or **L2** and press Down, Right,
✖, ⬤, ✖, ✖.

SANJI'S 3RD COSTUME
At the Title screen, hold **L1** or **L2** and press Up, Down,
✖, ⬤, ✖, ⬤.

J NAMI'S 3RD COSTUME
At the Title screen, hold **L1** or **L2** and press Left, Left,
✖, ⬤, ✖.

USOPP'S 3RD COSTUME
At the Title screen, hold **L1** or **L2** and press Right, Right,
✖, ⬤, ✖, △.

ZORO'S 3RD COSTUME
At the Title screen, hold **L1** or **L2** and press Down,
Down, ✖, ⬤, ✖, △.

OUTRUN 2006: COAST 2 COAST

100% COMPLETE/UNLOCK EVERYTHING
Edit your license and change the name to ENTIRETY.
Select Done, then back out of all menus.

1,000,000 OUTRUN MILES
Edit your license and change the name to MILESANDMILES. Select Done, then back out of all menus.

OVER THE HEDGE

COMPLETE LEVELS
Pause the game, hold **L1** + **R1** and press △, ⬤, △, ⬤, ⬤, ⬛.

ALL MINI-GAMES
Pause the game, hold **L1** + **R1** and press △, ⬤, △, △, ⬤, ⬛.

ALL MOVES
Pause the game, hold **L1** + **R1** and press △, ⬤, △, ⬛, ⬛, ⬤.

EXTRA DAMAGE

Pause the game, hold **L1** + **R1** and press ▲, ●, ▲, ●, ▲, ■.

MORE HP FROM FOOD

Pause the game, hold **L1** + **R1** and press ▲, ●, ▲, ●, ■, ▲.

ALWAYS POWER PROJECTILE

Pause the game, hold **L1** + **R1** and press ▲, ●, ●, ●, ■, ●.

BONUS COMIC 14

Pause the game, hold **L1** + **R1** and press ▲, ●, ■, ■, ●, ▲.

BONUS COMIC 15

Pause the game, hold **L1** + **R1** and press ▲, ▲, ■, ●, ■, ●.

PUMP IT UP: EXCEED

ARROWS DISAPPEAR

At the Song Select screen, press Up/Left, Up/Right, Down/Left, Down/Right, Center.

ARROW SPEED CHANGES THROUGHOUT SONG

At the Song Select screen, press Up/Left, Up/Right, Up/Left, Up/Right, Up/Left, Up/Right, Up/Left, Up/Right, Center.

DOUBLE SPEED

At the Song Select screen, press Up/Left Up/Right Up/Left Up/Right center 2X speed. Enter this code again to get 3x speed. A third time for 4x speed. A fourth time to get 8x speed.

DEACTIVATES THESE MODIFIERS

At the Song Select screen, press Down/Left, Down/Right, Down/Left, Down/Right, Down/Left, Down/Right.

RATATOUILLE

Select Gusteau's Shop from the Extras menu. Choose Secrets, select the appropriate code number, and then enter the code. Once the code is entered, select the cheat you want to activate it.

 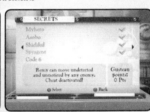

CODE NUMBER	CODE	EFFECT
1	Pieceocake	Very Easy difficulty mode
2	Myhero	No impact and no damage from enemies
3	Asobo	Plays the Asobo logo
4	Shielded	No damage from enemies
5	Spyagent	Move undetected by any enemy
6	Ilikeonions	Release air every time Remy jumps
7	Hardfeelings	Head butt when attacking instead of tailswipe
8	Slumberparty	Multiplayer mode
9	Gusteauart	All Concept Art
10	Gusteauship	All four championship modes
11	Mattelme	All single player and multiplayer mini-games
12	Gusteauvid	All Videos
13	Gusteaures	All Bonus Artworks
14	Gusteaudream	All Dream Worlds in Gusteau's Shop
15	Gusteauslide	All Slides in Gusteau's Shop
16	Gusteaulevel	All single player mini-games
17	Gusteaucombo	All items in Gusteau's Shop
18	Gusteaupot	5,000 Gusteau points
19	Gusteaujack	10,000 Gusteau points
20	Gusteauomni	50,000 Gusteau points

SHREK THE THIRD

10,000 GOLD COINS
At the gift shop, press Up, Up, Down, Up, Right, Left.

THE SIMS 2: CASTAWAY

CHEAT GNOME
During a game, press **R1**, **L1**, Down, ●, **R2**. You can now use this Gnome to get the following:

MAX ALL MOTIVES
During a game, press **R2**, Up, X, ●, **L1**.

MAX CURRENT INVENTORY
During a game, press Left, Right, ●, **R2**, ●.

MAX RELATIONSHIPS
During a game, press **L1**, Up, **R2**, Left, ▲.

ALL RESOURCES
During a game, press ●, ▲, Down, X, Left.

ALL CRAFTING PLANS
During a game, press X, ▲, **L2**, ●, **R1**.

ADD 1 TO SKILL
During a game, press ▲, **L1**, **L1**, Left, ▲.

THE SIMS 2: PETS

CHEAT GNOME
During a game, press **L1**, **L1**, **R1**, ✖, ✖, Up.

GIVE SIM PET POINTS
After activating the Cheat Gnome, press ▲, ●, ✖, ●, **L1**, **R1** during a game. Select the Gnome to access the cheat.

ADVANCE 6 HOURS
After activating the Cheat Gnome, press Up, Left, Down, Right, **R1** during a game. Select the Gnome to access the cheat.

GIVE SIM SIMOLEONS
After activating the Cheat Gnome, enter the Advance 6 Hours cheat. Access the Gnome and exit. Enter the cheat again. Now, Give Sim Simoleons should be available from the Gnome.

CAT AND DOG CODES
When creating a family, press ● to Enter Unlock Code. Enter the following for new fur patterns.

FUR PATTERN/CAT OR DOG	UNLOCK CODE
Bandit Mask Cats	EEGJ2YRQZZAIZ9QHA64
Bandit Mask Dogs	EEGJ2YRQZQARQ9QHA64
Black Dot Cats	EEGJ2YRZQQ1IQ9QHA64
Black Dot Dogs	EEGJ2YRZZZ1IQ9QHA64
Black Smiley Cats	EEGJ2YRQQZ1RQ9QHA64
Black Smiley Dogs	EEGJ2YRZQQARQ9QHA64
Blue Bones Cats	EEGJ2YRQZZARQ9QHA64
Blue Bones Dogs	EEGJ2YRZZZ1IZ9QHA64
Blue Camouflage Cats	EEGJ2YRZZQ1IQ9QHA64
Blue Camouflage Dogs	EEGJ2YRZZZ1RQ9QHA64
Blue Cats	EEGJ2YRQZZAIQ9QHA64
Blue Dogs	EEGJ2YRQQQ1IZ9QHA64
Blue Star Cats	EEGJ2YRQQZ1IZ9QHA64
Blue Star Dogs	EEGJ2YRZQZ1IZ9QHA64
Deep Red Cats	EEGJ2YRQQQAIQ9QHA64
Deep Red Dogs	EEGJ2YRZQZ1RQ9QHA64
Goofy Cats	EEGJ2YRQZQ1IZ9QHA64
Goofy Dogs	EEGJ2YRZZZARQ9QHA64
Green Cats	EEGJ2YRZQQAIZ9QHA64
Green Dogs	EEGJ2YRQZQAIQ9QHA64
Green Flower Cats	EEGJ2YRZQZAIQ9QHA64
Green Flower Dogs	EEGJ2YRQZZ1RQ9QHA64
Light Green Cats	EEGJ2YRZZQ1RQ9QHA64
Light Green Dogs	EEGJ2YRQQ1RQ9QHA64
Navy Hearts Cats	EEGJ2YRQZ1IQ9QHA64
Navy Hearts Dogs	EEGJ2YRQQZ1IQ9QHA64
Neon Green Cats	EEGJ2YRZZQAIQ9QHA64
Neon Green Dogs	EEGJ2YRZQQAIQ9QHA64
Neon Yellow Cats	EEGJ2YRZZQARQ9QHA64
Neon Yellow Dogs	EEGJ2YRQQQAIZ9QHA64
Orange Diagonal Cats	EEGJ2YRQQZAIQ9QHA64
Orange Diagonal Dogs	EEGJ2YRZQZ1IZ9QHA64
Panda Cats	EEGJ2YRQZQAIZ9QHA64
Pink Cats	EEGJ2YRQZZ1IZ9QHA64
Pink Dogs	EEGJ2YRZQZ1RQ9QHA64
Pink Vertical Strip Cats	EEGJ2YRQQQARQ9QHA64
Pink Vertical Strip Dogs	EEGJ2YRZZZAIQ9QHA64
Purple Cats	EEGJ2YRQQZARQ9QHA64
Purple Dogs	EEGJ2YRQQZAIZ9QHA64
Star Cats	EEGJ2YRZQZAQ9QHA64
Star Dogs	EEGJ2YRZQZAIZ9QHA64
White Paws Cats	EEGJ2YRQQQ1RQ9QHA64
White Paws Dogs	EEGJ2YRZQQ1IZ9QHA64
White Zebra Stripe Cats	EEGJ2YRZZQ1IZ9QHA64
White Zebra Stripe Dogs	EEGJ2YRZZZ1IQ9QHA64
Zebra Stripes Dogs	EEGJ2YRZZQAIZ9QHA64

SLY 3: HONOR AMONG THIEVES

TOONAMI PLANE
While flying the regular plane, pause the game and press **R1**, **R1**, Right, Down, Down, Right.

RESTART EPISODES
Pause the game during the Episode and enter the following codes to restart that Episode. You must first complete that part of the Episode to use the code.

EPISODE	CODE
Episode 1, Day 1	Left, R2, Right, L1, R2, L1
Episode 1, Day 2	Down, L2, Up, Left, R2, L2
Episode 2, Day 1	Right, L2, Left, Up, Right, Down
Episode 2, Day 2	Down, Up, R1, Up, R2, L2
Episode 3, Day 1	R2, R1, L1, Left, L1, Down
Episode 3, Day 2	L2, R1, R2, L2, L1, Up
Episode 4, Day 1	Left, Right, L1, R2, Right, R2
Episode 4, Day 2	L1, Left, L2, Left, Up, L1
Episode 5, Day 1	Left, R2, Right, Up, L1, R2
Episode 5, Day 2	R2, R1, L1, R1, R2, R1
Operation Laptop Retrieval	L2, Left, R1, L2, L1, Down
Operation Moon Crash	L2, Up, Left, L1, L2, L1
Operation Reverse Double Cross	Right, Left, Up, Left, R2, Left
Operation Tar Be-Gone	Down, L2, R1, L2, R1, Right
Operation Turbo Dominant Eagle	Down, Right, Left, L2, R1, Right
Operation Wedding Crasher	L2, R2, Right, Down, L1, R2

SPIDER-MAN: FRIEND OR FOE

NEW GREEN GOBLIN AS A SIDEKICK
While standing in the Helicarrier between levels, press Left, Down, Right, Right, Down, Left.

SANDMAN AS A SIDEKICK
While standing in the Helicarrier between levels, press Right, Right, Right, Up, Down, Left.

VENOM AS A SIDEKICK
While standing in the Helicarrier between levels, press Left, Left, Right, Up, Down, Down.

5000 TECH TOKENS
While standing in the Helicarrier between levels, press Up, Up, Down, Down, Left, Right.

SPLASHDOWN: RIDES GONE WILD

WAREHOUSE ITEMS
At the Options screen, press Down, Up, Down, Left, Right, Left, Right, Left, Down, Right, Up, Right, Down, Left, Up.

STAR TREK: ENCOUNTERS

ALL LEVELS AND SHIPS
Get a high score in Onslaught Mode and enter your name as 4jstudios.

ALL CREW CARDS
Get a high score in Onslaught Mode and enter your name as Bethesda.

STAR WARS: BATTLEFRONT II

INFINITE AMMO
Pause the game, hold **L2** + **R2** and press Up, Down, Left, Down, Down, Left, Down, Down, Left, Down, Down, Down, Left, Right.

INVINCIBILITY
Pause the game, hold **L2** + **R2** and press Up, Up, Up, Left, Down, Down, Down, Left, Up, Up, Up, Left, Right.

NO HUD
Pause the game, hold **L2** + **R2** and press Up, Up, Up, Up, Left, Up, Up, Down, Left, Down, Left, Down, Up, Up, Left, Right. Re-enter the code to enable the HUD again.

ALTERNATE SOLDIERS
Pause the game, hold **L2** + **R2** and press Down, Down, Down, Up, Up, Left, Down, Down, Down, Down, Down, Left, Up, Up, Up, Left.

ALTERNATE SOUNDS
Pause the game, hold **L2** + **R2** and press Up, Up, Up, Left, Up, Down, Up, Up, Left, Down, Down, Down, Down, Left, Up, Down, Down, Left, Right.

FUNNY MESSAGES WHEN REBELS DEFEATED
Pause the game, hold **L2** + **R2** and press Up, Down, Left, Down, Left, Right.

STRAWBERRY SHORTCAKE: THE SWEET DREAMS GAME

LEVEL SKIP
During a game, press Left, Left. Up, Up, Right, Right, Down, Down to skip the current level.

ALL BONUS AREAS
Load a saved game. At the Fantasy Garden or continue screen, press Down, Down, Right, Right, Up, Up, Left, Left.

STREET FIGHTER ALPHA ANTHOLOGY

Street Fighter Alpha
PLAY AS DAN
At the Character Select screen in Arcade Mode, hold the Start button and place the cursor on the Random Select space then input one of the following commands within 1 second:

LP LK MK HK HP MP

HP HK MK LK LP MP

LK LP MP HP HK MK

HK HP MP LP LK HK

PLAY AS M.BISON
At the Character Select screen, hold the Start button, place the cursor on the random select box, and input:

1P side: Down, Down, Back, Back, Down, Back, Back + LP + HP

2P side: Down, Down, Forward, Forward, Down, Forward, Forward + LP + HP

PLAY AS AKUMA
At the Character Select screen, hold the Start button, place the cursor on the random select box, and input:

1P side: Down, Down, Down, Back, Back, Back + LP + HP

2P side: Down, Down, Down, Forward, Forward, Forward + LP + HP

AKUMA MODE
Select your character in Arcade mode, then press and hold Start + MP + MK as the Character Selection screen ends.

RYU AND KEN VS. M.BISON

On both the 1p and 2p side in Arcade mode, press and hold Start, then:
1P side: place the cursor on Ryu and input Up, Up, release Start, Up, Up + LP
2P side: place the cursor on Ken and input Up, Up, release Start, Up, Up + HP

LAST BOSS MODE

Select Arcade mode while holding ⬤, ✖, and **R1**.

DRAMATIC BATTLE MODE

Select Dramatic Battle mode while holding ⬤, ✖, and **R2**.

RANDOM BATTLE MODE

Select Versus mode while holding ⬤, ✖, and **R2**.

Street Fighter Alpha 2

PLAY AS ORIGINAL CHUN-LI

Highlight Chun-Li on the Character Select screen, hold the Start button for 3 seconds, then select Chun-Li normally.

PLAY AS SHIN AKUMA

Highlight Akuma on the Character Select screen, hold the Start button for 3 seconds, then select Akuma normally.

PLAY AS EVIL RYU

Highlight Ryu on the Character Select screen, hold the Start button, input Forward, Up, Down, Back, then select Ryu normally.

PLAY AS EX DHALSIM

Highlight Dhalsim on the Character Select screen, hold the Start button, input Back, Down, Forward, Up, then select Dhalsim normally.

PLAY AS EX ZANGIEF

Highlight Zangief on the Character Select screen, hold the Start button, input Down, Back, Back, Back, Back, Up, Up, Forward, Forward, Forward, Forward, Down, then select Zangief normally.

LAST BOSS MODE

Select Arcade mode while holding the ⬤, ⬤, and **R1** buttons.

DRAMATIC BATTLE MODE

Select Dramatic Battle mode while holding the ⬤ + ✖ + **R2**.

SELECT SPECIAL ROUTE IN SURVIVAL MODE

Select Survival Battle while holding the **R1** or **R2**.

RANDOM BATTLE MODE

Select Versus mode while holding the ⬤ + ✖ + **R2**.

Street Fighter Alpha 2 Gold

PLAY AS EX RYU

Highlight Ryu and press the Start button once before selecting normally.

PLAY AS EVIL RYU

Highlight Ryu and press the Start button twice before selecting normally.

PLAY AS ORIGINAL CHUN-LI

Highlight Chun-Li and press the Start button once before selecting normally.

PLAY AS EX CHUN-LI

Highlight Chun-Li and press the Start button twice before selecting normally.

PLAY AS EX KEN

Highlight Ken and press the Start button once before selecting normally.

PLAY AS EX DHALSIM

Highlight Dhalsim and press the Start button once before selecting normally.

PLAY AS EX ZANGIEF
Highlight Zangief and press the Start button once before selecting normally.

PLAY AS EX SAGAT
Highlight Sagat and press the Start button once before selecting normally.

PLAY AS EX M.BISON
Highlight M.Bison and press the Start button once before selecting normally.

PLAY USING SAKURA'S ALTERNATE COLORS
Highlight Sakura and press the Start button five times before selecting normally.

PLAY AS SHIN AKUMA
Highlight Akuma and press the Start button five times before selecting normally.

PLAY AS CAMMY
Highlight M.Bison and press the Start button twice before selecting normally.

LAST BOSS MODE
Select Arcade mode while holding ⬤ + ⬤ + R1.

SELECT SPECIAL ROUTE IN SURVIVAL MODE
Select Survival Battle while holding the R1 or R2.

DRAMATIC BATTLE MODE
Select Dramatic Battle mode while holding ⬤ + ✖ + R2.

RANDOM BATTLE MODE
Select Versus mode while holding ⬤ + ✖ + R2.

Street Fighter Alpha 3
PLAY AS BALROG
Highlight Karin for one second, then move the cursor to the random select box and hold Start before selecting normally.

PLAY AS JULI
Highlight Karin for one second, then move the cursor to the random select box and press Up, or Down, while selecting normally.

PLAY AS JUNI
Highlight Karin for one second, then move the cursor to the random select box and press Back, or Forward, while selecting normally.

CLASSICAL MODE
Press and hold HP + HK while starting game.

SPIRITED MODE
Press and hold MP + MK while starting game.

SAIKYO MODE
Press and hold LP + LK while starting game.

SHADALOO MODE
Press and hold LK + MK + HK while starting game.

SELECT SPECIAL ROUTE IN SURVIVAL MODE
Select Survival mode while holding R1 or R2.

DRAMATIC BATTLE MODE
Select Dramatic Battle mode while holding ⬤ + ✖ + R2.

RANDOM BATTLE MODE
Select Versus mode while holding ⬤ + ✖ + R2.

STUNTMAN IGNITION

3 PROPS IN STUNT CREATOR MODE
Select Cheats from Extras and enter COOLPROP.

ALL ITEMS UNLOCKED FOR CONSTRUCTION MODE
Select Cheats from Extras and enter NOBLEMAN.

MVX SPARTAN
Select Cheats from Extras and enter fastride.

ALL CHEATS
Select Cheats from Extras and enter Wearefrozen. This unlocks the following cheats: Slo-mo Cool, Thrill Cam, Vision Switcher, Nitro Addiction, Freaky Fast, and Ice Wheels.

ALL CHEATS
Select Cheats from Extras and enter Kungfoopete.

ICE WHEELS CHEAT
Select Cheats from Extras and enter IceAge.

NITRO ADDICTION CHEAT
Select Cheats from Extras and enter TheDuke.

VISION SWITCHER CHEAT
Select Cheats from Extras and enter GFXMODES.

SUPERMAN RETURNS

GOD MODE
Pause the game, select Options and press Up, Up, Down, Down, Left, Right, Left, Right, ●, ●.

INFINITE CITY HEALTH
Pause the game, select Options and press ●, Right, ●, Right, Up, Left, Right, ●.

ALL POWER-UPS
Pause the game, select Options and press Left, ●, Right, ●, Down, ●, Up, Down, ●, ●, ●.

ALL UNLOCKABLES
Pause the game, select Options and press Left, Up, Right, Down, ●, ●, ●, Up, Right, ●.

FREE ROAM AS BIZARRO
Pause the game, select Options and press Up, Right, Down, Right, Up, Left, Down, Right, Up.

TAITO LEGENDS

EXTRA GAMES
At the Title screen, press L1, R1, R2, L2, Select, Start.

TAK: THE GREAT JUJU CHALLENGE

BONUS SOUND EFFECTS
In Juju's Potions, select Universal Card and enter 20, 17, 5 for Bugs, Crystals and Fruits respectively.

BONUS SOUND EFFECTS 2
In Juju's Potions, select Universal Card and enter 50, 84, 92 for Bugs, Crystals and Fruits respectively.

BONUS MUSIC TRACK 1
In Juju's Potions, select Universal Card and enter 67, 8, 20 for Bugs, Crystals and Fruits respectively.

BONUS MUSIC TRACK 2
In Juju's Potions, select Universal Card and enter 6, 18, 3 for Bugs, Crystals and Fruits respectively.

MAGIC PARTICLES
In Juju's Potions, select Universal Card and enter 24, 40, 11 for Bugs, Crystals and Fruits respectively.

MORE MAGIC PARTICLES
In Juju's Potions, select Universal Card and enter 48, 57, 57 for Bugs, Crystals and Fruits respectively.

VIEW JUJU CONCEPT ART
In Juju's Potions, select Universal Card and enter Art 33, 22, 28 for Bugs, Crystals and Fruits respectively.

VIEW VEHICLE ART
In Juju's Potions, select Universal Card and enter 11, 55, 44 for Bugs, Crystals and Fruits respectively.

VIEW WORLD ART
In Juju's Potions, select Universal Card and enter 83, 49, 34 for Bugs, Crystals and Fruits respectively.

TEENAGE MUTANT NINJA TURTLES 3: MUTANT NIGHTMARE

INVINCIBILITY
Select Passwords from the Options screen and enter MDLDSSLR.

HEALTH POWER-UPS BECOME SUSHI
Select Passwords from the Options screen and enter SLLMRSLD.

NO HEALTH POWER-UPS
Select Passwords from the Options screen and enter DMLDMRLD.

ONE HIT DEFEATS TURTLE
Select Passwords from the Options screen and enter LDMSLRDD.

MAX OUGI
Select Passwords from the Options screen and enter RRDMLSDL.

UNLIMITED SHURIKEN
Select Passwords from the Options screen and enter LMDRRMSR.

NO SHURIKEN
Select Passwords from the Options screen and enter LLMSRDMS.

DOUBLE ENEMY ATTACK
Select Passwords from the Options screen and enter MSRLSMML.

DOUBLE ENEMY DEFENSE
Select Passwords from the Options screen and enter SLRMLSSM.

TEST DRIVE UNLIMITED

ALL CARS AND MONEY
At the Main menu, press ▲, ◉, L1, R1, ▲.

THRILLVILLE

$50,000
During a game, press ■, ◉, ▲, ■, ◉, ▲, ✖. Repeat this code as much as desired.

ALL PARKS
During a game, press ■, ◉, ▲, ■, ◉, ▲, ■.

ALL RIDES
During a game, press ■, ◉, ▲, ■, ◉, ▲, ▲. Some rides still need to be researched.

COMPLETE MISSIONS
During a game, press ■, ◉, ▲, ■, ◉, ▲, ◉. Then, at the Missions menu, highlight a mission and press ■ to complete that mission. Some missions have Bronze, Silver, and Gold objectives. For these missions the first press of ■ earns the Bronze, the second earns the Silver, and the third earns the Gold.

THRILLVILLE: OFF THE RAILS

ALL PARKS
While in a park, press ■, ●, ▲, ■, ●, ▲, ■.

ALL RIDES IN PARK
While in a park, press ■, ●, ▲, ■, ●, ▲, ▲.

$50,000
While in a park, press ■, ●, ▲, ■, ●, ▲, ✕.

MISSION COMPLETE
While in a park, press ■, ●, ▲, ■, ●, ▲, ●.

TIGER WOODS PGA TOUR 07

ALL CHARACTERS
Select Password from the Options menu and enter gameface.

UNLOCK ADIDAS ITEMS
Select Password from the Options menu and enter three stripes.

UNLOCK BRIDGESTONE ITEMS
Select Password from the Options menu and enter shojiro.

UNLOCK COBRA ITEMS
Select Password from the Options menu and enter snakeking.

UNLOCK EA SPORTS ITEMS
Select Password from the Options menu and enter inthegame.

UNLOCK GRAFALLOYE ITEMS
Select Password from the Options menu and enter just shafts.

UNLOCK MACGREGOR ITEMS
enter mactec.

UNLOCK MIZUNO ITEMS
Select Password from the Options menu and enter rihachinrzo.

UNLOCK NIKE ITEMS
Select Password from the Options menu and enter justdoit.

UNLOCK OAKLEY ITEMS
Select Password from the Options menu and enter jannard.

UNLOCK PGA TOUR ITEMS
Select Password from the Options menu and enter lightning.

UNLOCK PING ITEMS
Select Password from the Options menu and enter solheim.

UNLOCK PRECEPT ITEMS
Select Password from the Options menu and enter guys are good.

UNLOCK TAYLORMADE ITEMS
Select Password from the Options menu and enter mradams.

TIGER WOODS PGA TOUR 08

ALL GOLFERS
Select Passwords from the Options and enter GAMEFACE.

BRIDGESTONE ITEMS
Select Passwords from the Options and enter SHOJIRO.

COBRA ITEMS
Select Passwords from the Options and enter SNAKEKING.

GRAFALLOY ITEMS
Select Passwords from the Options and enter JUSTSHAFTS.

MACGREGOR ITEMS
Select Passwords from the Options and enter MACTEC.

MIZUNO ITEMS
Select Passwords from the Options and enter RIHACHINRIZO.

NIKE ITEMS
Select Passwords from the Options and enter JUSTDOIT.

OAKLEY ITEMS
Select Passwords from the Options and enter JANNARD.

PING ITEMS
Select Passwords from the Options and enter SOLHEIM.

PRECEPT ITEMS
Select Passwords from the Options and enter GUYSAREGOOD.

TAYLORMADE ITEMS
Select Passwords from the Options and enter MRADAMS.

TIM BURTON'S THE NIGHTMARE BEFORE CHRISTMAS: OOGIE'S REVENGE

ALL LEVELS
At the Title screen, press L1, L2, L1, L2, L3, R1, R2, R1, R2, R3.

INVINCIBILITY
During a game, press Right, Left, L3, R3, Left, Right, R3, L3.

OPEN PUMKIN JACK AND SANTA JACK COUSTUMES
During a game, press Down, Up, Right, Left, L3, R3.

TMNT

DON'S BIG HEAD GOODIE
At the Main menu, hold L1 and press ●, ▲, ✕, ●.

CHALLENGE MAP 2
At the Main menu, hold L1 and press ✕, ✕, ●, ✕.

TOKYO XTREME RACER DRIFT 2

START WITH EXTRA CP

Enter the following as your name to get the corresponding amount of CP to start the game.

CP	NAME	CP	NAME
1,700,000	Ikentani	2,910,000	Hachiroku
1,950,000	Wataru	2,960,000	Takeshi
2,840,000	Toshiya	2,960,000	Bunta
2,850,000	Fujiwara	2,960,000	Takahashi
2,880,000	Tomoyuki	2,960,000	Tsuchiya
2,900,000	Richard	2,980,000	DRIFT
2,900,000	Ryosuke	2,990,000	Takumi
2,910,000	Nakazato		

TONY HAWK'S DOWNHILL JAM

CHEAT CODES

Select Cheat Codes from the Options menu and enter the following cheats. Select Toggle Cheats to enable/disable them.

FREE BOOST
Enter OOTBAGHFOREVER.

ALWAYS SPECIAL
Enter POINTHOGGER.

UNLOCK MANUALS
Enter IMISSMANUALS.

PERFECT RAIL
Enter LIKETILTINGAPLATE.

PERFECT MANUAL
Enter TIGHTROPEWALKER.

PERFECT STATS
Enter IAMBOB.

FIRST-PERSON SKATER
Enter FIRSTPERSONJAM.

SHADOW SKATER
Enter CHIMNEYSWEEP.

DEMON SKATER
Enter EVILCHIMNEYSWEEP.

MINI SKATER
Enter DOWNTHERABBITHOLE.

GIGANTO-SKATER
Enter IWANNABETALLTALL.

INVISIBLE SKATER
Enter NOWYOUSEEME.

SKATE AS A WORK OF ART
Enter FOURLIGHTS.

DISPLAY COORDINATES
Enter DISPLAYCOORDINATES.

LARGE BIRDS
Enter BIRDBIRDBIRDBIRD.

ESPECIALLY LARGE BIRDS
Enter BIRDBIRDBIRDBIRDBIRD.

TINY PEOPLE
Enter SHRINKTHEPEOPLE.

There is no need to toggle on the following cheats. They take effect after entering them.

ALL EVENTS
Enter ADVENTURESOFKWANG.

ALL SKATERS
Enter IMINTERFACING.

ALL BOARDS/OUTFITS
Enter RAIDTHEWOODSHED.

ALL MOVIES
Enter FREEBOZZLER.

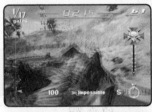

TONY HAWK'S PROJECT 8

SPONSOR ITEMS

As you progress through Career mode and move up the rankings, you gain sponsors and each comes with its own Create-a-skater item.

RANK REQUIRED	C-A-S ITEM UNLOCKED
Rank 040	Adio Kenny V2 Shoes
Rank 050	Quiksilver_Hoody_3
Rank 060	Birdhouse Tony Hawk Deck
Rank 080	Vans No Skool Gothic Shoes
Rank 100	Volcom Scallero Jacket
Rank 110	eS Square One Shoes
Rank 120	Almost Watch What You Say Deck
Rank 140	DVS Adage Shoe
Rank 150	Element Illuminate Deck
Rank 160	Etnies Sheckler White Lavender Shoes
Complete Skateshop Goal	Stereo Soundwave Deck

SKATERS

All of the skaters, except for Tony Hawk, must be unlocked by completing challenges in the Career Mode. They are useable in Free Skate and 2-Player modes.

SKATER	HOW THEY ARE UNLOCKED
Tony Hawk	Always Unlocked
Lyn-z Adams Hawkins	Complete Pro Challenge
Bob Burquist	Complete Pro Challenge
Dustin Dollin	Complete Pro Challenge
Nyjah Huston	Complete Pro Challenge
Bam Margera	Complete Pro Challenge
Rodney Mullen	Complete Pro Challenge
Paul Rodriguez	Complete Pro Challenge
Ryan Sheckler	Complete Pro Challenge
Daewon Song	Complete Pro Challenge
Mike Vallely	Complete Pro Challenge
Stevie Williams	Complete Pro Challenge
Travis Barker	Complete Pro Challenge
Kevin Staab	Complete Pro Challenge
Zombie	Complete Pro Challenge
Christaian Hosoi	Animal Chin Challenge
Jason Lee	Complete Final Tony Hawk Goal
Photographer	Unlock Shops
Security Guard	Unlock School
Bum	Unlock Car Factory
Beaver Mascot	Unlock High School
Real Estate Agent	Unlock Downtown
Filmer	Unlock High School
Skate Jam Kid	Rank #4
Dad	Rank #1
Colonel	All Gaps
Nerd	Complete School Spirit Goal

CHEAT CODES

Select Cheat Codes from the Options and enter the following codes. While playing, you can access some codes from the Options menu.

CHEAT CODE	RESULTS	CHEAT CODE	RESULTS
plus44	Unlocks Travis Barker	allthebest	Full Stats
hohohosoi	Unlocks Christian Hosoi	needaride	All decks unlocked and free, except for inkblot deck and gamestop deck
notmono	Unlocks Jason Lee		
mixitup	Unlocks Kevin Staab	yougotitall	All specials unlocked and in player's special list and set as owned in skate shop
strangefellows	Unlocks Dad & Skater Jam Kid		
themedia	Unlocks Photog Girl & Filmer	enterandwin	Unlocks Bum
militarymen	Unlocks Colonel & Security Guard	wearelosers	Unlocks Nerd
		manineedadate	Unlocks Mascot
jammypack	Unlocks Always Special	suckstobedead	Unlocks Zombie
balancegalore	Unlocks Perfect Rail	sellsellsell	Unlocks Skinny real estate agent
frontandback	Unlocks Perect Manual		
shellshock	Unlocks Unlimited Focus	newshound	Unlocks Anchor man
shescaresme	Unlocks Big Realtor	badverybad	Unlocks Twin
birdhouse	Unlocks Inkblot deck		

TONY HAWK'S PROVING GROUND

CHEAT CODES

Select Cheat Codes from the Options and enter the following cheats. Some codes need to be enabled by selecting Cheats from the Options during a game.

UNLOCK	CHEAT
Unlocks Bosco	MOREMILK
Unlocks Cam	NOTACAMERA
Unlocks Cooper	THECOOP
Unlocks Eddie X	SKETCHY
Unlocks El Patinador	PILEDRIVER
Unlocks Eric	FLYAWAY
Unlocks Judy Nails	LOVEROCKNROLL
Unlocks Mad Dog	RABBIES
Unlocks MCA	INTERGALACTIC
Unlocks Mel	NOTADUDE
Unlocks Rube	LOOKSSMELLY
Unlocks Spence	DAPPER
Unlocks Shayne	MOVERS
Unlocks TV Producer	SHAKER
Unlock FDR	THEPREZPARK
Unlock Lansdowne	THELOCALPARK
Unlock Air & Space Museum	THEINDOORPARK
Unlocks all Fun Items	OVERTHETOP
Unlock all Game Movies	WATCHTHIS
Unlock all Rigger Pieces	IMGONNABUILD
All specials unlocked and in player's special list	LOTSOFTRICKS
Full Stats	BEEFEDUP
Give player +50 skill points	NEEDSHELP
Unlocks Perfect Manual	STILLAINTFALLIN
Unlocks Perfect Rail	AINTFALLIN
Unlocks Unlimited Focus	MYOPIC
Invisible Man	THEMISSING
Mini Skater	TINYTATER

TRANSFORMERS: THE GAME

INFINITE HEALTH
At the Main menu, press Left, Left, Up, Left, Right, Down, Right.

INFINITE AMMO
At the Main menu, press Up, Down, Left, Right, Up, Up, Down.

NO MILITARY OR POLICE
At the Main menu, press Right, Left, Right, Left, Right, Left, Right.

ALL MISSIONS
At the Main menu, press Down, Up, Left, Right, Right, Right, Up, Down.

BONUS CYBERTRON MISSIONS
At the Main menu, press Right, Up, Up, Down, Right, Left, Left.

GENERATION 1 SKIN: JAZZ
At the Main menu, press Left, Up, Down, Down, Left, Up, Right.

GENERATION 1 SKIN: MEGATRON
At the Main menu, press Down, Left, Left, Down, Right, Right, Up.

GENERATION 1 SKIN: OPTIMUS PRIME
At the Main menu, press Down, Right, Left, Up, Down, Down, Left.

GENERATION 1 SKIN: ROBOVISION OPTIMUS PRIME
At the Main menu, press Down, Down, Up, Up, Right, Right, Right.

GENERATION 1 SKIN: STARSCREAM
At the Main menu, press Right, Down, Left, Left, Down, Up, Up.

TY THE TASMANIAN TIGER 3: NIGHT OF THE QUINKAN

100,000 OPALS
During a game, press Start, Start, ●, Start, Start, ▲, ●, ✕, ●, ✕.

ALL 'RANG CHASSIS
During a game, press Start, Start, ●, Start, Start, ▲, ●, ■, ●, ■.

ULTIMATE SPIDER-MAN

ALL CHARACTERS
Pause the game and select Controller Setup from the Options. Press Right, Down, Right, Down, Left, Up, Left, Right.

ALL COVERS
Pause the game and select Controller Setup from the Options. Press Left, Left, Right, Left, Up, Left, Left, Down.

ALL CONCEPT ART
Pause the game and select Controller Setup from the Options. Press Down, Down, Down, Up, Down, Up, Left, Left.

ALL LANDMARKS
Pause the game and select Controller Setup from the Options. Press Up, Right, Down, Left, Down, Up, Right, Left.

VICTORIOUS BOXERS 2: FIGHTING SPRIRT

EXTRA CHARACTERS IN EXHIBITION
Select Password from the Options and enter NEL SAZ UMA.

BROCCOMAN IN EXHIBITION MODE
Select Password from the Options and enter BRC MAN EXH.

LUNSAKU PAUDY, JUNICHI HOTTA AND HIROSHI YAMANAKA
Select Password from the Options and enter ALL *ST ARS.

KAMOGAWA, NEKOTA AND HAMA IN EXHIBITION MODE
Select Password from the Options and enter MRS AND MAN.

DATE VS. RAMIREZ MATCH IN STORY MODE
Select Password from the Options and enter DAT EVS RMZ.

TAKAMURA VS. YAJIMA MATCH IN STORY MODE
Select Password from the Options and enter ASA CT3 CLR.

EXTRA STAGES
Select Password from the Options and enter DAM ATA MAQ.

X-MEN: THE OFFICIAL GAME

DANGER ROOM ICEMAN
At the Cerebro Files menu, press Right, Right, Left, Left, Down, Up, Down, Up, Start.

DANGER ROOM NIGHTCRAWLER
At the Cerebro Files menu, press Up, Up, Down, Down, Left, Right, Left, Right, Start.

DANGER ROOM WOLVERINE
At the Cerebro Files menu, press Down, Down, Up, Up, Right, Left, Right, Left, Start.

PLAYSTATION® 3

EVERYONE

MADDEN NFL 07

MAJOR LEAGUE BASEBALL 2K7

MLB 07: THE SHOW

NASCAR 08

NBA 07

NBA 2K7

NBA 2K8

NBA LIVE 07

NBA STREET HOMECOURT

NHL 08

RATATOUILLE

SUPER PUZZLE FIGHTER II TURBO HD REMIX

TIGER WOODS PGA TOUR 08

EVERYONE 10+

SURF'S UP

TEEN

BLAZING ANGELS: SQUADRONS OF WWII

FULL AUTO 2: BATTLELINES

GUITAR HERO III: LEGENDS OF ROCK

JUICED 2: HOT IMPORT NIGHTS

LAIR

MARVEL ULTIMATE ALLIANCE

MOTORSTORM

SKATE

STUNTMAN IGNITION

TONY HAWK'S PROJECT 8

TONY HAWK'S PROVING GROUND

TRANSFORMERS: THE GAME

VIRTUA FIGHTER 5

Playstation® 3 Contents

BLAZING ANGELS: SQUADRONS OF WWII

ALL MISSIONS, MEDALS & PLANES
At the Main menu, hold **L2** + **R2** and press ●, **L1**, **R1**, ●, ▲, **R1**, **L1**, ●.

GOD MODE
Pause the game, hold **L2** and press ●, ▲, ▲, ●. Release **L2**, hold **R2** and press ▲, ●, ●, ▲.
Re-enter the code to disable it.

INCREASED DAMAGE
Pause the game, hold **L2** and press **L1**, **L1**, **R1**. Release **L2**, hold **R2** and press **R1**, **R1**, **L1**.
Re-enter the code to disable it.

FULL AUTO 2: BATTLELINES

ALL CARS
Select Cheat Codes from Extras and enter 47GIV3MECARS.

ALL MISSIONS
Select Cheat Codes from Extras and enter IMFEDUPWITHTHIS.

SCEPTRE AND MINI-ROCKETS
Select Cheat Codes from Extras and enter 10E6CUSTOMER. This vehicle and weapon become available in Arcade
Mode and Head to Head.

VULCAN AND FLAMETHROWER
Select Cheat Codes from Extras and enter 5FINGERDISCOUNT. This vehicle and weapon become available in Arcade
Mode and Head to Head.

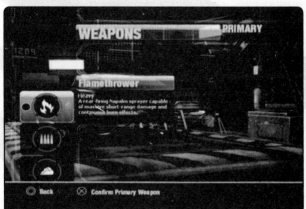

GUITAR HERO III: LEGENDS OF ROCK

To enter the following cheats, strum the guitar with the given buttons held. For example, if it says Yellow + Orange, hold Yellow and Orange as you strum. Air Guitar, Precision Mode and Performance Mode can be toggled on and off from the Cheats menu. You can also change between five different levels of Hyperspeed at this menu.

ALL SONGS

Select Cheats from the Options. Choose Enter Cheat and enter Yellow + Orange, Red + Blue, Red + Orange, Green + Blue, Red + Yellow, Yellow + Orange, Red + Yellow, Red + Blue, Green + Yellow, Green + Yellow, Yellow + Blue, Yellow + Blue, Yellow + Orange, Yellow + Orange, Yellow + Blue, Yellow, Red, Red + Yellow, Red, Yellow, Orange.

AIR GUITAR

Select Cheats from the Options. Choose Enter Cheat and enter Blue + Yellow, Green + Yellow, Green + Yellow, Red + Blue, Red + Blue, Red + Yellow, Red + Yellow, Blue + Yellow, Green + Yellow, Green + Yellow, Red + Blue, Red + Blue, Red + Yellow, Red + Yellow, Green + Yellow, Green + Yellow, Red + Yellow, Red + Yellow.

PRECISION MODE

Select Cheats from the Options. Choose Enter Cheat and enter Green + Red, Green + Red, Green + Red, Red + Yellow, Red + Yellow, Red + Blue, Red + Blue, Yellow + Blue, Yellow + Orange, Yellow + Orange, Green + Red, Green + Red, Green + Red, Red + Yellow, Red + Yellow, Red + Blue, Red + Blue, Yellow + Blue, Yellow + Orange, Yellow + Orange.

HYPERSPEED

Select Cheats from the Options. Choose Enter Cheat and enter Orange, Blue, Orange, Yellow, Orange, Blue, Orange, Yellow.

PERFORMANCE MODE

Select Cheats from the Options. Choose Enter Cheat and enter Red + Yellow, Red + Blue, Red + Orange, Red + Blue, Red + Yellow, Green + Blue, Red + Yellow, Red + Blue.

JUICED 2: HOT IMPORT NIGHTS

ASCARI KZ1

Select Cheats and Codes from the DNA Lab menu and enter KNOX. Defeat the challenge to earn the car.

AUDI TT 1.8L QUATTRO

Select Cheats and Codes from the DNA Lab menu and enter YTHZ. Defeat the challenge to earn the car.

BMW Z4 ROADSTER

Select Cheats and Codes from the DNA Lab menu and enter GVDL. Defeat the challenge to earn the car.

FRITO-LAY INFINITI G35

Select Cheats and Codes from the DNA Lab menu and enter MNCH. Defeat the challenge to earn the car.

HOLDEN MONARO

Select Cheats and Codes from the DNA Lab menu and enter RBSG. Defeat the challenge to earn the car.

HYUNDAI COUPE 2.7L V6

Select Cheats and Codes from the DNA Lab menu and enter BSLU. Defeat the challenge to earn the car.

INFINITI G35

Select Cheats and Codes from the DNA Lab menu and enter MRHC. Defeat the challenge to earn the car.

KOENIGSEGG CCX

Select Cheats and Codes from the DNA Lab menu and enter KDTR. Defeat the challenge to earn the car.

MITSUBISHI PROTOTYPE X

Select Cheats and Codes from the DNA Lab menu and enter DOPX. Defeat the challenge to earn the car.

NISSAN 350Z

Select Cheats and Codes from the DNA Lab menu and enter PRGN. Defeat the challenge to earn the car.

NISSAN SKYLINE R34 GT-R

Select Cheats and Codes from the DNA Lab menu and enter JWRS. Defeat the challenge to earn the car.

SALEEN S7

Select Cheats and Codes from the DNA Lab menu and enter WIKF. Defeat the challenge to earn the car.

SEAT LEON CUPRA R

Select Cheats and Codes from the DNA Lab menu and enter FAMQ. Defeat the challenge to earn the car.

LAIR

CHICKEN VIDEO
At the cheat menu, enter chicken.

COFFEE VIDEO
At the cheat menu, enter 686F7420636F66666565.

UNLOCKS STABLE OPTION FOR ALL LEVELS
At the cheat menu, enter koelsch. Saving is disabled with this code.

MADDEN NFL 07

MADDEN CARDS
Select Madden Cards from My Madden. Then select Madden Codes and enter the following:

CARD	PASSWORD	CARD	PASSWORD
#199 Gold Lame Duck Cheat	5LAWOO	#245 1993 Bills Gold	DLA3I7
#200 Gold Mistake Free Cheat	XL7SP1	#246 1994 49ers Gold	DR7EST
#210 Gold QB on Target Cheat	WROA0R	#247 1996 Packers Gold	F8LUST
#220 Super Bowl XLI Gold	RLA9R7	#248 1998 Broncos Gold	FIES95
#221 Super Bowl XLII Gold	WRLUF8	#249 1999 Rams Gold	S9OUSW
#222 Super Bowl XLIII Gold	NIEV4A	#250 Bears Pump Up the Crowd	B1OUPH
#223 Super Bowl XLIV Gold	M5AB7L	#251 Bengals Cheerleader	DRL2SW
#224 Aloha Stadium Gold	YI8P8U	#252 Bills Cheerleader	1PLUYO
#225 1958 Colts Gold	B57QLU	#253 Broncos Cheerleader	3ROUJO
#226 1966 Packers Gold	1PL1FL	#254 Browns Pump Up the Crowd	T1UTOA
#227 1968 Jets Gold	MIE6WO	#255 Buccaneers Cheerleader	S9EWRI
#228 1970 Browns Gold	CL2TOE	#256 Cardinals Cheerleader	57IEPI
#229 1972 Dolphins Gold	NOEB7U	#257 Chargers Cheerleader	F7UHL8
#230 1974 Steelers Gold	YOOFLA	#258 Chiefs Cheerleader	PRI5SL
#231 1976 Raiders Gold	MOA11I	#259 Colts Cheerleader	1R5AMI
#232 1977 Broncos Gold	C8UM7U	#260 Cowboys Cheerleader	Z2ACHL
#233 1978 Dolphins Gold	VIUOO7	#261 Dolphins Cheerleader	C5AHLE
#234 1980 Raiders Gold	NLAPH3	#262 Eagles Cheerleader	PO7DRO
#235 1981 Chargers Gold	COAGI4	#263 Falcons Cheerleader	37USPO
#236 1982 Redskins Gold	WL8BRI	#264 49ers Cheerleader	KLOCRL
#237 1983 Raiders Gold	HOEW71	#265 Giants Pump Up the Crowd	C4USPI
#238 1984 Dolphins Gold	M1AM1E	#266 Jaguars Cheerleader	MIEH7E
#239 1985 Bears Gold	QOET08	#267 Jets Pump Up the Crowd	COLUXI
#240 1986 Giants Gold	ZI8S2L	#268 Lions Pump Up the Crowd	3LABLU
#241 1988 49ers Gold	SP2A8H	#269 Packers Pump Up the Crowd	4HO7VO
#242 1990 Eagles Gold	2L4TRO	#270 Panthers Cheerleader	F2IASP
#243 1991 Lions Gold	J1ETRI	#282 All AFC Team Gold	PRO9PH
#244 1992 Cowboys Gold	W9UVI9	#283 All NFC Team Gold	RLATH7

MAJOR LEAGUE BASEBALL 2K7

MICKEY MANTLE ON THE FREE AGENTS LIST

Select Enter Cheat Code from the My 2K7 menu and enter themick.

ALL CHEATS

Select Enter Cheat Code from the My 2K7 menu and enter Black Sox.

ALL EXTRAS

Select Enter Cheat Code from the My 2K7 menu and enter Game On.

UNLOCK EVERYTHING

Select Enter Cheat Code from the My 2K7 menu and enter Derek Jeter. This does not unlock the Topps cheats.

MIGHTY MICK CHEAT

Select Enter Cheat Code from the My 2K7 menu and enter mightymick.

TRIPLE CROWN CHEAT

Select Enter Cheat Code from the My 2K7 menu and enter triplecrown.

BIG BLAST CHEAT

Select Enter Cheat Code from the My 2K7 menu and enter m4murder.

MARVEL ULTIMATE ALLIANCE

UNLOCK ALL SKINS
At the Team Menu, press Up, Down, Left, Right, Left, Right, Start.

UNLOCKS ALL HERO POWERS
At the Team Menu, press Left, Right, Up, Down, Up, Down, Start.

ALL HEROES TO LEVEL 99
At the Team Menu, press Up, Left, Up, Left, Down, Right, Down, Right, Start.

UNLOCK ALL HEROES
At the Team Menu, press Up, Up, Down, Down, Left, Left, Left, Start.

UNLOCK DAREDEVIL
At the Team Menu, press Left, Left, Right, Right, Up, Down, Up, Down, Start.

UNLOCK ALL CONCEPT ART
At the Review menu, press Down, Down, Down, Right, Right, Left, Down, Start.

UNLOCK SILVER SURFER
At the Team Menu, press Down, Left, Left, Up, Right, Up, Down, Left, Start.

GOD MODE
During gameplay, press Up, Down, Up, Down, Up, Left, Down, Right, Start.

TOUCH OF DEATH
During gameplay, press Left, Right, Down, Down, Right, Left, Start.

SUPER SPEED
During gameplay, press Up, Left, Up, Right, Down, Right, Start.

UNLOCK ALL CINEMATICS
At the Review menu, press Up, Left, Left, Up, Right, Right, Up, Start.

FILL MOMENTUM
During gameplay, press Left, Right, Right, Left, Up, Down, Down, Up, Start.

UNLOCK ALL LOAD SCREENS
At the Review menu, press Up, Down, Right, Left, Up, Up Down, Start.

UNLOCK ALL COMICS
At the Review menu, press Left, Right, Right, Left, Up, Up, Right, Start.

UNLOCK ALL COURSES
At the Comic Missions menu, press Up, Right, Left, Down, Up, Right, Left, Down, Start.

MLB 07: THE SHOW

CLASSIC STADIUMS
At the Main Menu, press Down, Up, Right, Down, Up, Left, Down, Up.

GOLDEN/SLIVER ERA PLAYERS
At the Main Menu, press Left, Up, Right, Down, Down, Left, Up, Down.

MOTORSTORM

UNLOCK EVERYTHING
At the Main menu, hold **L1** + **L2** + **R1** + **R2** + **R3** (while pressed Up) + **L3** (while pressed Down).

BIG HEADS ON ATVS AND BIKES
Pause the game and hold **L1** + **L2** + **R1** + **R2** + **R3** (while pressed Right), + **L3** (while pressed Left).

NASCAR 08

ALL CHASE MODE CARS
Select cheat codes from the options menu and enter checkered flag.

EA SPORTS CAR
Select cheat codes from the options menu and enter ea sports car.

FANTASY DRIVERS
Select cheat codes from the options menu and enter race the pack.

WALMART CAR AND TRACK
Select cheat codes from the options menu and enter walmart everyday.

NBA 07

2006 CHARLOTTE BOBCATS ALTERNATE JERSEY
Select NBA.com from the Trophy Room. Press ● to bring up the Enter Code screen. Enter JKL846ETK5.

2006 NOK HORNETS ALTERNATE JERSEY
Select NBA.com from the Trophy Room. Press ● to bring up the Enter Code screen. Enter EL2E3T8H58.

2006 NEW JERSEY NETS ALTERNATE JERSEY
Select NBA.com from the Trophy Room. Press ● to bring up the Enter Code screen. Enter NB79D965D2.

2006 UTAH JAZZ ALTERNATE JERSEY
Select NBA.com from the Trophy Room. Press ● to bring up the Enter Code screen. Enter 228GG7585G.

2006 WAS WIZARDS ALTERNATE JERSEY
Select NBA.com from the Trophy Room. Press ● to bring up the Enter Code screen. Enter PL5285F37F.

2007 EASTERN ALL STARS
Select NBA.com from the Trophy Room. Press ● to bring up the Enter Code screen. Enter 5F89RE3H8G.

2007 WESTERN ALL STARS
Select NBA.com from the Trophy Room. Press ● to bring up the Enter Code screen. Enter 2H5E89EH8C.

NBA 2K7

ABA BALL
Select Codes from the Features menu and enter payrespect.

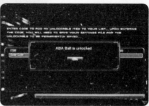

ALL-STAR BALL
Select Codes from the Features menu and enter ply8mia.

MAXIMUM DURABILITY
Select Codes from the Features menu and enter ironman.

UNLIMITED STAMINA
Select Codes from the Features menu and enter norest.

+10 DEFENSIVE AWARENESS
Select Codes from the Features menu and enter getstops.

+10 OFFENSIVE AWARENESS
Select Codes from the Features menu and enter inthezone.

2007 ALL-STAR UNIFORMS
Select Codes from the Features menu and enter syt6cii.

BOBCATS SECONDARY
Select Codes from the Features menu and enter bcb8sta.

JAZZ SECONDARY
Select Codes from the Features menu and enter zjb3lau.

NETS SECONDARY
Select Codes from the Features menu and enter nrd4esj.

WIZARDS SECONDARY
Select Codes from the Features menu and enter zw9idla.

ST. PATRICK'S DAY UNIFORMS
Select Codes from the Features menu and enter tpk7sgn.

VALENTINE'S DAY UNIFORMS
Select Codes from the Features menu and enter vdr5lya.

INTERNATIONAL ALL-STARS
Select Codes from the Features menu and enter tns9roi.

NBA 2K TEAM
Select Codes from the Features menu and enter bestsim.

SUPERSTARS
Select Codes from the Features menu and enter rta1spe.

TOPPS 2K SPORTS ALL-STARS
Select Codes from the Features menu and enter topps2ksports.

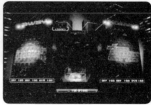

NBA 2K8

2KSPORTS TEAM
Select Codes from the Features menu and enter 2ksports.

VISUAL CONCEPTS TEAM
Select Codes from the Features menu and enter Vcteam.

ABA BALL
Select Codes from the Features menu and enter Payrespect.

NBA LIVE 07

AIR JORDAN V
Select NBA Codes from My NBA Live 07 and enter PNBBX1EVT5.

AIR JORDAN V
Select NBA Codes from My NBA Live 07 and enter VIR13PC451.

AIR JORDAN V
Select NBA Codes from My NBA Live 07 and enter IB7G8NN91Z.

JORDAN MELO M3
Select NBA Codes from My NBA Live 07 and enter JUL38TC485.

C-BILLUPS ALL-STAR EDITION
Select NBA Codes from My NBA Live 07 and enter BV6877HB9N.

ADIDAS C-BILLUPS VEGAS EDITION
Select NBA Codes from My NBA Live 07 and enter 85NVLDMWS5.

ADIDAS GARNETT BOUNCE ALL-STAR EDITION
Select NBA Codes from My NBA Live 07 and enter HYIOUHCAAN.

ADIDAS GARNETT BOUNCE VEGAS EDITION
Select NBA Codes from My NBA Live 07 and enter KDZ2MQL17W.

ADIDAS GIL-ZERO ALL-STAR EDITION
Select NBA Codes from My NBA Live 07 and enter 23DN1PPOG4.

ADIDAS GIL-ZERO VEGAS EDITION
Select NBA Codes from My NBA Live 07 and enter QQQ3JCUYQ7.

ADIDAS GIL-ZERO MID
Select NBA Codes from My NBA Live 07 and enter 1GSJC8JWRL.

ADIDAS GIL-ZERO MID
Select NBA Codes from My NBA Live 07 and enter 369V6RVU3G.

ADIDAS STEALTH ALL-STAR EDITION
Select NBA Codes from My NBA Live 07 and enter FE454DFJCC.

ADIDAS T-MAC 6 ALL-STAR EDITION
Select NBA Codes from My NBA Live 07 and enter MCJK843NNC.

ADIDAS T-MAC 6 VEGAS EDITION
Select NBA Codes from My NBA Live 07 and enter 84GF7EJG8V.

CHARLOTTE BOBCATS SECOND ROAD JERSEY
Select NBA Codes from My NBA Live 07 and enter WEDX671H7S.

UTAH JAZZ SECOND ROAD JERSEY
Select NBA Codes from My NBA Live 07 and enter VCBI89FK83.

NEW JERSEY NETS SECOND ROAD JERSEY
Select NBA Codes from My NBA Live 07 and enter D4SAA98U5H.

WASHINGTON WIZARDS SECOND ROAD JERSEY
Select NBA Codes from My NBA Live 07 and enter QV93NLKXQC.

EASTERN ALL-STARS 2007 ROAD JERSEY
Select NBA Codes from My NBA Live 07 and enter WOCNW4KL7L.

EASTERN ALL-STARS 2007 HOME JERSEY
Select NBA Codes from My NBA Live 07 and enter 5654ND43N6.

WESTERN ALL-STARS 2007 ROAD JERSEY
Select NBA Codes from My NBA Live 07 and enter XX93BVL20U.

WESTERN ALL-STARS 2007 HOME JERSEY
Select NBA Codes from My NBA Live 07 and enter 993NSKL199.

NBA STREET HOMECOURT

ALL TEAMS
At the Main menu, hold **R1** + **L1** and press Left, Right, Left, Right.

ALL COURTS
At the Main menu, hold **R1** + **L1** and press Up, Right, Down, Left.

BLACK/RED BALL
At the Main menu, hold **R1** + **L1** and press Up, Down, Left, Right.

NHL 08

ALL RBK EDGE JERSEYS
At the RBK Edge Code option, enter h3oyxpwksf8ibcgt.

RATATOUILLE

Select Gusteau's Shop from the Extras menu. Choose Secrets, select the appropriate code number, and then enter the code. Once the code is entered, select the cheat you want to activate it.

CODE NUMBER	CODE	EFFECT
1	Pieceocake	Very Easy difficulty mode
2	Myhero	no impact and no damage from enemies
3	Shielded	No damage from enemies
4	Spyagent	Move undetected by any enemy
5	Ilikeonions	Fart every time Remy jumps
6	Hardfeelings	Head butt when attacking instead of tailswipe
7	Slumberparty	Multiplayer mode
8	Gusteauart	All Concept Art
9	Gusteauship	All four championship modes
10	Mattelme	All single player and multiplayer minigames
11	Gusteauvid	All Videos
12	Gusteaures	All Bonus Artworks
13	Gusteaudream	All Dream Worlds in Gusteau's Shop
14	Gusteauslide	All Slides in Gusteau's Shop
15	Gusteaulevel	All single player minigames
16	Gusteaucombo	All items in Gusteau's Shop
17	Gusteaupot	5,000 Gusteau points
18	Gusteaujack	10,000 Gusteau points
19	Gusteauomni	50,000 Gusteau points

SKATE

BEST BUY CLOTHES
At the Main menu, press Up, Down, Left, Right, ⬤, R1, ⬤, L1.

STUNTMAN IGNITION

3 PROPS IN STUNT CREATOR MODE
Select Cheats from Extras and enter COOLPROP.

ALL ITEMS UNLOCKED FOR CONSTRUCTION MODE
Select Cheats from Extras and enter NOBLEMAN.

MVX SPARTAN
Select Cheats from Extras and enter fastride.

ALL CHEATS
Select Cheats from Extras and enter Wearefrozen.
This unlocks the following cheats: Slo-mo Cool, Thrill Cam, Vision Switcher, Nitro Addiction, Freaky Fast, and Ice Wheels.

ALL CHEATS
Select Cheats from Extras and enter Kungfoopete.

ICE WHEELS CHEAT
Select Cheats from Extras and enter IceAge.

NITRO ADDICTION CHEAT
Select Cheats from Extras and enter TheDuke.

VISION SWITCHER CHEAT
Select Cheats from Extras and enter GFXMODES.

SUPER PUZZLE FIGHTER II TURBO HD REMIX

PLAY AS AKUMA
At the character select, highlight Hsien-Ko and press Down.

PLAY AS DAN
At the character select, highlight Donovan and press Down.

PLAY AS DEVILOT
At the character select, highlight Morrigan and press Down.

PLAY AS ANITA
At the character select, hold **L1** + **R1** and choose Donovan.

PLAY AS HSIEN-KO'S TALISMAN
At the character select, hold **L1** + **R1** and choose Hsien-Ko.

PLAY AS MORRIGAN AS A BAT
At the character select, hold **L1** + **R1** and choose Morrigan.

SURF'S UP

ALL CHAMPIONSHIP LOCATIONS
Select Cheat Codes from the Extras menu and enter FREEVISIT.

ALL LEAF SLIDE STAGES
Select Cheat Codes from the Extras menu and enter GOINGDOWN.

ALL MULTIPLAYER LEVELS
Select Cheat Codes from the Extras menu and enter MULTIPASS.

ALL BOARDS
Select Cheat Codes from the Extras menu and enter MYPRECIOUS.

ASTRAL BOARD
Select Cheat Codes from the Extras menu and enter ASTRAL.

MONSOON BOARD
Select Cheat Codes from the Extras menu and enter MONSOON.

TINE SHOCKWAVE BOARD
Select Cheat Codes from the Extras menu and enter TINYSHOCKWAVE.

ALL CHARACTER CUSTOMIZATIONS
Select Cheat Codes from the Extras menu and enter TOPFASHION.

PLAY AS ARNOLD
Select Cheat Codes from the Extras menu and enter TINYBUTSTRONG.

PLAY AS ELLIOT
Select Cheat Codes from the Extras menu and enter SURPRISEGUEST.

PLAY AS GEEK
Select Cheat Codes from the Extras menu and enter SLOWANDSTEADY.

PLAY AS TANK EVANS
Select Cheat Codes from the Extras menu and enter IMTHEBEST.

PLAY AS TATSUHI KOBAYASHI
Select Cheat Codes from the Extras menu and enter KOBAYASHI.

PLAY AS ZEKE TOPANGA
Select Cheat Codes from the Extras menu and enter THELEGEND.

ALL VIDEOS AND SPEN GALLERY
Select Cheat Codes from the Extras menu and enter WATCHAMOVIE.

ART GALLERY
Select Cheat Codes from the Extras menu and enter NICEPLACE.

TIGER WOODS PGA TOUR 08

ALL COURSES
Select Password from EA Sports Extras and enter greensfees.

ALL GOLFERS
Select Password from EA Sports Extras and enter allstars.

WAYNE ROONEY
Select Password from EA Sports Extras and enter playfifa08.

INFINITE MONEY
Select Password from EA Sports Extras and enter cream.

TONY HAWK'S PROJECT 8

SPONSOR ITEMS

As you progress through Career mode and move up the rankings, you gain sponsors and each comes with its own Create-a-skater item.

RANK REQUIRED	CAS ITEM UNLOCKED
Rank 040	Adio Kenny V2 Shoes
Rank 050	Quiksilver_Hoody_3
Rank 060	Birdhouse Tony Hawk Deck
Rank 080	Vans Na Skool Gothic Shoes
Rank 100	Volcom Scallero Jacket
Rank 110	eS Square One Shoes
Rank 120	Almost Watch What You Say Deck
Rank 140	DVS Adage Shoe
Rank 150	Element Illuminate Deck
Rank 160	Etnies Sheckler White Lavender Shoes
Complete Skateshop Goal	Stereo Soundwave Deck

SKATERS

All of the skaters, except for Tony Hawk, must be unlocked by completing challenges in the Career Mode. They are useable in Free Skate and 2 Player modes.

SKATER	HOW TO UNLOCK
Tony Hawk	Always Unlocked
Lyn-z Adams Hawkins	Complete Pro Challenge
Bob Burquist	Complete Pro Challenge
Dustin Dollin	Complete Pro Challenge
Nyjah Huston	Complete Pro Challenge
Bam Margera	Complete Pro Challenge
Rodney Mullen	Complete Pro Challenge
Paul Rodriguez	Complete Pro Challenge
Ryan Sheckler	Complete Pro Challenge
Daewon Song	Complete Pro Challenge
Mike Vallely	Complete Pro Challenge
Stevie Willams	Complete Pro Challenge
Travis Barker	Complete Pro Challenge
Kevin Staab	Complete Pro Challenge
Zombie	Complete Pro Challenge
Christiaan Hosoi	Rank #1
Jason Lee	Complete Final Tony Hawk Goal
Photographer	Unlock Shops
Security Guard	Unlock School
Bum	Unlock Car Factory
Beaver Mascot	Unlock High School

SKATER	HOW TO UNLOCK
Real Estate Agent	Unlock Downtown
Filmer	Unlock High School
Skate Jam Kid	Rank #4
Dad	Rank #1
Colonel	All Gaps
Nerd	Complete School Spirit Goal

CHEAT CODES

Select Cheat Codes from the Options and enter the following codes. In game you can access some codes from the Options menu.

CHEAT CODE	RESULTS
plus44	Unlocks Travis Barker
hohohosoi	Unlocks Christian Hosoi
notmono	Unlocks Jason Lee
mixitup	Unlocks Kevin Staab
strangefellows	Unlocks Dad & Skater Jam Kid
themedia	Unlocks Photog Girl & Filmer
militarymen	Unlocks Colonel & Security Guard
jammypack	Unlocks Always Special
balancegalore	Unlocks Perfect Rail
frontandback	Unlocks Perect Manual
shellshock	Unlocks Unlimited Focus
shescaresme	Unlocks Big Realtor
birdhouse	Unlocks Inkblot deck
allthebest	Full stats
needaride	All decks unlocked and free, except for Inkblot Deck and Gamestop Deck
yougotitall	All specials unlocked and in player's special list and set as owned in skate shop
wearelosers	Unlocks Nerd and a Bum
manineedadate	Unlocks Beaver Mascot
suckstobedead	Unlocks Officer Dick
HATEDANDPROUD	Unlocks the Vans item

TONY HAWK'S PROVING GROUND

Select Cheat Codes from the Options and enter the following cheats. Some codes need to be enabled by selecting Cheats from the Options during a game.

UNLOCK	CHEAT	UNLOCK	CHEAT
Unlocks Boneman	CRAZYBONEMAN	Unlock Lansdowne	THELOCALPARK
Unlocks Bosco	MOREMILK	Unlock Air & Space Museum	THEINDOORPARK
Unlocks Cam	NOTACAMERA	Unlocks all Fun Items	OVERTHETOP
Unlocks Cooper	THECOOP	Unlocks all CAS items	GIVEMESTUFF
Unlocks Eddie X	SKETCHY	Unlocks all Decks	LETSGOSKATE
Unlocks El Patinador	PILEDRIVER	Unlock all Game Movies	WATCHTHIS
Unlocks Eric	FLYAWAY	Unlock all Lounge Bling Items	SWEETSTUFF
Unlocks Mad Dog	RABBIES	Unlock all Lounge Themes	LAIDBACKLOUNGE
Unlocks MCA	INTERGALACTIC	Unlock all Rigger Pieces	IMGONNABUILD
Unlocks Mel	NOTADUDE	Unlock all Video Editor Effects	TRIPPY
Unlocks Rube	LOOKSSMELLY	Unlock all Video Editor Overlays	PUTEMONTOP
Unlocks Spence	DAPPER	All specials unlocked and in player's special list	LOTSOFTRICKS
Unlocks Shayne	MOVERS	Full Stats	BEEFEDUP
Unlocks TV Producer	SHAKER	Give player +50 skill points	NEEDSHELP
Unlock FDR	THEPREZPARK		

UNLOCK	CHEAT		UNLOCK	CHEAT
Unlock all Lounge Themes	LAIDBACKLOUNGE		All specials unlocked and in player's special list	LOTSOFTRICKS
Unlock all Rigger Pieces	IMGONNABUILD		Full Stats	BEEFEDUP
Unlock all Video Editor Effects	TRIPPY		Give player +50 skill points	NEEDSHELP
Unlock all Video Editor Overlays	PUTEMONTOP			

The following cheats lock you out of the Leaderboards:

UNLOCK	CHEAT		UNLOCK	CHEAT
Unlocks Perfect Manual	STILLAINTFALLIN		Unlock Unlimited Slash Grind	SUPERSLASHIN
Unlocks Perfect Rail	AINTFALLIN		Unlocks 100% branch completion in NTT	FOREVERNAILED
Unlock Super Check	BOOYAH		No Bails	ANDAINTFALLIN
Unlocks Unlimited Focus	MYOPIC			

You can not use the Video Editor with the following cheats:

UNLOCK	CHEAT
Unlocks Invisible Man	THEMISSING
Mini Skater	TINYTATER
No Board	MAGICMAN

TRANSFORMERS: THE GAME

INFINITE HEALTH
At the Main menu, press Left, Left, Up, Left, Right, Down, Right.

INFINITE AMMO
At the Main menu, press Up, Down, Left, Right, Up, Up, Down.

NO MILITARY OR POLICE
At the Main menu, press Right, Left, Right, Left, Right, Left, Right.

ALL MISSIONS
At the Main menu, press Down, Up, Left, Right, Right, Right, Up, Down.

BONUS CYBERTRON MISSIONS
At the Main menu, press Right, Up, Up, Down, Right, Left, Left.

GENERATION 1 SKIN: JAZZ
At the Main menu, press Left, Up, Down, Down, Left, Up, Right.

GENERATION 1 SKIN: MEGATRON
At the Main menu, press Down, Left, Left, Down, Right, Right, Up.

GENERATION 1 SKIN: OPTIMUS PRIME
At the Main menu, press Down, Right, Left, Up, Down, Down, Left.

GENERATION 1 SKIN: ROBOVISION OPTIMUS PRIME
At the Main menu, press Down, Down, Up, Up, Right, Right, Right.

GENERATION 1 SKIN: STARSCREAM
At the Main menu, press Right, Down, Left, Left, Down, Up, Up.

VIRTUA FIGHTER 5

WATCH MODE
Select Exhibition Mode, then at the character select, hold **L1** + **R1** and press ✖.

PLAYSTATION® PORTABLE

EVERYONE

ATV OFFROAD FURY: BLAZIN' TRAILS

BURNOUT LEGENDS

CAPCOM PUZZLE WORLD

CARS

EXIT

FROGGER HELMET CHAOS

GRADIUS COLLECTION

HOT SHOTS GOLF 2

HOT SHOTS GOLF: OPEN TEE

LEGO STAR WARS II: THE ORIGINAL TRILOGY

MAJOR LEAGUE BASEBALL 2K7

MLB 07: THE SHOW

MTX MOTOTRAX

NBA BALLERS: REBOUND

NEOPETS PETPET ADVENTURE: THE WAND OF WISHING

OUTRUN 2006: COAST 2 COAST

POPOLOCROIS

STAR TREK: TACTICAL ASSAULT

VIRTUA TENNIS: WORLD TOUR

WRC: FIA WORLD RALLY CHAMPIONSHIP

YU-GI-OH! GX TAG FORCE

YU-GI-OH! GX TAG FORCE 2

EVERYONE 10+

BATTLEZONE

FULL AUTO 2: BATTLELINES

SHREK THE THIRD

THRILLVILLE: OFF THE RAILS

WORMS: OPEN WARFARE

TEEN

CAPCOM CLASSICS COLLECTION REMIXED

CASTLEVANIA: THE DRACULA X CHRONICLES

DEATH JR.

DISGAEA: AFTERNOON OF DARKNESS

DRAGON BALL Z: SHIN BUDOKAI

EA REPLAY

FINAL FANTASY TACTICS: THE WAR OF THE LIONS

JUICED: ELIMINATOR

JUSTICE LEAGUE HEROES

MARVEL TRADING CARD GAME

MARVEL ULTIMATE ALLIANCE

MEDIEVIL: RESURRECTION

PIRATES OF THE CARIBBEAN: DEAD MAN'S CHEST

SEGA GENESIS COLLECTION

THE SIMS 2

THE SIMS 2: PETS

STAR WARS: BATTLEFRONT II

STAR WARS: LETHAL ALLIANCE

TOMB RAIDER: LEGEND

TONY HAWK'S PROJECT 8

WORLD CHAMPIONSHIP POKER 2: FEATURING HOWARD LEDERER

X-MEN LEGENDS II: RISE OF APOCALYPSE

Table of Contents

ATV OFFROAD FURY: BLAZIN' TRAILS

UNLOCK EVERYTHING EXCEPT THE FURY BIKE
Select Player Profile from Options. Choose Enter Cheat and enter All Access.

1500 CREDITS

Select Player Profile from Options. Choose Enter Cheat and enter $moneybags$.

ALL RIDER GEAR

Select Player Profile from Options. Choose Enter Cheat and enter Duds.

TIRES

Select Player Profile from Options. Choose Enter Cheat and enter Dubs.

MUSIC VIDEOS

Select Player Profile from Options. Choose Enter Cheat and enter Billboards.

BATTLEZONE

Select cheats from the options menu. Highlight the following cheats and enter the appropriate cheat. Press ⊗ to exit the cheat menu. Press ⊙ to disable all cheats.

INVISIBLE
L, Left, Right, ⊙, ⊚, R.

INSTA GIB
L, ⊙, ⊚, Right, ⊚, R.

MAX PLAYERS
Right, Left, Right, Left, Right, Left.

MORTAR ONLY
⊚, L, ⊙, ⊙, Right, Left.

NO AUTO HEAL
Start, Right, Left, select, Right, ⊙.

PICK UP DOUBLE TIME
⊙, Right, ⊚, Right, R, L

TEAM SPECIAL RECHARGE
Right, Right, Left. ⊙, R, L

UNLIMITED AMMO
Left, R, L, ⊚, Right, ⊙.

BURNOUT LEGENDS

COP RACER
Earn a Gold in all Pursuit events.

FIRE TRUCK
Earn a Gold on all Crash Events.

GANGSTER BOSS
Earn Gold in all Race events.

CAPCOM CLASSICS COLLECTION REMIXED

UNLOCK EVERYTHING
At the title screen, press Left on D-pad, Right on D-pad, Left on Analog stick, Right on Analog stick, ⊙, ⊙, Up on D-pad, Down on D-pad.

CAPCOM PUZZLE WORLD

SUPER BUSTER BROS.

LEVEL SELECT IN TOUR MODE
At the Main menu, highlight Tour Mode, hold Down and press ✖.

SUPER PUZZLE FIGHTER

PLAY AS AKUMA
At the character select, highlight Hsien-Ko and press Down.

PLAY AS DAN
At the character select, highlight Donovan and press Down.

PLAY AS DEVILOT
At the character select, highlight Morrigan and press Down.

PLAY AS ANITA
At the character select, hold L + R and choose Donovan.

PLAY AS HSIEN-KO'S TALISMAN
At the character select, hold L + R and choose Hsien-Ko.

PLAY AS MORRIGAN AS A BAT
At the character select, hold L + R and choose Morrigan.

CASTLEVANIA: THE DRACULA X CHRONICLES

Symphony of the Night
After clearing the game as Alucard, select New Game and enter the following as your name:

PLAY AS ALUCARD, WITH 99 LUCK AND THE LAPIS LAZULI
X-X!V''Q

PLAY AS ALUCARD, WITH THE AXE LORD ARMOR
AXEARMOR

PLAY AS MARIA RENARD
MARIA

PLAY AS RICHTER BELMONT
RICHTER

CARS

BONUS SPEEDWAY (REVERSED) IN CUSTOM RACE
At the Main menu hold L and press ✖, ⬤, ⬤, ✖, ⬤, ⬤.

EATH JR.

AN'T TOUCH THIS (INVINCIBILITY)
use the game, hold L + R and press Up, Up, Down, Down, Left, Left, Right, Right, ●, ▲.

CREASED HEALTH
use the game, hold L + R and press Up, Up, Down, Down, ✖, ●, ▲, ●, ✖, ✖.

EAPONS UPGRADED (GIVES ALL WEAPONS)
use the game, hold L + R and press Up, Up, Down, Down, Left, Right, Left, Right, ✖, ●.

MMO REFILLED
use the game, hold L + R and press ▲, ▲, ✖, ✖, ●, ●, ●, ●, Down, Right.

NLIMITED AMMO
use the game, hold L + R and press ▲, ▲, ✖, ✖, ●, ●, ●, ●, Right, Down.

MY HEAD FEELS FUNNY (BIG HEAD)
Pause the game, hold L + R and press ▲, ●, ✖, ●, ▲, Up, Right, Down, Left, Up. Re-enter the code for normal head.

ANT BLADE (BIG SCYTHE)
use the game, hold L + R and press ▲, ●, ✖, ●, , Up, Left, Down, Right, Up.

FREE SEEP
Pause the game, hold L + R and press Left, Left, Right, Right, Left, Right, Left, Right, ✖, ✖.

A LITTLE MORE HELP (ASSIST EXTENDER)
Pause the game, hold L + R and press Up, Up, Down, Down, ●, ▲, ✖, ✖, ▲, ●.

EE WIDGET
use the game, hold L + R and press Right, Up, Down, , Up, Left, ●, ●, Right.

L LEVELS AND FREE ALL ARACTERS
use the game, hold L + R and press Up, Up, Up, Up, wn, Down, Down, Down, ✖, ✖. Enter a stage and t back to the museum for code to take effect.

I'D BUY THAT FOR A DOLLAR (FILL PANDORA ASSIST METER)

Pause the game, hold L + R and press Up, Up, Down, Down, Up, Right, Down, Left, ✖, ✖.

THIS WAS JED'S IDEA (ATTACKS HAVE DIFFERENT NAMES)

Pause the game, hold L + R and press Up, Up, Down, Left, ▲, ▲, ●, ✖, ●, ■.

WEAPON NAMES = NORMAL (WEAPONS HAVE DIFFERENT NAMES)

Pause the game, hold L + R and press Down, Down, Up, Up, Left, Right, Left, Right, ●, ▲.

EYEDOOR SOLIDITY QUESTIONABLE (NO LONGER REQUIRE SOULS)

Pause the game, hold L + R and press Up, Left, Down, Right, Left, ▲, ●, ✖, ●, ■.

BUDDY DECALS (BULLET HOLES BECOME PICTURES)

Pause the game, hold L + R and press Up, Right, Down, Left, Up, ▲, ✖, ●, ■, ▲.

STAGE WARP

Pause the game, hold L + R and enter the following codes to warp to that stage.

STAGE	CODE
Advanced Training	Down, ✖, Down, ✖, Down, ✖, Down, ✖, Down, ●
The Basement	Down, ✖, Down, ✖, Down, ✖, Down, ✖, Up, ▲
Basic Training	Up, ▲, Up, ✖, Down, ✖, Down, ✖, Down, ✖
Big Trouble in Little Downtown	Up, ▲, Down, ✖, Down, ✖, Down, ✖, Down, ✖
Bottom of the Bell Curve	Down, ✖, Down, ✖, Down, ✖, Down, ✖, Down, ▲
The Burger Tram	Down, ✖, Down, ✖, Down, ✖, Up, ✖, Down, ✖
Burn it Down	Down, ✖, Up, ▲, Down, ✖, Down, ✖, Down, ✖
The Corner Store	Down, ✖, Up, ✖, Down, ✖, Down, ✖, Down, ✖
Final Battle	Down, ✖, Down, ✖, Down, ✖, Down, ✖, Up, ▲
Growth Spurt	Down, ✖, Down, ✖, Down, ✖, Down, ✖, Up, ✖
Happy Trails Insanitarium	Down, ✖, Down, ▲, Up, ✖, Down, ✖, Down, ✖
Higher Learning	Down, ✖, Down, ✖, Down, ✖, Down, ✖, Down, ✖
How a Cow Becomes a Steak	Down, ✖, Down, ▲, Down, ✖, Down, ✖, Down, ✖
Inner Madness	Down, ✖, Down, ✖, Up, ▲, Down, ✖, Down, ✖
Into the Box	Down, ✖, Down, ✖, Down, ✖, Up, ▲, Down, ✖
Moving on Up	Down, ▲, Up, ✖, Down, ✖, Down, ✖, Down, ✖
The Museum	Up, ✖, Down ✖, Down, ✖, Down, ✖, Down, ✖
My House	Down, ✖, Down, ✖, Down, ✖, Down, ✖, Down, ✖
Seep's Hood	Down, ▲, Down, ✖, Down, ✖, Down, ✖, Down, ✖
Shock Treatment	Down, ✖, Down, ✖, Down, ▲, Up, ✖, Down, ✖
Udder Madness	Down, ✖, Down, ✖, Up, ✖, Down, ✖, Down, ✖

DISGAEA: AFTERNOON OF DARKNESS

ETNA MODE

At the Main menu, highlight New Game and press ▲, ■, ●, ▲, ▲, ■, ●, ✖.

DRAGON BALL Z: SHIN BUDOKAI

MINI-GAME
At the Main menu, press L and then press R to begin the mini-game.

EA REPLAY

DESERT STRIKE

10 LIVES
At the Desert Strike menu, press ● to bring up the Password screen. Enter BQQQAEZ.

JUNGLE STRIKE

PASSWORDS
Press ● at the Jungle Strike menu to bring up the Password screen. Enter the following:

LEVEL	PASSWORD	LEVEL	PASSWORD
Mountains	7LSPFBVWTWP	River Raid	TGB76MGCZCC
Night Strike	X4MFB4MHPH4	Training Ground	9NHDXMGCZCG
Puloso City	V6HGY39XVXL	Washington D.C	BXYTNMGCYDB
Return Home	N4MK9N6MHM7		

WING COMMANDER

INVINCIBILITY AND STAGE SELECT
At the Wing Commander menu, press ✕, ●, ✕, ●, ✕, ●, L, ●, R, ●, Start.

EXIT

SITUATION 8
Complete Situation 1. Then at the Title screen, press L, R, Left, Right, ●, ●, ✕, ▲.

SITUATION 9
Complete Situation 1 and unlock Situation 8. Then at the Title screen, press ▲, Down, ●, Left, ✕, Up, ●, Right.

SITUATION 10
Complete Situation 1 and unlock Situations 8 and 9. Then at the Title screen, press Right, Down, Up, Left, ●, ✕, R, L.

FINAL FANTASY TACTICS: THE WAR OF THE LIONS

MUSIC TEST MODE
Enter the main character's name as PolkaPolka at the name entry screen.

FROGGER HELMET CHAOS

MOHAWK WIG
Enter Berry, Lily, Lumpy, Lily as a password.

AFRO WIG
Enter Finnius, Frogger, Frogger, Wani as a password.

SANTA HAT
Enter Lily, Lily, Wani, Wani as a password.

PIRATE HAT
Enter Frogger, Berry, Finnius, Frogger as a password.

BASEBALL CAP
Enter Frogger, Frogger, Frogger, Berry as a password.

CROC HAT
Enter Lily, Lily, Wani, Lumpy as a password.

BUNNY EARS
Enter Lily, Frogger, Frogger, Lumpy as a password.

CAMOUFLAGE COSTUME
Enter Lily, Wani, Lily, Wani as a password.

COWBOY COSTUME
Enter Frogger, Lily, Lily, Lily as a password.

SANTA COSTUME
Play the game for four hours.

PIRATE COSTUME
Play the game for six hours.

PUNK COSTUME
Pause the game and press Up, Up, Down, Down, Left, Right, Left, Right, ●, ●, Start.

FULL AUTO 2: BATTLELINES

ALL CARS
Select Cheats from the Options and press Up, Up, Up, Up, Left, Down, Up, Right, Down, Down, Down, Down.

ALL EVENTS
Select Cheats from the Options and press Start, Left, Select, Right, Right, ●, ✖, ●, Start, R, Down, Select.

GRADIUS COLLECTION

ALL WEAPONS & POWER-UPS ON EASY DIFFICULTY
Pause the game and press Up, Up, Down, Down, Left, Right, Left, Right, ✖, ●.

HOT SHOTS GOLF 2

UNLOCK EVERYTHING
Enter 2gsh as your name.

HOT SHOTS GOLF: OPEN TEE

UNLOCK EVERYTHING
Start a new game with the name 5TNEPO.

EASY DIFFICULTY FOR CHALLENGE MODE
Lose two matches or tournaments in a row. This can be changed in the Options.

AUTUMN PAGODA COURSE
Reach Beginner level in Challenge Mode.

GOLDEN DESERT COURSE
Reach Senior level in Challenge Mode.

OLIVE COAST COURSE
Reach Mid-Rank level in Challenge Mode.

5TH LOYALTY HEART
Defeat the character with a Super Win to get the 5th Loyalty Heart.

MANUAL REPLAY MODE
Reach Senior level in Challenge Mode.

JUICED: ELIMINATOR

ALL CARS AND TRACKS IN ARCADE MODE
Select Cheats from the Extras menu and enter PIES.

JUSTICE LEAGUE HEROES

UNLOCK EVERYTHING
Pause the game, hold L + R and press Down, Left, Up, Right.

INVINCIBLE
Pause the game, hold L + R and press Left, Down, Right, Up, Left, Down, Right, Up.

UNLIMITED ENERGY
Pause the game, hold L + R and press Down, Down, Right, Right, Up, Up, Left, Left.

MAX ABILITIES
Pause the game, hold L + R and press Right, Down, Right, Down.

20 FREE SHIELDS
Pause the game, hold L + R and press Up, Up, Down, Down.

25 BOOSTS
Pause the game, hold L + R and press Left, Right, Left, Right.

LEGO STAR WARS II: THE ORIGINAL TRILOGY

BEACH TROOPER
At Mos Eisley Canteena, select Enter Code and enter UCK868. You still need to select Characters and purchase this character for 20,000 studs.

BEN KENOBI (GHOST)
At Mos Eisley Canteena, select Enter Code and enter BEN917. You still need to select Characters and purchase this character for 1,100,000 studs.

BESPIN GUARD
At Mos Eisley Canteena, select Enter Code and enter VHY832. You still need to select Characters and purchase this character for 15,000 studs.

BIB FORTUNA
At Mos Eisley Canteena, select Enter Code and enter WTY721. You still need to select Characters and purchase this character for 16,000 studs.

BOBA FETT
At Mos Eisley Canteena, select Enter Code and enter HLP221. You still need to select Characters and purchase this character for 175,000 studs.

DEATH STAR TROOPER
At Mos Eisley Canteena, select Enter Code and enter BNC332. You still need to select Characters and purchase this character for 19,000 studs.

EWOK
At Mos Eisley Canteena, select Enter Code and enter TTT289. You still need to select Characters and purchase this character for 34,000 studs.

GAMORREAN GUARD
At Mos Eisley Canteena, select Enter Code and enter YZF999. You still need to select Characters and purchase this character for 40,000 studs.

GONK DROID
At Mos Eisley Canteena, select Enter Code and enter NFX582. You still need to select Characters and purchase this character for 1,550 studs.

GRAND MOFF TARKIN
At Mos Eisley Canteena, select Enter Code and enter SMG219. You still need to select Characters and purchase this character for 38,000 studs.

GREEDO
At Mos Eisley Canteena, select Enter Code and enter NAH118. You still need to select Characters and purchase this character for 60,000 studs.

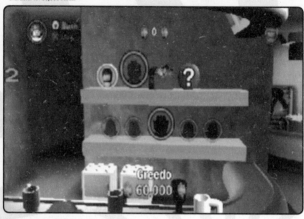

HAN SOLO (HOOD)
At Mos Eisley Canteena, select Enter Code and enter YWM840. You still need to select Characters and purchase this character for 20,000 studs.

IG-88
At Mos Eisley Canteena, select Enter Code and enter NXL973. You still need to select Characters and purchase this character for 30,000 studs.

IMPERIAL GUARD
At Mos Eisley Canteena, select Enter Code and enter MMM111. You still need to select Characters and purchase this character for 45,000 studs.

IMPERIAL OFFICER
At Mos Eisley Canteena, select Enter Code and enter BBV889. You still need to select Characters and purchase this character for 28,000 studs.

IMPERIAL SHUTTLE PILOT
At Mos Eisley Canteena, select Enter Code and enter VAP664. You still need to select Characters and purchase this character for 29,000 studs.

IMPERIAL SPY
At Mos Eisley Canteena, select Enter Code and enter CVT125. You still need to select Characters and purchase this character for 13,500 studs.

JAWA
At Mos Eisley Canteena, select Enter Code and enter JAW499. You still need to select Characters and purchase this character for 24,000 studs.

LOBOT
At Mos Eisley Canteena, select Enter Code and enter UUB319. You still need to select Characters and purchase this character for 11,000 studs.

PALACE GUARD
At Mos Eisley Canteena, select Enter Code and enter SGE549. You still need to select Characters and purchase this character for 14,000 studs.

REBEL PILOT
At Mos Eisley Canteena, select Enter Code and enter CYG336. You still need to select Characters and purchase this character for 15,000 studs.

REBEL TROOPER (HOTH)
At Mos Eisley Canteena, select Enter Code and enter EKU849. You still need to select Characters and purchase this character for 16,000 studs.

SANDTROOPER
At Mos Eisley Canteena, select Enter Code and enter YDV451. You still need to select Characters and purchase this character for 14,000 studs.

SKIFF GUARD
At Mos Eisley Canteena, select Enter Code and enter GBU888. You still need to select Characters and purchase this character for 12,000 studs.

SNOWTROOPER
At Mos Eisley Canteena, select Enter Code and enter NYU989. You still need to select Characters and purchase this character for 16,000 studs.

STROMTROOPER
At Mos Eisley Canteena, select Enter Code and enter PTR345. You still need to select Characters and purchase this character for 10,000 studs.

THE EMPEROR
At Mos Eisley Canteena, select Enter Code and enter HHY382. You still need to select Characters and purchase this character for 275,000 studs.

TIE FIGHTER
At Mos Eisley Canteena, select Enter Code and enter HDY739. You still need to select Characters and purchase this character for 60,000 studs.

TIE FIGHTER PILOT
At Mos Eisley Canteena, select Enter Code and enter NNZ316. You still need to select Characters and purchase this character for 21,000 studs.

TIE INTERCEPTOR
At Mos Eisley Canteena, select Enter Code and enter QYA828. You still need to select Characters and purchase this character for 40,000 studs.

TUSKEN RAIDER
At Mos Eisley Canteena, select Enter Code and enter PEJ821. You still need to select Characters and purchase this character for 23,000 studs.

UGNAUGHT
At Mos Eisley Canteena, select Enter Code and enter UGN694. You still need to select Characters and purchase this character for 36,000 studs.

MAJOR LEAGUE BASEBALL 2K7

MICKEY MANTLE ON THE FREE AGENTS LIST
Select Enter Cheat Code from the My 2K7 menu and enter themick.

MICKEY PINCH HITS
Select Enter Cheat Code from the My 2K7 menu and enter phmantle.

UNLOCK EVERYTHING
Select Enter Cheat Code from the My 2K7 menu and enter Derek Jeter. This does not unlock the Topps cheats.

ALL CHEATS
Select Enter Cheat Code from the My 2K7 menu and enter Black Sox.

ALL EXTRAS
Select Enter Cheat Code from the My 2K7 menu and enter Game On.

MIGHTY MICK CHEAT
Select Enter Cheat Code from the My 2K7 menu and enter mightymick.

TRIPLE CROWN CHEAT
Select Enter Cheat Code from the My 2K7 menu and enter triplecrown.

BIG BLAST CHEAT
Select Enter Cheat Code from the My 2K7 menu and enter m4murder.

MARVEL TRADING CARD GAME

COMPLETE CARD LIBRARY
At the Deck menu, select new deck and name it BLVRTRSK

ALL PUZZLES
At the Deck menu, select new deck and name it WHOWANTSPIE

MARVEL ULTIMATE ALLIANCE

UNLOCK ALL SKINS
At the Team menu, press Up, Down, Left, Right, Left, Right, Start.

UNLOCKS ALL HERO POWERS
At the Team menu, press Left, Right, Up, Down, Up, Down, Start.

ALL HEROES TO LEVEL 99
At the Team menu, press Up, Left, Up, Left, Down, Right, Down, Right, Start.

UNLOCK ALL HEROES
At the Team menu, press Up, Up, Down, Down, Left, Left, Left, Start.

UNLOCK DAREDEVIL
At the Team menu, press Left, Left, Right, Right, Up, Down, Up, Down, Start.

UNLOCK SILVER SURFER
At the Team menu, press Down, Left, Left, Up, Right, Up, Down, Left, Start.

GOD MODE
During gameplay, press Up, Down, Up, Down, Up, Left, Down, Right, Start.

TOUCH OF DEATH
During gameplay, press Left, Right, Down, Down, Right, Left, Start.

SUPER SPEED
During gameplay, press Up, Left, Up, Right, Down, Right, Start.

FILL MOMENTUM
During gameplay, press Left, Right, Right, Left, Up, Down, Down, Up, Start.

UNLOCK ALL COMICS
At the Review menu, press Left, Right, Right, Left, Up, Up, Right, Start.

UNLOCK ALL CONCEPT ART
At the Review menu, press Down, Down, Down, Right, Right, Left, Down, Start.

UNLOCK ALL CINEMATICS
At the Review menu, press Up, Left, Left, Up, Right, Right, Up, Start.

UNLOCK ALL LOAD SCREENS
At the Review menu, press Up, Down, Right, Left, Up, Up Down, Start.

UNLOCK ALL COURSES
At the Comic Missions menu, press Up, Right, Left, Down, Up, Right, Left, Down, Start.

MEDIEVIL: RESURRECTION

CHEAT MENU
Pause the game, hold R and press Down, Up, ●, ▲, ●, Down, Up, ● + ▲. This gives you invincibility and all weapons.

ALL ARTIFACTS AND KEYS
Pause the game and press L + R, ✖, ✖, ●, ●, ▲, ✖.

MLB 07: THE SHOW

SILVER ERA AND GOLD ERA TEAMS
At the Main menu, press Left, Up, Right, Down, Down, Left, Up, Down.

MAX BREAK PITCHES
Pause the game and press Right, Up, Right, Down, Up, Left, Left, Down.

MAX SPEED PITCHES
Pause the game and press Up, Left, Down, Up, Left, Right, Left, Down.

MTX MOTOTRAX

ALL TRACKS
Enter BA7H as a password.

ALL BONUSES
Enter 2468GOA7 as a password.

SUPER SPEED
Enter JIH345 as a password.

MAXIMUM AIR
Enter BFB0020 as a password.

BUTTERFINGER GEAR
Enter B77393 as a password.

LEFT FIELD GEAR
Enter 12345 as a password.

SOBE GEAR
Enter 5OBE as a password.

NBA BALLERS: REBOUND

VERSUS SCREEN CHEATS

You can enter the following codes at the Vs screen. The ● button corresponds to the first number in the code, the ▲ is the second number, and the ● button corresponds to the last number. Press the D-pad in any direction to enter the code. The name of the code will appear if entered correctly. Some of the codes will give you the wrong code name when entered.

EFFECT	CODE
Big Head	1 3 4
Pygmy	4 2 5
Alternate Gear	1 2 3
Show Shot Percentage	0 1 2
Expanded Move Set	5 1 2
Super Push	3 1 5
Super Block Ability	1 2 4
Great Handles	3 3 2
Unlimited Juice	7 6 3
Super Steals	2 1 5
Perfect Free Throws	3 2 7
Better Free Throws	3 1 7
Speedy Players	2 1 3
Alley-Oop Ability	7 2 5
Back-In Ability	1 2 2
Hotspot Ability	6 2 7

EFFECT	CODE
Pass 2 Friend Ability	5 3 6
Put Back Ability	3 1 3
Stunt Ability	3 7 4
2x Juice Replenish	4 3 1
Legal Goal Tending	7 5 6
Play As Afro Man	5 1 7
Play As Agent	5 5 7
Play As Business-A	5 3 7
Play As Business-B	5 2 7
Play As Coach	5 6 7
Play As Secretary	5 4 7
Super Back-Ins	2 3 5
Half House	3 6 7
Random Moves	3 0 0
Tournament Mode	0 1 1

PHRASE-OLOGY CODES

Select Phrase-ology from the Inside Stuff option and enter the following to unlock that bonus.

BONUS	PHRASE
All Players and Cinemas	NBA BALLERS TRUE PLAYA
Special Shoe #2	COLD STREAK
Special Shoe #3	LOST YA SHOES

CRIBS

Select Phrase-ology from the Inside Stuff option and enter the following to unlock player cribs.

CRIB	PHRASE
Allen Iverson's Recording Studio	THE ANSWER
Karl Malone's Devonshire Estate	ICE HOUSE
Kobe Bryant's Italian Estate	EURO CRIB
Ben Gordon's Yacht	NICE YACHT
Yao Ming's Childhood Grade School	PREP SCHOOL

NEOPETS PETPET ADVENTURE: THE WAND OF WISHING

START GAME WITH 5 CHOCOLATE TREATS

Enter treat4u as your Petpet's name. You can then rename name your character. The chocolate treats are shaped according to the character you chose.

OUTRUN 2006: COAST 2 COAST

100% COMPLETE/UNLOCK EVERYTHING

Edit your license and change the name to ENTIRETY. Select Done, then back out of all menus.

1000000 OUTRUN MILES

Edit your license and change the name to MILESANDMILES. Select Done, then back out of all menus.

PIRATES OF THE CARIBBEAN: DEAD MAN'S CHEST

GOD MODE

During a game, press ▲, ●, ●, ▲, ▲, ●, ✕, ✕.

FULL HEALTH

During a game, press ▲, ●, ▲, ●, ▲, ●, ●, ✕.

UNLIMITED POWER MOVES

During a game, press ▲, ▲, ▲, ■, ●, ✕, ●, ●.

ONE-SHOT KILL

During a game, press ▲, ●, ●, ▲, ▲, ●, ■, ■.

ALL TREASURE LEVELS

During a game, press ●, ●, ●, ▲, ▲, ✕, ✕.

KRAKEN BATTLE

During a game, press ●, ●, ●, ▲, ▲, ■, ■.

POPOLOCROIS

HIDDEN LEVEL SELECT

At the Main menu hold L + R and press ▲, ▲, ■, ■.

SEGA GENESIS COLLECTION

Before using the following cheats, select the ABC Control option. This sets the controller to the following: ⬤ is A, ⬤ is B, ⬤ is C.

ALTERED BEAST

OPTIONS MENU
At the title screen, hold ✖ and press Start.

LEVEL SELECT
After enabling the Options menu, select a level from the menu. At the title screen, hold ⬤ and press Start.

BEAST SELECT
At the title screen, hold ⬤ + ✖ + ⬤ + Down/Left and then press Start

SOUND TEST
At the title screen, hold ⬤ + ⬤ + Up/Right and press Start.

COMIX ZONE

INVINCIBILITY
At the jukebox screen, press C on the following sounds:
3, 12, 17, 2, 2, 10, 2, 7, 7, 11

LEVEL SELECT
At the jukebox screen, press C on the following sounds:
14, 15, 18, 5, 13, 1, 3, 18, 15, 6
Press C on the desired level.

ECCO THE DOLPHIN

INVINCIBILITY
When the level name appears, hold ⬤ + Start until the level begins.

DEBUG MENU
Pause the game with Ecco facing the screen and press Right, ✖,⬤, ✖,⬤, Down,⬤, Up.

INFINITE AIR
Enter LIFEFISH as a password

PASSWORDS

LEVEL	PASSWORD		LEVEL	PASSWORD	
The Undercaves	WEFIDNMP		Deep City	DDXPQQLJ	
The Vents	BQDPXJDS		City of Forever	MSDBRQLA	
The Lagoon	JNSBRIKY		Jurassic Beach	IYCBUNLB	
Ridge Water	NTSBZTKB		Pteranodon Pond		DMXEUNLI
Open Ocean	YWGTTJNI		Origin Beach	EGRIUNLB	
Ice Zone	HZIFZBMF		Trilobite Circle	IELMUNLB	
Hard Water	LRFJRQLI		Dark Water	RKEQUNLN	
Cold Water	UYNFRQLC		City of Forever 2		HPQIGPLA
Island Zone	LYTIOQLZ		The Tube	JUMFKMLB	
Deep Water	MNOPOQLR		The Machine	GXUBKMLF	
The Marble	RJNTQQLZ		The Last Fight	TSONLMLU	
The Library	RTGXQQLE				

FLICKY

ROUND SELECT
Begin a new game. Before the first round appears, hold ⬤ + ⬤ + Up + Start. Press Up or Down to select a Round

GAIN GROUND

LEVEL SELECT
At the Options screen, press ⬤, ⬤, ✖, ⬤.

GOLDEN AXE

LEVEL SELECT
Select Arcade Mode. At the character select, hold Down/Left + ✖ and press Start. Press Up or Down to select a lev

RISTAR

Select Passwords from the Options menu and enter the following:

LEVEL SELECT
ILOVEU

BOSS RUSH MODE
MUSEUM

TIME ATTACK MODE
DOFEEL

TOUGHER DIFFICULTY
SUPER

ONCHI MUSIC
MAGURO. Activate this from the Sound Test.

CLEARS PASSWORD
XXXXXX

GAME COPYRIGHT INFO
AGES

SONIC THE HEDGEHOG

LEVEL SELECT
At the title screen, press Up, Down, Left, Right. Hold ● and press Start.

SONIC THE HEDGEHOG 2

LEVEL SELECT
Select Sound Test from the options. Press C on the following sounds in order: 19, 65, 09, 17. At the title screen, hold ● and press Start.

VECTORMAN

DEBUG MODE
At the options screen, press ●, ✖, ✖, ●, Down, ●, ✖, ✖, ●.

REFILL LIFE
Pause the game and press ●, ✖, Right, ●, ●, ●, Down, ●, ✖, Right, ●.

VECTORMAN 2

LEVEL SELECT
Pause the game and press Up, Right, ●, ✖, ●, Down, Left, ●, Down.

EXTRA LIFE
Pause the game and press Right, Up, ✖, ●, Down, Up, ✖, Down, Up, ✖. Repeat for more lives.

FULL ENERGY
Pause the game and press ✖, ●, ✖, ●, Left, Up, Up.

NEW WEAPON
Pause the game and press ●, ●, Left, Left, Down, ●, Down. Repeat for more weapons.

SHREK THE THIRD

10,000 BONUS COINS
Press Up, Up, Down, Up, Right, Left at the Gift Shop.

THE SIMS 2

PERK CHEAT
At the Buy Perks screen, hold L + R +●. Buy the Cheat Perk to get some money, skills and more.

THE SIMS 2: PETS

CHEAT GNOME
During a game, press L, L, R, ✕, ✕, Up. Now you can enter the following cheats:

ADVANCE TIME 6 HOURS
During a game, press Up, Left, Down, Right, R.

GIVE SIM PET POINTS
During a game, press ▲, ●, ✕, ■, L, R.

$10,000
During a game, press ▲, Up, Left, Down, Right.

STAR TREK: TACTICAL ASSAULT

5 UPGRADE POINTS
At the Crew Screen, press Up, Down, Left, Right, Select, Start, Select.

ALL SHIPS FOR SKIRMISH AND MULTIPLAYER
At the skirmish screen, press Up, Down, Left, Right, Select, Start, ●.

STAR WARS: BATTLEFRONT II

INFINITE AMMO
Pause the game and press Up, Down, Left, Down, Down, Left, Down, Down, Left, Down, Down, Down Left, Right.

INVINCIBILITY
Pause the game and press Up, Up, Left, Down, Down, Down, Left, Up, Up, Up, Left, Right.

NO H.U.D.
Pause the game and press Up, Up, Up, Up, Left, Up, Up, Down, Left, Down, Up, Up, Left, Right.

LOW-RES CHARACTERS
Pause the game and press Down, Down, Down, Up, Left, Down, Down, Down, Down, Down, Left, Up, Up, Up, Left.

STAR WARS: LETHAL ALLIANCE

ALL LEVELS
Select Create Profile from the Profiles menu and enter HANSOLO.

ALL LEVELS AND REFILL HEALTH WHEN DEPLETED
Select Create Profile from the Profiles menu and enter JD1MSTR.

REFILL HEALTH WHEN DEPLETED
Select Create Profile from the Profiles menu and enter B0BAF3T.

THRILLVILLE: OFF THE RAILS

ALL PARKS
While in a park, press ■, ●, ▲, ■, ●, ▲, ■.

ALL RIDES IN PARK
While in a park, press ■, ●, ▲, ■, ●, ▲, ▲.

$50.000
While in a park, press ■, ●, ▲, ■, ●, ▲, ✕.

MISSION COMPLETE
While in a park, press ■, ●, ▲, ■, ●, ▲, ●.

TOMB RAIDER: LEGEND

BULLETPROOF
During a game, hold L and press ✕, R, ▲, R, ●, R.

DRAW ENEMY HEALTH
During a game, hold L and press ■, ●, ✕, R, R, ▲.

INFINITE ASSUALT RIFLE AMMO
During a game, hold L and press ✕, ○, ✕, R, ■, ▲.

INFINITE GRENADE LAUNCHER
During a game, hold L and press R, ▲, R, ●, R, ■.

INFINITE SHOTGUN AMMO
During a game, hold L and press R, ●, ■, R, ●, ✕.

INFINITE SMG AMMO
During a game, hold L and press ●, ▲, R, R, ✕, ●.

ONE SHOT KILL
During a game, hold L and press ▲, ✕, ▲, ■, R, ●.

TEXTURELESS MODE
hold L and press R, ✕, ●, ✕, ▲, R.

WIELD EXCALIBUR
During a game, hold L and press ▲, ✕, ●, R, ▲, R.

TONY HAWK'S PROJECT 8

CHEAT CODES

Select Cheat Codes from the Options and enter the following codes. In game you can access some codes from the Options menu.

CHEAT CODE	RESULTS
plus44	Unlocks Travis Barker
hohohosoi	Unlocks Christian Hosoi
notmono	Unlocks Jason Lee
mixitup	Unlocks Kevin Staab
strangefellows	Unlocks Dad & Skater Jam Kid
themedia	Unlocks Photog Girl & Filmer
militarymen	Unlocks Colonel & Security Guard
jammypack	Unlocks Always Special
balancegalore	Unlocks Perfect Rail
frontandback	Unlocks Perect Manual
shellshock	Unlocks Unlimited Focus
shescaresme	Unlocks Big Realtor
birdhouse	Unlocks Inkblot deck
allthebest	Full Stats
needaride	All Decks unlocked and free, except for inkblot deck and gamestop deck
yougotitall	All specials unlocked and in player's special list and set as owned in skate shop
enterandwin	Unlocks Bum
wearelosers	Unlocks Nerd
manineedadate	Unlocks Mascot
sellsellsell	Unlocks Skinny real estate agent
newshound	Unlocks Anchor man

VIRTUA TENNIS: WORLD TOUR

KING & QUEEN
At the Main menu, hold L and press Up, Down, Up, Down, ⦿, ▲, ⦿.

ALL RACQUETS AND CLOTHING
At the Main menu, hold L and press Right, Left, Right, Right, Up, Up, Up.

ALL STADIUMS
At the Main menu, hold L and press Up, Down, Left, Right, ⦿, ⦿, ⦿.

BEGIN WORLD TOUR WITH $1,000,000
At the Main menu, hold L and press Up, Down, Left, Down, ▲, ▲, ▲.

$2000 A WEEK IN WORLD TOUR
At the Main menu, hold L and press Up, Down, Right, Down, ▲, ⦿, ▲.

SEPIA MODE
At the Main menu, hold L and press Up, Down, Left, Right, Left, Left, Left.

WORLD CHAMPIONSHIP POKER 2: FEATURING HOWARD LEDERER

SKIP WEEK AND MONEY CHEATS
At the career world map, hold **R1**. Hold **L1** and release **R1**. Hold Up and release **L1**. Hold **L1** and release Up. Hold **R1** and release **L1**. While still holding **R1**, press Up/Down to skip weeks and Right/Left for money.

WORMS: OPEN WARFARE

FULL HEALTH
Pause the game, hold L + R, and press ▲, Down, ✖, Up.

WRC: FIA WORLD RALLY CHAMPIONSHIP

UNLOCK EVERYTHING
Create a new profile with the name PADLOCK.

EXTRA AVATARS
Create a new profile with the name UGLYMUGS.

GHOST CAR
Create a new profile with the name SPOOKY.

SUPERCHARGER
Create a new profile with the name MAXPOWER.

TIME TRIAL GHOST CARS
Create a new profile with the name AITRIAL.

BIRD CAMERA
Create a new profile with the name dovecam.

REVERSES CONTROLS
Create a new profile with the name REVERSE.

X-MEN LEGENDS II: RISE OF APOCALYPSE

ALL CHARACTERS
At the Team Management screen, press Right, Left, Left, Right, Up, Up, Up, Start.

LEVEL 99 CHARACTERS
At the Team Management screen, press Up, Down, Up, Down, Left, Up, Left, Right, Start.

ALL SKILLS
At the Team Management screen, press Left, Right, Left, Right, Down, Up, Start.

SUPER SPEED
Pause the game and press Up, Up, Up, Down, Up, Down, Start.

UNLIMITED XTREME POWER
Pause the game and press Left, Down, Right, Down, Up, Up, Down, Up Start.

100,000 TECHBITS
At Forge or Beast's equipment screen, press Up, Up, Up, Down, Right, Right, Start.

ALL CINEMATICS
A the Review menu, press Left, Right, Right, Left, Down, Down, Left, Start.

ALL COMIC BOOKS
At the Review menu, press Right, Left, Left, Right, Up, Up, Right, Start.

YU-GI-OH! GX TAG FORCE

BOOSTER PACK

At the card shop, press Up, Up, Down, Down, Left, Right, Left, Right, ✖, ●.

YU-GI-OH! GX TAG FORCE 2

MIDDDAY CONSTELLATION BOOSTER PACK

When buying booster packs, press Up, Up, Down, Down, Left, Right, Left, Right, ✖, ●.

YU-GI-OH! CARD PASSWORDS

Enter the following in the Password Machine to obtain for rental:

CARD	PASSWORD	CARD	PASSWORD
30,000-Year White Turtle	11714098	Amphibious Bugroth MK-3	64342551
4-Starred Ladybug of Doom	83994646	Amplifier	00303660
7	67048711	An Owl of Luck	23927567
7 Colored Fish	23771716	Ancient Elf	93221206
7 Completed	86198326	Ancient Gear	31557782
A Cat of Ill Omen	24140059	Ancient Gear Beast	10509340
A Deal with Dark Ruler	06850209	Ancient Gear Cannon	80045583
A Feather of the Phoenix	49140998	Ancient Gear Castle	92001300
A Feint Plan	68170903	Ancient Gear Drill	67829249
A Hero Emerges	21597117	Ancient Gear Golem	83104731
A Legendary Ocean	00295517	Ancient Gear Soldier	56094445
A Man with Wdjat	51351302	Ancient Lamp	54912977
A Rival Appears!	05728014	Ancient Lizard Warrior	43230671
A Wingbeat of Giant Dragon	28596933	Andro Sphinx	15013468
A-Team: Trap Disposal Unit	13026402	Anteatereatingant	13250922
Abare Ushioni	89718302	Anti-Aircraft Flower	65064143
Absolute End	27744077	Anti-Spell	53112492
Absorbing Kid From the Sky	49771608	Apprentice Magician	09156135
Abyss Soldier	18318842	Appropriate	48539234
Abyssal Designator	89801755	Aqua Madoor	85639257
Acid Rain	21323861	Aqua Spirit	40916023
Acid Trap Hole	41356845	Arcane Archer of the Forest	55001420
Acrobat Monkey	47372349	Archfiend of Gilfer	50287060
Adhesion Trap Hole	62325062	Archfiend Soldier	49881766
Adhesive Explosive	53828396	Archlord Zerato	18378582
After the Struggle	25345186	Armaill	53153481
Agido	16135253	Armed Changer	90374791
Airknight Parshath	18036057	Armed Dragon LV 3	00980973
Aitsu	48202661	Armed Dragon LV 5	46384672
Alkana Knight Joker	06150044	Armed Dragon LV 7	73879377
Alpha the Magnet Warrior	99785935	Armed Dragon LV 10	59464593
Altar for Tribute	21070956	Armed Ninja	09076207
Amazon Archer	91869203	Armed Samurai - Ben Kei	84430950
Amazoness Archers	67987611	Armor Axe	07180418
Amazoness Blowpiper	73574678	Armor Break	79649195
Amazoness Chain Master	29654737	Armored Lizard	15480588
Amazoness Paladin	47480070	Armored Starfish	17535588
Amazoness Swords Woman	94004268	Armored Zombie	20277860
Amazoness Tiger	10979723	Array of Revealing Light	69296555
Ambulance Rescueroid	98927491	Arsenal Bug	42364374
Ambulanceroid	36378213	Arsenal Robber	55348096
Ameba	95174353	Arsenal Summoner	85489096
Amphibian Beast	67371383	Assault on GHQ	62633180

CARD	PASSWORD	CARD	PASSWORD
Astral Barrier	37053871	Black Illusion Ritual	41426869
Asura Priest	02134346	Black Luster Soldier - Envoy of the Beginning	72989439
Aswan Apparition	88236094		
Atomic Firefly	87340664	Black Pendant	65169794
Attack and Receive	63689843	Black Tyranno	38670435
Attack Reflector Unit	91989718	Blackland Fire Dragon	87564352
Aussa the Earth Charmer	37970940	Blade Knight	39507162
Autonomous Action Unit	71453557	Blade Rabbit	58268433
Avatar of the Pot	99284890	Blade Skater	97023549
Axe Dragonute	84914462	Bladefly	28470714
Axe of Despair	40619825	Blast Held By a Tribute	89041555
B. Skull Dragon	11901678	Blast Magician	21051146
B.E.S. Covered Core	15317640	Blast with Chain	98239899
B.E.S. Crystal Core	22790789	Blasting the Ruins	21466326
B.E.S. Tetran	44954628	Blazing Inpachi	05464695
Baby Dragon	88819587	Blind Destruction	32015116
Back to Square One	47453433	Blindly Loyal Goblin	35215622
Backfire	82705573	Block Attack	25880422
Backup Soldier	36280194	Blockman	48115277
Bad Reaction to Simochi	40633297	Blowback Dragon	25551951
Bait Doll	07165085	Blue-Eyes Shining Dragon	53347303
Ballista of Rampart Smashing	00242146	Blue-Eyes Toon Dragon	53183600
Banisher of the Light	61528025	Blue-Eyes Ultimate Dragon	23995346
Bark of Dark Ruler	41925941	Blue-Eyes White Dragon	89631139
Barrel Dragon	81480460	Blue-Winged Crown	41396436
Basic Insect	89091579	Bokoichi the Freightening Car	08715625
Battery Charger	61181383	Bombardment Beetle	57409948
Batteryman AA	63142001	Bonding - H2O	45898858
Batteryman C	19733961	Boneheimer	98456117
Batteryman D	55401221	Book of Life	02204140
Battle Footballer	48094997	Book of Moon	14087893
Battle Ox	05053103	Book of Taiyou	38699854
Battle-Scarred	94463200	Boss Rush	66947414
Bazoo The Soul-Eater	40133511	Bottom Dweller	81386177
Beast Soul Swap	35149085	Bottomless Shifting Sand	76532077
Beaver Warrior	32452818	Bottomless Trap Hole	29401950
Beckoning Light	16255442	Bountiful Artemis	32296881
Beelze Frog	49522489	Bowganian	52090844
Begone, Knave	20374520	Bracchio-Raidus	16507828
Behemoth the King of All Animals	22996376	Brain Control	87910978
Beige, Vanguard of Dark World	33731070	Brain Jacker	40267580
Berserk Dragon	85605684	Branch	30548775
Berserk Gorilla	39168895	Breaker the Magical Warrior	71413901
Beta the Magnet Warrior	39256679	Broww, Huntsman of Dark World	79126789
Bickuribox	25655502	Brron, Mad King of Dark World	06214884
Big Bang Shot	61127349	Bubble Blaster	53586134
Big Burn	95472621	Bubble Illusion	80075749
Big Core	14148099	Bubble Shuffle	61968753
Big Eye	16768387	Bubonic Vermin	06104968
Big Koala	42129512	Burning Algae	41859700
Big Shield Gardna	65240384	Burning Beast	59364406
Big Wave Small Wave	51562916	Burning Land	24294108
Big-Tusked Mammoth	59380081	Burst Breath	80163754
Bio-Mage	58696829	Burst Return	27191436
Birdface	45547649	Burst Stream of Destruction	17655904
		Buster Blader	78193831

CARD	PASSWORD	CARD	PASSWORD
Buster Rancher	84740193	Compulsory Evacuation Device	94192409
Butterfly Dagger - Elma	69243953	Confiscation	17375316
Byser Shock	17597059	Conscription	31000575
Call of The Haunted	97077563	Continuous Destruction Punch	68057622
Call of the Mummy	04861205	Contract With Exodia	33244944
Cannon Soldier	11384280	Contract With the Abyss	69035382
Cannonball Spear Shellfish	95614612	Contract with the Dark Master	96420087
Card of Safe Return	57953380	Convulsion of Nature	62966332
Card Shuffle	12183332	Cost Down	23265313
Castle of Dark Illusions	00062121	Covering Fire	74458486
Cat's Ear Tribe	95841282	Crab Turtle	91782219
Catapult Turtle	95727991	Crass Clown	93889755
Cathedral of Nobles	29762407	Creature Swap	31036355
Catnipped Kitty	96501677	Creeping Doom Manta	52571838
Cave Dragon	93220472	Crimson Ninja	14618326
Ceasefire	36468556	Criosphinx	18654201
Celtic Guardian	91152256	Cross Counter	37083210
Cemetery Bomb	51394546	Crush D. Gandra	64681432
Centrifugal	01801154	Cure Mermaid	85802526
Ceremonial Bell	20228463	Curse of Aging	41398771
Cetus of Dagala	28106077	Curse of Anubis	66742250
Chain Burst	48276469	Curse of Darkness	84970821
Chain Destruction	01248895	Curse of Dragon	28279543
Chain Disappearance	57139487	Curse of the Masked Beast	94377247
Chain Energy	79323590	Curse of Vampire	34294855
Chain Thrasher	88190453	Cyberdark Dragon	40418351
Chainsaw Insect	77252217	Cyberdark Horn	41230939
Change of Heart	04031928	Cyberdark Keel	03019642
Chaos Command Magician	72630549	D - Sheild	62868900
Chaos Emperor Dragon-Envoy of the End	82301904	D - Time	99075257
Chaos End	61044390	D. D. Assailant	70074904
Chaos Greed	97439308	D. D. Borderline	60912752
Chaos Necromancer	01434352	D. D. Trainer	86498013
Chaos Sorcerer	09596126	D. D. Warrior Lady	07572887
Chaosrider Gutaph	47829960	D.D. Crazy Beast	48148828
Charcoal Inpachi	13179332	D.D. Dynamite	08628798
Charm of Shabti	50412166	D.D. Trap Hole	05606466
Charubin the Fire Knight	37421579	D.D.M. - Different Dimension Master	82112775
Chiron the Mage	16956455	Dancing Fairy	90925163
Chopman the Desperate Outlaw	40884383	Dangerous Machine TYPE-6	76895648
Chorus of Sanctuary	81380218	Dark Artist	72520073
Chthonian Alliance	46910446	Dark Bat	67049542
Chthonian Blast	18271561	Dark Blade	11321183
Chthonian Polymer	72287557	Dark Blade the Dragon Knight	86805855
Chu-Ske the Mouse Fighter	08508055	Dark Driceratops	65287621
Clay Charge	22479888	Dark Dust Spirit	89111398
Cliff the Trap Remover	06967870	Dark Elf	21417692
Cobra Jar	86801871	Dark Energy	04614116
Cobraman Sakuzy	75109441	Dark Factory of Mass Production	90928333
Cold Wave	60682203	Dark Flare Knight	13722870
Collected Power	07565547	Dark Hole	53129443
Combination Attack	08964854	Dark Magic Attack	02314238
Command Knight	10375182	Dark Magic Ritual	76792184
Commander Covington	22666164	Dark Magician	46986414
Commencement Dance	43417563	Dark Magician Girl	38033121

CARD	PASSWORD	CARD	PASSWORD
Dark Magician of Chaos	40737112	Doitsu	57062206
Dark Magician's Tome of Black Magic	67227834	Dokurorider	99721536
Dark Master - Zorc	97642679	Dokuroyaiba	30325729
Dark Mirror Force	20522190	Don Turtle	03493978
Dark Paladin	98502113	Don Zaloog	76922029
Dark Paladin	98502113	Doriado	84916669
Dark Room of Nightmare	85562745	Doriado's Blessing	23965037
Dark Sage	92377303	Dragon Seeker	28563545
Dark Snake Syndrome	47233801	Dragon Treasure	01435851
Dark-Piercing Light	45895206	Dragon Zombie	66672569
Darkfire Dragon	17881964	Dragon's Mirror	71490127
Darkfire Soldier #1	05388481	Dragon's Rage	54178050
Darkfire Soldier #2	78861134	Dragoness the Wicked Knight	70681994
Darkworld Thorns	43500484	Draining Shield	43250041
De-Spell	19159413	Dream Clown	13215230
Deal of Phantom	69122763	Drillago	99050989
Decayed Commander	10209545	Drillroid	71218746
Dedication Through Light And Darkness	69542930	Dunames Dark Witch	12493482
Deepsea Shark	28593363	Dust Tornado	60082867
Dekoichi the Battlechanted Locomotive	87621407	Earth Chant	59820352
Delinquent Duo	44763025	Earthbound Spirit	67105242
Demotion	72575145	Earthquake	82828051
Des Counterblow	39131963	Eatgaboon	42578427
Des Croaking	44883830	Ebon Magician Curran	46128076
Des Dendle	12965761	Electro-Whip	37820550
Des Feral Imp	81985784	Elegant Egotist	90219263
Des Frog	84451804	Element Dragon	30314994
Des Kangaroo	78613627	Elemental Burst	61411502
Des Koala	69579761	Elemental Hero Avian	21844576
Des Lacooda	02326738	Elemental Hero Bladedge	59793705
Des Wombat	09637706	Elemental Hero Bubbleman	79979666
Desert Sunlight	93747864	Elemental Hero Burstinatrix	58932615
Destertapir	13409151	Elemental Hero Clayman	84327329
Destiny Board	94212438	Elemental Hero Electrum/Erekshieler	29343734
Destiny Hero - Captain Tenacious	77608643	Elemental Hero Flame Wingman	35809262
Destiny Hero - Diamond Dude	13093792	Elemental Hero Mariner	14225239
Destiny Hero - Doom Lord	41613948	Elemental Hero Necroid Shaman	81003500
Destiny Hero - Dreadmaster	40591390	Elemental Hero Neos	89943723
Destiny Signal	35464895	Elemental Hero Phoenix Enforcer	41436536
Destroyer Golem	73481154	Elemental Hero Shining Flare Wingman	25366484
Destruction Ring	21219755	Elemental Hero Shining Phoenix Enforcer	88820235
Dian Keto the Cure Master	84257639	Elemental Hero Sparkman	20721928
Dice Jar	03549275	Elemental Hero Thunder Giant	61204971
Dimension Distortion	95194279	Elemental Mistress Doriado	99414158
Dimensional Warrior	37043180	Elemental Recharge	36586443
Dimenional Fissure	816747482	Elf's Light	39897277
Disappear	24623598	Emblem of Dragon Destroyer	06390406
Disarmament	20727787	Embodiment of Apophis	28649820
Disc Fighter	19612721	Emergency Provisions	53046408
Dissolverock	40826495	Emes the Infinity	43580269
Divine Dragon Ragnarok	62113340	Empress Judge	15237615
Divine Wrath	49010598	Empress Mantis	58818411
DNA Surgery	74701381	Enchanted Javelin	96355986
DNA Transplant	56769674	Enchanting Mermaid	75376965

CARD	PASSWORD	CARD	PASSWORD
Enraged Battle Ox	76909279	Frenzied Panda	98818516
Enraged Muka Muka	91862578	Frozen Soul	57069605
Eradicating Aerosol	94716515	Fruits of Kozaky's Studies	49998907
Eternal Draught	56606928	Fuh-Rin-Ka-Zan	01781310
Eternal Rest	95051344	Fuhma Shuriken	09373534
Exhausting Spell	95451366	Fulfillment of the Contract	48206762
Exile of the Wicked	26725158	Fushi No Tori	38538445
Exiled Force	74131780	Fusion Gate	33550694
Exodia Necross	12600382	Fusion Recovery	18511384
Exodia the Forbidden One	33396948	Fusion Sage	26902560
Fairy Box	21598948	Fusion Weapon	27967615
Fairy Dragon	20315854	Fusionist	01641883
Fairy King Truesdale	45425051	Gadget Soldier	86281779
Fairy Meteor Crush	97687912	Gagagigo	49003308
Faith Bird	75582395	Gaia Power	56594520
Fatal Abacus	77910045	Gaia the Dragon Champion	66889139
Fenrir	00218704	Gaia the Fierce Knight	06368038
Feral Imp	41392891	Gale Dogra	16229315
Fiber Jar	78706415	Gale Lizard	77491079
Fiend Comedian	81172176	Gamble	37313786
Fiend Scorpion	26566878	Gamma the Magnet Warrior	11549357
Fiend's Hand	52800428	Garma Sword	90844184
Fiend's Mirror	31890399	Garma Sword Oath	78577570
Final Countdown	95308449	Garoozis	14977074
Final Destiny	18591904	Garuda the Wind Spirit	12800777
Final Flame	73134081	Gatling Dragon	87751584
Final Ritual of the Ancients	60369732	Gazelle the King of Mythical Beasts	05818798
Fire Darts	43061293	Gear Golem the Moving Fortress	30190809
Fire Eye	88435542	Gearfried the Iron Knight	00423705
Fire Kraken	46534755	Gearfried the Swordmaster	57046845
Fire Princess	64752646	Gemini Elf	69140098
Fire Reaper	53581214	Getsu Fuhma	21887179
Fire Sorcerer	27132350	Giant Axe Mummy	78266168
Firegrass	53293545	Giant Germ	95178994
Firewing Pegasus	27054370	Giant Kozaky	58185394
Fireyarou	71407486	Giant Orc	73698349
Fissure	66788016	Giant Rat	97017120
Five God Dragon (Five-Headed Dragon)	99267150	Giant Red Seasnake	58831685
Flame Cerebrus	60862676	Giant Soldier of Stone	13039848
Flame Champion	42599677	Giant Trunade	42703248
Flame Dancer	12883044	Gift of the Mystical Elf	98299011
Flame Ghost	58528964	Giga Gagagigo	43793530
Flame Manipulator	34460851	Giga-Tech Wolf	08471389
Flame Swordsman	45231177	Gigantes	47606319
Flame Viper	02830619	Gigobyte	53776525
Flash Assailant	96890582	Gil Garth	38445524
Flower Wolf	95952802	Gilasaurus	45894482
Flying Fish	31987274	Giltia the D. Knight	51828629
Flying Kamakiri #1	84834865	Girochin Kuwagata	84620194
Flying Kamakiri #2	03134241	Goblin Attack Force	78658564
Follow Wind	98252586	Goblin Calligrapher	12057781
Foolish Burial	81439173	Goblin Elite Attack Force	85306040
Forest	87430998	Goblin Thief	45311864
Fortress Whale	62337487	Goblin's Secret Remedy	11868825
Fortress Whale's Oath	77454922	Gogiga Gagagigo	39674352

CARD	PASSWORD	CARD	PASSWORD
Golem Sentry	82323207	Headless Knight	05434080
Good Goblin Housekeeping	09744376	Heart of Clear Water	64801562
Gora Turtle	80233946	Heart of the Underdog	35762283
Graceful Charity	79571449	Heavy Mech Support Platform	23265594
Graceful Dice	74137509	Heavy Storm	19613556
Gradius	10992251	Helios - the Primordial Sun	54493213
Gradius' Option	14291024	Helios Duo Megistus	80887952
Granadora	13944422	Helios Tris Megiste	17286057
Grand Tiki Elder	13676474	Helping Robo for Combat	47025270
Granmarg the Rock Monarch	60229110	Hero Barrier	44676200
Gravedigger Ghoul	82542267	HERO Flash!	00191749
Gravekeeper's Cannonholder	99877698	Hero Heart	67951831
Gravekeeper's Curse	50712728	Hero Kid	32679370
Gravekeeper's Guard	37101832	Hero Ring	26647858
Gravekeeper's Servant	16762927	Hero Signal	22020907
Gravekeeper's Spear Soldier	63695531	Hidden Book of Spell	21840375
Gravekeeper's Spy	24317029	Hidden Soldier	02047519
Gravekeeper's Vassal	99690140	Hieracosphinx	82260502
Graverobber's Retribution	33737664	Hieroglyph Lithograph	10248192
Gravity Bind	85742772	High Tide Gyojin	54579801
Gray Wing	29618570	Hiita the Fire Charmer	00759393
Great Angus	11813953	Hino-Kagu-Tsuchi	75745607
Great Long Nose	02356994	Hinotama Soul	96851799
Great Mammoth of Goldfine	54622031	Hiro's Shadow Scout	81863068
Green Gadget	41172955	Hitotsu-Me Giant	76184692
Gren Maju Da Eiza	36584821	Holy Knight Ishzark	57902462
Ground Attacker Bugroth	58314394	Homunculus the Alchemic Being	40410110
Ground Collapse	90502999	Horn of Heaven	98069388
Gruesome Goo	65623423	Horn of Light	38552107
Gryphon Wing	55608151	Horn of the Unicorn	64047146
Gryphon's Feather Duster	34370473	Horus The Black Flame Dragon LV 4	75830094
Guardian Angel Joan	68007326	Horus The Black Flame Dragon LV 6	11224103
Guardian of the Labyrinth	89272878	Horus The Black Flame Dragon LV 8	48229808
Guardian of the Sea	85448931	Hoshiningen	67629977
Guardian Sphinx	40659562	House of Adhesive Tape	15083728
Guardian Statue	75209824	Howling Insect	93107608
Gust Fan	55321970	Huge Revolution	65396880
Gyaku-Gire Panda	09817927	Human-Wave Tactics	30353551
Gyroid	18325492	Humanoid Slime	46821314
Hade-Hane	28357177	Humanoid Worm Drake	05600127
Hamburger Recipe	80811661	Hungry Burger	30243636
Hammer Shot	26412047	Hydrogeddon	22587018
Hamon	32491822	Hyena	22873798
Hand of Nephthys	98446407	Hyozanryu	62397231
Hane-Hane	07089711	Hyper Hammerhead	02671330
Hannibal Necromancer	05640330	Hysteric Fairy	21297224
Hard Armor	20060230	Icarus Attack	53567095
Harpie Girl	34100324	Illusionist Faceless Mage	28546905
Harpie Lady 1	91932350	Impenetrable Formation	96631852
Harpie Lady 2	27927359	Imperial Order	61740673
Harpie Lady 3	54415063	Inaba White Rabbit	77084837
Harpie Lady Sisters	12206212	Incandescent Ordeal	33031674
Harpie's Brother	30532390	Indomitable Fighter Lei Lei	84173492
Harpies' Hunting Ground	75782277	Infernal Flame Emperor	19847532
Hayabusa Knight	21015833	Infernal Queen Archfiend	08581705

CARD	PASSWORD
Inferno	74823665
Inferno Fire Blast	52684508
Inferno Hammer	17185260
Inferno Reckless Summon	12247206
Inferno Tempest	14391920
Infinite Cards	94163677
Infinite Dismissal	54109233
Injection Fairy Lily	79575620
Inpachi	97923414
Insect Armor with Laser Cannon	03492538
Insect Barrier	23615409
Insect Imitation	96965364
Insect Knight	35052053
Insect Princess	37957847
Insect Queen	91512835
Insect Soldiers of the Sky	07019529
Inspection	16227556
Interdimensional Matter Transporter	36261276
Invader From Another Dimension	28450915
Invader of Darkness	56647086
Invader of the Throne	03056267
Invasion of Flames	26082229
Invigoration	98374133
Iron Blacksmith Kotetsu	73431236
Island Turtle	04042268
Jack's Knight	90876561
Jade Insect Whistle	95214051
Jam Breeding Machine	21770260
Jam Defender	21558682
Jar of Greed	83968380
Jar Robber	33784505
Javelin Beetle	26932788
Javelin Beetle Pact	41182875
Jellyfish	14851496
Jerry Beans Man	23635815
Jetroid	43697559
Jinzo	77585513
Jinzo #7	32809211
Jirai Gumo	94773007
Jowgen the Spiritualist	41855169
Jowls of Dark Demise	05257687
Judge Man	30113682
Judgment of Anubis	55256016
Just Desserts	24068492
KA-2 Des Scissors	52768103
Kabazauls	51934376
Kagemusha of the Blue Flame	15401633
Kaibaman	34627841
Kaiser Dragon	94566432
Kaiser Glider	52824910
Kaiser Sea Horse	17444133
Kaminari Attack	09653271
Kaminote Blow	97570038
Kamionwizard	41544074
Kangaroo Champ	95789089

CARD	PASSWORD
Karate Man	23289281
Karbonala Warrior	54541900
Karma Cut	71587526
Kelbek	54878498
Keldo	80441106
Killer Needle	88979991
Kinetic Soldier	79853073
King Dragun	13756293
King Fog	84686841
King of the Skull Servants	36021814
King of the Swamp	79109599
King of Yamimakai	69455834
King Tiger Wanghu	83986578
King's Knight	64788463
Kiryu	84814897
Kiseitai	04266839
Kishido Spirit	60519422
Knight's Title	87210505
Koitsu	69456283
Kojikocy	01184620
Kotodama	19406822
Kozaky	99171160
Kozaky's Self-Destruct Button	21908319
Kryuel	82642348
Kumootoko	56283725
Kurama	85705804
Kuriboh	40640057
Kuwagata Alpha	60802233
Kwagar Hercules	95144193
Kycoo The Ghost Destroyer	88240808
La Jinn The Mystical Genie of The Lamp	97590747
Labyrinth of Nightmare	66526672
Labyrinth Tank	99551425
Lady Assailant of Flames	90147755
Lady Ninja Yae	82005435
Lady of Faith	17358176
Larvas	94675535
Laser Cannon Armor	77007920
Last Day of Witch	90330453
Last Turn	28566710
Launcher Spider	87322377
Lava Battleguard	20394040
Lava Golem	00102380
Layard the Liberator	67468948
Left Arm of the Forbidden One	07902349
Left Leg of the Forbidden One	44519536
Legendary Black Belt	96438440
Legendary Flame Lord	60258960
Legendary Jujitsu Master	25773409
Legendary Sword	61854111
Leghul	12472242
Lekunga	62543393
Lesser Dragon	55444629
Lesser Fiend	16475472
Level Conversion Lab	84397023

CARD	PASSWORD	CARD	PASSWORD
el Limit - Area A	54976796	Magnet Circle	94940436
el Limit - Area B	03136426	Maha Vailo	93013676
el Modulation	61850482	Maharaghi	40695128
el Up	25290459	Maiden of the Aqua	17214465
a-Dragon	37721209	Maji-Gire Panda	60102563
a-Dragon - Daedalus	37721209	Maju Garzett	08794435
t of Intervention	62867251	Makiu	27827272
t of Judgment	44595286	Makyura the Destructor	21593977
ten the Load	37231841	Malevolent Nuzzler	99597615
tforce Sword	49587034	Malfunction	06137095
tning Blade	55226821	Malice Ascendant	14255590
tning Conger	27671321	Malice Dispersion	13626450
tning Vortex	69162969	Mammoth Graveyard	40374923
ter Removal	23171610	Man Eater	93553943
d Beast	93108297	Man-Eater Bug	54652250
e Chimera	68658728	Man-Eating Black Shark	80727036
e-Winguard	90790253	Man-Eating Treasure Chest	13723605
rd Soldier	20831168	Man-Thro' Tro	43714890
of the Lamp	99510761	Manga Ryu-Ran	38369349
Guardian	45871897	Manju of the Ten Thousand Hands	95492061
nous Soldier	57282479	Manticore of Darkness	77121851
nous Spark	81777047	Marauding Captain	02460565
er Dragon	11091375	Marie the Fallen One	57579381
er Dragon #2	17658803	Marine Beast	29929832
arrior #1	56342351	Marshmallon	31305911
arrior #2	92731455	Marshmallon Glasses	66865880
ine Conversion Factory	25769732	Maryokutai	71466592
ine Duplication	63995093	Masaki the Legendary Swordsman	44287299
ine King	46700124	Mask of Brutality	82432018
ine King Prototype	89222931	Mask of Darkness	28933734
iners Defender	96384007	Mask of Restrict	29549364
iners Force	58054262	Mask of Weakness	57882509
iners Sniper	23782705	Masked Dragon	39191307
iners Soldier	60999392	Masked of the Accursed	56948373
Dog of Darkness	79182538	Masked Sorcerer	10189126
Lobster	97240270	Mass Driver	34906152
Sword Beast	79870141	Master Kyonshee	24530661
Power	83746708	Master Monk	49814180
c Drain	59344077	Master of Dragon Knight	62873545
c Jammer	77414722	Master of Oz	27134689
cal Cylinder	62279055	Mataza the Zapper	22609617
cal Dimension	28553439	Mavelus	59036972
cal Explosion	32723153	Maximum Six	30707994
cal Hats	81210420	Mazera DeVille	06133894
cal Labyrinth	64389297	Mech Mole Zombie	63545455
cal Marionette	08034697	Mecha-Dog Marron	94667532
cal Merchant	32362575	Mechanical Hound	22512237
cal Plant Mandragola	07802006	Mechanical Snail	34442949
al Scientist	34206604	Mechanical Spider	45688586
al Thorn	53119267	Mechanicalchaser	07359741
cian of Black Chaos	30208479	Meda Bat	76211194
ian of Faith	31560081	Medusa Worm	02694423
ian's Circle	00050755	Mefist the Infernal General	46820049
ian's Unite	36045450	Mega Thunderball	21817254
an's Valkyrie	80304126	Mega Ton Magical Cannon	32062913

CARD	PASSWORD	CARD	PASSWORD
Megamorph	22046459	Monster Egg	36121917
Megarock Dragon	71544954	Monster Eye	84133008
Melchid the Four-Face Beast	86569121	Monster Gate	43040603
Memory Crusher	48700891	Monster Reborn	83764718
Mermaid Knight	24435369	Monster Recovery	93108433
Messenger of Peace	44656491	Monster Reincarnation	74848038
Metal Armored Bug	65957473	Mooyan Curry	58074572
Metal Dragon	09293977	Morale Boost	93671934
Metallizing Parasite	07369217	Morphing Jar	33508719
Metalmorph	68540058	Morphing Jar #2	79106360
Metalzoa	50705071	Mother Grizzly	57839750
Metamorphosis	46411259	Mountain	50913601
Meteor B. Dragon	90660762	Mr. Volcano	31477025
Meteor Dragon	64271667	Mudora	82108372
Meteor of Destruction	33767325	Muka Muka	46657337
Meteorain	64274292	Multiplication of Ants	22493811
Michizure	37580756	Multiply	40703222
Micro-Ray	18190572	Musician King	56907389
Mid Shield Gardna	75487237	Mustering of the Dark Scorpions	68191243
Mighty Guard	62327910	Mysterious Puppeteer	54098121
Mikazukinoyaiba	38277918	Mystic Horseman	68516705
Millennium Golem	47986555	Mystic Lamp	98049915
Millennium Scorpion	82482194	Mystic Plasma Zone	18161786
Millennium Shield	32012841	Mystic Swordsman LV 2	47507260
Milus Radiant	07489323	Mystic Swordsman LV 4	74591968
Minar	32539892	Mystic Swordsman LV 6	60482781
Mind Control	37520316	Mystic Tomato	83011277
Mind Haxorz	75392615	Mystic Wok	80161395
Mind on Air	66690411	Mystical Beast Serket	89194033
Mind Wipe	52718046	Mystical Elf	15025844
Mine Golem	76321376	Mystical Knight of Jackal	98745000
Minefield Eruption	85519211	Mystical Moon	36607978
Minor Goblin Official	01918087	Mystical Sand	32751480
Miracle Dig	06343408	Mystical Sheep #	30451366
Miracle Fusion	45906428	Mystical Shine Ball	39552864
Miracle Kid	55985014	Mystical Space Typhoon	05318639
Miracle Restoring	68334074	Mystik Wok	80161395
Mirage Dragon	15960641	Mythical Beast Cerberus	55424270
Mirage Knight	49217579	Nanobreaker	70948327
Mirage of Nightmare	41482598	Necklace of Command	48576971
Mirror Force	44095762	Necrovalley	47355498
Mirror Wall	22359980	Needle Ball	94230224
Misfortune	01036974	Needle Burrower	98162242
Mispolymerization	58392024	Needle Ceiling	38411870
Mistobody	47529357	Needle Wall	38299233
Moai Interceptor Cannons	45159319	Needle Worm	81843628
Mobius the Frost Monarch	04929256	Negate Attack	14315573
Moisture Creature	75285069	Nemuriko	90963488
Mokey Mokey	27288416	Neo Aqua Madoor	49563947
Mokey Mokey King	13803864	Neo Bug	16587243
Mokey Mokey Smackdown	01965724	Neo the Magic Swordsman	50930991
Molten Behemoth	17192817	Neo-Space	40215635
Molten Destruction	19384334	Neo-Spacian Aqua Dolphin	17955766
Molten Zombie	04732017	Newdoria	04335645
Monk Fighter	03810071	Next to be Lost	07076131

CARD	PASSWORD	CARD	PASSWORD
Night Assailant	16226786	Parasitic Ticky	87978805
Nightmare Horse	59290628	Patrician of Darkness	19153634
Nightmare Penguin	81306586	Patroid	71930383
Nightmare Wheel	54704216	Penguin Knight	36039163
Nightmare's Steelcage	58775978	Penumbral Soldier Lady	64751286
Nimble Momonga	22567609	People Running About	12143771
Nin-Ken Dog	11987744	Perfect Machine King	18891691
Ninja Grandmaster Sasuke	04041838	Performance of Sword	04849037
Ninjitsu Art of Decoy	89628781	Petit Angel	38142739
Ninjitsu Art of Transformation	70861343	Petit Dragon	75356564
Nitro Unit	23842445	Petit Moth	58192742
Niwatori	07805359	Phantasmal Martyrs	93224848
Nobleman of Crossout	71044499	Pharaoh's Servant	52550973
Nobleman of Extermination	17449108	Pharonic Protector	89959682
Nobleman-Eater Bug	65878864	Phoenix Wing Wind Blast	63356631
Non Aggression Area	76848240	Photon Generator Unit	66607691
Non-Fusion Area	27581098	Pikeru's Circle of Enchantment	74270067
Non-Spellcasting Area	20065549	Pikeru's Second Sight	58015506
Novox's Prayer	43694075	Pinch Hopper	26185991
Nubian Guard	51616747	Pineapple Blast	90669991
Numinous Healer	02130625	Piranha Army	50823978
Nutrient Z	29389368	Pitch-Black Power Stone	34029630
Nuvia the Wicked	12953226	Pitch-Black Warwolf	88975532
0 - Oversoul	63703130	Pitch-Dark Dragon	47415292
Obnoxious Celtic Guardian	52077741	Poison Draw Frog	56840658
Ocubeam	86088138	Poison Fangs	76539047
Offerings to the Doomed	19230407	Poison Mummy	43716289
Ojama Black	79335209	Poison of the Old Man	08842266
Ojama Delta Hurricane	08251996	Polymerization	24094653
Ojama Green	12482652	Possessed Dark Soul	52860176
Ojama King	90140980	Pot of Avarice	67169062
Ojama Trio	29843091	Pot of Generosity	70278545
Ojama Yellow	42941100	Pot of Greed	55144522
Ojamagic	24643836	Power Bond	37630732
Ojamuscle	98259197	Power Capsule	54289683
Old Vindictive Magician	45141844	Precious Card from Beyond	68304813
Ominous Fortunetelling	56995655	Premature Burial	70828912
Oni Tank T-3	66927994	Prepare to Strike Back	04483989
Opti-Camaflauge Armor	44762290	Prevent Rat	00549481
Opticlops	14531242	Prickle Fairy	91559748
Option Hunter	33248692	Primal Seed	23701465
Orca Mega-Fortress of Darkness	63120904	Princess Curran	02316186
Ordeal of a Traveler	39537362	Princess of Tsurugi	51371017
Order to Charge	78986941	Princess Pikeru	75917088
Order to Smash	39019325	Protective Soul Ailin	11678191
Otohime	39751093	Protector of the Sanctuary	24221739
Outstanding Dog Marron	11548522	Protector of the Throne	10071456
Overdrive	02311603	Proto-Cyber Dragon	26439287
Oxygeddon	58071123	Pumpking the King of Ghosts	29155212
Painful Choice	74191942	Punished Eagle	74703140
Paladin of White Dragon	73398797	Pyramid of Light	53569894
Pale Beast	21263083	Pyramid Turtle	77044671
Pandemonium	94585852	Queen's Knight	25652259
Pandemonium Watchbear	75375465	Rabid Horseman	94905343
Parasite Paracide	27911549	Rafflesia Seduction	31440542

CARD	PASSWORD	CARD	PASSWORD
Raging Flame Sprite	90810762	Robbin' Zombie	83258273
Raigeki	12580477	Robolady	92421852
Raigeki Break	04178474	Robotic Knight	44203504
Rain Of Mercy	66719324	Roboyarou	38916461
Rainbow Flower	21347810	Rock Bombardment	20781762
Rancer Dragonute	11125718	Rock Ogre Grotto	68846917
Rapid-Fire Magician	06337436	Rocket Jumper	53890795
Rare Metalmorph	12503902	Rocket Warrior	30860696
Raregold Armor	07625614	Rod of the Mind's Eye	94793422
Raviel, Lord of Phantasms	69890967	Roll Out	91597389
Ray & Temperature	85309439	Root Water	39004808
Ray of Hope	82529174	Rope of Life	93382620
Re-Fusion	74694807	Rope of Spirit	37383714
Ready For Intercepting	31785398	Roulette Barrel	46303688
Really Eternal Rest	28121403	Royal Command	33950246
Reaper of the Cards	33066139	Royal Decree	51452091
Reaper of the Nightmare	85684223	Royal Keeper	16509093
Reasoning	58577036	Royal Knight	68280530
Reborn Zombie	23421244	Royal Magical Library	70791313
Reckless Greed	37576645	Royal Surrender	56058888
Recycle	96316857	Royal Tribute	72405967
Red Archery Girl	65570596	Ruin, Queen of Oblivion	46427957
Red Gadget	86445415	Rush Recklessly	70046172
Red Medicine	38199696	Ryu Kokki	57281778
Red Moon Baby	56387350	Ryu Senshi	49868263
Red-Eyes B. Chick	36262024	Ryu-Kishin Clown	42647539
Red-Eyes B. Dragon	74677422	Ryu-Kishin Powered	24611934
Red-Eyes Black Metal Dragon	64335804	Saber Beetle	49645921
Red-Eyes Darkness Dragon	96561011	Sacred Crane	30914564
Reflect Bounder	02851070	Sacred Phoenix of Nephthys	61441708
Regenerating Mummy	70821187	Saggi the Dark Clown	66602787
Reinforcement of the Army	32807846	Sakuretsu Armor	56120475
Release Restraint	75417459	Salamandra	32268901
Relinquished	64631466	Salvage	96947648
Reload	22589918	Samsara	44182827
Remove Trap	51482758	Sand Gambler	50593156
Rescue Cat	14878871	Sand Moth	73648243
Rescueroid	24311595	Sangan	26202165
Reshef the Dark Being	62420419	Sanwitch	53539634
Respect Play	08951260	Sasuke Samurai	16222645
Return from the Different Dimension	27174286	Sasuke Samurai 2#	11760174
Return of the Doomed	19827717	Sasuke Samurai 3#	77379481
Reversal of Graves	17484499	Sasuke Samurai 4#	64538655
Reversal Quiz	05990062	Satellite Cannon	50400231
Revival Jam	31709826	Scapegoat	73915051
Right Arm of the Forbidden One	70903634	Scarr, Scout of Dark World	05498296
Right Leg of the Forbidden One	08124921	Science Soldier	67532912
Ring of Destruction	83555666	Scroll of Bewitchment	10352095
Ring of Magnetism	20436034	Scyscraper	63035430
Riryoku Field	70344351	Sea Serpent Warrior of Darkness	42071342
Rising Air Current	45778932	Sealmaster Meisei	02468169
Rising Energy	78211862	Second Coin Toss	36562627
Rite of Spirit	30450531	Second Goblin	19086954
Ritual Weapon	54351224	Secret Barrel	27053506
Robbin' Goblin	88279736	Self-Destruct Button	57585212

CARD	PASSWORD	CARD	PASSWORD
Senri Eye	60391791	Solar Ray	44472639
Serial Spell	49398568	Solemn Judgment	41420027
Serpent Night Dragon	66516792	Solemn Wishes	35346968
Serpentine Princess	71829750	Solomon's Lawbook	23471572
Servant of Catoblisam	02792265	Sonic Duck	84696266
Seven Tools of the Bandit	03819470	Sonic Jammer	84550200
Shadow Ghoul	30778711	Sorcerer of Dark Magic	88619463
Shadow Of Eyes	58621589	Soul Absorption	68073522
Shadow Tamer	37620434	Soul Exchange	68005187
Shadowknight Archfiend	09603356	Soul of Purity and Light	77527210
Shadowslayer	20939559	Soul Release	05758500
Share the Pain	56830749	Soul Resurrection	92924317
Shield & Sword	52097679	Soul Reversal	78864369
Shield Crash	30683373	Soul Tiger	15734813
Shien's Spy	07672244	Soul-Absorbing Bone Tower	63012333
Shift	59560625	Souleater	31242786
Shifting Shadows	59237154	Souls Of The Forgotten	04920010
Shinato's Ark	60365591	Space Mambo	36119641
Shinato, King of a Higher Plane	86327225	Spark Blaster	97362768
Shining Abyss	87303357	Sparks	76103675
Shining Angel	95956346	Spatial Collapse	20644748
Shooting Star Bow - Ceal	95638658	Spear Cretin	58551308
Silent Insect	40867519	Spear Dragon	31553716
Silent Magician Lv 4	73665146	Spell Canceller	84636823
Silent Magician Lv 8	72443568	Spell Economics	04259068
Silent Swordsman LV 3	01995985	Spell Purification	01669772
Silent Swordsman LV 5	74388798	Spell Reproduction	29228529
Silent Swordsman LV 7	37267041	Spell Shield Type-8	38275183
Silva, Warlord of Dark World	32619583	Spell Vanishing	29735721
Silpheed	73001017	Spell-Stopping Statute	10069180
Silver Fang	90357090	Spellbinding Circle	18807108
Simultaneous Loss	92219931	Spherous Lady	52121290
Sinister Serpent	08131171	Sphinx Teleia	51402177
Sixth Sense	03280747	Spiral Spear Strike	49328340
Skill Drain	82732705	Spirit Barrier	53239672
Skilled Dark Magician	73752131	Spirit Caller	48659020
Skilled White Magician	46363422	Spirit Message "A"	94772232
Skull Archfiend of Lightning	61370518	Spirit Message "I"	31893528
Skull Descovery Knight	78700060	Spirit Message "L"	30170981
Skull Dog Marron	86652646	Spirit Message "N"	67287533
Skull Invitation	98139712	Spirit of Flames	13522325
Skull Lair	06733059	Spirit of the Breeze	53530069
Skull Mariner	05265750	Spirit of the Harp	80770678
Skull Red Bird	10202894	Spirit of the Pharaoh	25343280
Skull Servant	32274490	Spirit Reaper	23205979
Skull Zoma	79852326	Spirit Ryu	67957315
Skull-Mark Ladybug	64306248	Spiritual Earth Art - Kurogane	70156997
Skyscraper	63035430	Spiritual Energy Settle Machine	99173029
Slate Warrior	78636495	Spiritual Fire Art - Kurenai	42945701
Smashing Ground	97169186	Spiritual Water Art - Aoi	06540606
Smoke Grenade of the Thief	63789924	Spiritual Wind Art - Miyabi	79333300
Snatch Steal	45986603	Spiritualism	15866454
Sogen	86318356	St. Joan	21175632
Soitsu	60246171	Stamping Destruction	81385346
Solar Flare Dragon	45985838	Star Boy	08201910

CARD	PASSWORD
Statue of the Wicked	65810489
Staunch Defender	92854392
Stealth Bird	03510565
Steam Gyroid	05368615
Steamroid	44729197
Steel Ogre Grotto #1	29172562
Steel Ogre Grotto #2	90908427
Stim-Pack	83225447
Stop Defense	63102017
Storming Wynn	29013526
Stray Lambs	60764581
Strike Ninja	41006930
Stronghold	13955608
Stumbling	34646691
Success Probability 0%	06859683
Summon Priest	00423585
Summoned Skull	70781052
Summoner of Illusions	14644902
Super Conductor Ttranno	85520851
Super Rejuvenation	27770341
Super Robolady	75923050
Super Roboyarou	01412158
Supply	44072894
Susa Soldier	40473581
Swarm of Locusts	41872150
Swarm of Scarabs	15383415
Swift Gaia the Fierce Knight	16589042
Sword Hunter	51345461
Sword of Deep-Seated	98495314
Sword of Dragon's Soul	61405855
Sword of the Soul Eater	05371656
Swords of Concealing Light	12923641
Swords of Revealing Light	72302403
Swordsman of Landstar	03573512
Symbol of Heritage	45305419
System Down	18895832
T.A.D.P.O.L.E	10456559
Tactical Espionage Expert	89698120
Tailor of the Fickle	43641473
Taunt	90740329
Tenkabito Shien	41589166
Terra the Terrible	63308047
Terraforming	73628505
Terrorking Archfiend	35975813
Terrorking Salmon	78060096
Teva	16469012
The Agent of Creation - Venus	64734921
The Agent of Force - Mars	91123920
The Agent of Judgment - Saturn	91345518
The Agent of Wisdom - Mercury	38730226
The All-Seeing White Tiger	32269855
The Big March of Animals	01689516
The Bistro Butcher	71107816
The Cheerful Coffin	41142615
The Creator	61505339

CARD	PASSWORD
The Creator Incarnate	97093037
The Dark - Hex Sealed Fusion	52101615
The Dark Door	30606547
The Dragon Dwelling in the Cave	93346024
The Dragon's Bead	92408984
The Earl of Demise	66989694
The Earth - Hex Sealed Fusion	88696724
The Emperor's Holiday	68400115
The End of Anubis	65403020
The Eye Of Truth	34694160
The Fiend Megacyber	66362965
The Flute of Summoning Dragon	43973174
The Flute of Summoning Kuriboh	20065322
The Forceful Sentry	42829885
The Forces of Darkness	29826127
The Forgiving Maiden	84080938
The Furious Sea King	18710707
The Graveyard in the Fourth Dimension	88089103
The Gross Ghost of Fled Dreams	68049471
The Hunter With 7 Weapons	01525329
The Illusionary Gentleman	83764996
The Immortal of Thunder	84926738
The Kick Man	90407382
The Last Warrior From Another Planet	86099788
The Law of the Normal	66926224
The League of Uniform Nomenclature	55008284
The Legendary Fisherman	03643300
The Light - Hex Sealed Fusion	15717011
The Little Swordsman of Aile	25109950
The Masked Beast	49064413
The Portrait's Secret	32541773
The Regulation of Tribe	00296499
The Reliable Guardian	16430187
The Rock Spirit	76305638
The Sanctuary in the Sky	56433456
The Second Sarcophagus	04081094
The Secret of the Bandit	99351431
The Shallow Grave	43434803
The Spell Absorbing Life	99517131
The Thing in the Crater	78243409
The Third Sarcophagus	78697395
The Trojan Horse	38479725
The Unhappy Girl	27618634
The Unhappy Maiden	51275027
The Warrior returning alive	95281259
Theban Nightmare	51838385
Theinen the Great Sphinx	87997872
Thestalos the Firestorm Monarch	26205777
Thousand Dragon	41462083
Thousand Energy	05703682
Thousand Needles	33977496
Thousand-Eyes Idol	27125110
Thousand-Eyes Restrict	63519819

CARD	PASSWORD	CARD	PASSWORD
Threatening Roar	36361633	Twin-Headed Wolf	88132637
Three-Headed Geedo	78423643	Twinheaded Beast	82035781
Throwstone Unit	76075810	Two Thousand Needles	83228073
Thunder Crash	69196160	Two-Man Cell Battle	25578802
Thunder Dragon	31786629	Two-Mouth Darkruler	57305373
Thunder Nyan Nyan	70797118	Two-Pronged Attack	83887306
Thunder of Ruler	91781589	Tyhone	72842870
Time Seal	35316708	Type Zero Magic Crusher	21237481
Time Wizard	71625222	Tyranno Infinity	83235263
Timeater	44913552	Tyrant Dragon	94568601
Timidity	40350910	UFOroid	07602840
Token Festevil	83675475	UFOroid Fighter	32752319
Token Thanksgiving	57182235	Ultimate Insect LV 1	49441499
Tongyo	69572024	Ultimate Insect LV 3	34088136
Toon Cannon Soldier	79875176	Ultimate Insect LV 5	34830502
Toon Dark Magician Girl	90960358	Ultimate Insect LV 7	19877898
Toon Defense	43509019	Ultimate Obedient Fiend	32240937
Toon Gemini Elf	42386471	Ultimate Tyranno	15894048
Toon Goblin Attack Force	15270885	Ultra Evolution Pill	22431243
Toon Masked Sorcerer	16392422	Umi	22702055
Toon Mermaid	65458948	Umiiruka	82999629
Toon Summoned Skull	91842653	Union Attack	60399954
Toon Table of Contents	89997728	United Resistance	85936485
Toon World	15259703	United We Stand	56747793
Tornado Bird	71283180	Unity	14731897
Tornado Wall	18605135	Unshaven Angler	92084010
Torpedo Fish	90337190	Upstart Goblin	70368879
Torrential Tribute	53582587	Uraby	01784619
Total Defense Shogun	75372290	Uria, Lord of Sealing Flames	06007213
Tower of Babel	94256039	V-Tiger Jet	51638941
Tradgedy	35686187	Valkyrion the Magna Warrior	75347539
Transcendent Wings	25573054	Vampire Genesis	22056710
Trap Dustshoot	64697231	Vampire Lord	53839837
Trap Hole	04206964	Vampire Orchis	46571052
Trap Jammer	19252988	Vengeful Bog Spirit	95220856
Treeborn Frog	12538374	Victory D	44910027
Tremendous Fire	46918794	Vilepawn Archfiend	73219648
Tri-Horned Dragon	39111158	VW-Tiger Catapult	58859575
Triage	30888893	VWXYZ-Dragon Catapult Cannon	84243274
Trial of Nightmare	77827521	W-Wing Catapult	96300057
Trial of the Princesses	72709014	Waboku	12607053
Triangle Ecstasy Spar	12181376T	Wall of Revealing Light	17078030
Triangle Power	32298781	Wandering Mummy	42994702
Tribe-Infecting Virus	33184167	Warrior Dai Grepher	75953262
Tribute Doll	02903036	Warrior of Zera	66073051
Tribute to The Doomed	79759861	Wasteland	23424603
Tripwire Beast	45042329	Water Dragon	85066822
Troop Dragon	55013285	Water Omotics	02483611
Tsukuyomi	34853266	Wave Motion Cannon	38992735
Turtle Oath	76806714	Weed Out	28604635
Turtle Tiger	37313348	Whiptail Crow	91996584
Twin Swords of Flashing Light	21900719	Whirlwind Prodigy	15090429
Twin-Headed Behemoth	43586926	White Dragon Ritual	09786492
Twin-Headed Fire Dragon	78984772	White Horn Dragon	73891874
Twin-Headed Thunder Dragon	54752875	White Magical Hat	15150365

CARD	PASSWORD	CARD	PASSWORD
White Magician Pikeru	81383947	X-Head Cannon	62651957
White Ninja	01571945	Xing Zhen Hu	76515293
Wicked-Breaking Flameberge-Baou	68427465	XY-Dragon Cannon	02111707
Wild Nature's Release	61166988	XYZ-Dragon Cannon	91998119
Winged Dragon, Guardian of the Fortress #1	87796900	XZ-Tank Cannon	99724761
Winged Kuriboh	57116033	Y-Dragon Head	65622692
Winged Kuriboh LV1	98585345	Yamata Dragon	76862289
Winged Minion	89258225	Yami	59197169
Winged Sage Falcos	87523462	Yata-Garasu	03078576
Wingweaver	31447217	Yellow Gadget	13839120
Witch Doctor of Chaos	75946257	Yellow Luster Shield	04542651
Witch of the Black Forest	78010363	Yomi Ship	51534754
Witch's Apprentice	80741828	YZ-Tank Dragon	25119460
Witty Phantom	36304921	Z-Metal Tank	64500000
Wolf Axwielder	56369281	Zaborg the Thunder Monarch	51945556
Woodborg Inpachi	35322812	Zero Gravity	83133491
Woodland Sprite	06979239	Zoa	24311372
Worm Drake	73216412	Zolga	16268841
Wroughtweiler	06480253	Zombie Tiger	47693640
Wynn the Wind Charmer	37744402	Zombyra the Dark	88472456
		Zure, Knight of Dark World	07459013

XBOX®

EVERYONE

AVATAR: THE LAST AIRBENDER

BRATZ: FOREVER DIAMONDZ

CARS

CHICKEN LITTLE

DANCE DANCE REVOLUTION ULTRAMIX 3

EA SPORTS ARENA FOOTBALL

FORZA MOTORSPORT

ICE AGE 2: THE MELTDOWN

LEGO STAR WARS II: THE ORIGINAL TRILOGY

MADDEN NFL 07

MAJOR LEAGUE BASEBALL 2K7

NASCAR 07

NBA 2K7

NBA BALLERS: PHENOM

NBA LIVE 07

NCAA FOOTBALL 07

NEED FOR SPEED CARBON

NFL HEAD COACH

OUTRUN 2006: COAST 2 COAST

OVER THE HEDGE

RALLISPORT CHALLENGE 2

TEENAGE MUTANT NINJA TURTLES 3: MUTANT NIGHTMARE

TIGER WOODS PGA TOUR 07

TIM BURTON'S THE NIGHTMARE BEFORE CHRISTMAS: OOGIE'S REVENGE

WORLD RACING 2

YU-GI-OH! THE DAWN OF DESTINY

EVERYONE 10+

THRILLVILLE

TEEN

ALIEN HOMINID

BLAZING ANGELS: SQUADRONS OF WWII

CABELA'S DANGEROUS HUNTS 2

CAPCOM CLASSICS COLLECTION

THE DA VINCI CODE

DESTROY ALL HUMANS! 2

DIGIMON RUMBLE ARENA 2

ERAGON

FLATOUT 2

JUICED

L.A. RUSH

MARVEL ULTIMATE ALLIANCE

PETER JACKSON'S KING KONG: THE

OFFICIAL GAME OF THE MOVIE

SHATTERED UNION

SID MEIER'S PIRATES!

THE SIMS 2

STAR WARS: BATTLEFRONT II

STAR WARS KNIGHTS OF THE OLD REPUBLIC II: THE SITH LORDS

SUPERMAN RETURNS: THE VIDEOGAME

TOMB RAIDER: LEGEND

TONY HAWK'S PROJECT 8

ULTIMATE SPIDER-MAN

X-MEN: THE OFFICIAL GAME

XBOX®

Table of Contents

ALIEN HOMINID

ALL LEVELS, MINI-GAMES, AND HATS
Select Player 1 Setup or Player 2 Setup and change the name to ROYGBIV.

HATS FOR 2-PLAYER GAME
Go to the Options menu and rename your alien one of the following:

ABE	Top Hat	#11
APRIL	Blond Wig	#4
BEHEMOTH	Red Cap	#24
CLETUS	Hunting Hat	#3
DANDY	Flower Petal Hat	#13
GOODMAN	Black Curly Hair	#7
GRRL	Flowers	#10
PRINCESS	Tiara	#12
SUPERFLY	Afro	#6
TOMFULP	Brown Messy Hair	#2

AVATAR: THE LAST AIRBENDER

ALL TREASURE MAPS
Select Code Entry from Extras and enter 37437.

1 HIT DISHONOR
Select Code Entry from Extras and enter 54641.

DOUBLE DAMAGE
Select Code Entry from Extras and enter 34743.

UNLIMITED COPPER
Select Code Entry from Extras and enter 23637.

UNLIMITED CHI
Select Code Entry from Extras and enter 24463.

UNLIMITED HEALTH
Select Code Entry from Extras and enter 94677.

NEVERENDING STEALTH
Select Code Entry from Extras and enter 53467.

CHARACTER CONCEPT ART GALLERY
Select Code Entry from Extras and enter 97831.

BLAZING ANGELS: SQUADRONS OF WWII

ALL MISSIONS, MEDALS, & PLANES
At the Main menu, hold Left Trigger + Right Trigger and press ❌, White, Black, ❤, ❤, Black, White, ❌.

GOD MODE
Pause the game, hold Left Trigger and press ❌, ❤, ❤, ❌. Release Left Trigger, hold Right Trigger and press ❤, ❌, ❌, ❤. Re-enter the code to disable it.

DAMAGE INCREASED
Pause the game, hold Left Trigger and press White, White, Black. Release Left Trigger, hold Right Trigger and press Black, Black, White. Re-enter the code to disable it.

BRATZ: FOREVER DIAMONDZ

1000 BLINGZ
While in the Bratz Office, use the Cheat computer to enter SIZZLN.

2000 BLINGZ
While in the Bratz Office, use the Cheat computer to enter FLAUNT.

PET TREATS
While in the Bratz Office, use the Cheat computer to enter TREATZ.

GIFT SET A
While in the Bratz Office, use the Cheat computer to enter STYLIN.

GIFT SET B
While in the Bratz Office, use the Cheat computer to enter SKATIN.

GIFT SET C
While in the Bratz Office, use the Cheat computer to enter JEWELZ.

GIFT SET E
While in the Bratz Office, use the Cheat computer to enter DIMNDZ.

CABELA'S DANGEROUS HUNTS 2

DOUBLE HEALTH
Select Codes and enter Eye, Bolt, Skull, Hand, Boot.

HEALTH REGENERATES FASTER
Select Codes and enter Skull, Eye, Boot, Bolt, Hand.

DOUBLE DAMAGE
Select Codes and enter Hand, Boot, Skull, Eye, Bolt.

INFINITE AMMO
Select Codes and enter Bolt, Hand, Eye, Boot, Skull.

CAPCOM CLASSICS COLLECTION

ALL LOCKS OPENED
At the Title screen, press Left Trigger, Right Trigger, Up on Right Thumbstick, Down on Right Thumbstick, Left Trigger, Right Trigger, Up on Left Thumbstick, Down on Left Thumbstick, Left Trigger, Right Trigger, Up, Down.

CARS

UNLOCK EVERYTHING
Select Cheat Codes from the Options and enter IF900HP.

ALL CHARACTERS
Select Cheat Codes from the Options and enter YAYCARS.

ALL CHARACTER SKINS
Select Cheat Codes from the Options and enter R4MONE.

ALL MINI-GAMES AND COURSES
Select Cheat Codes from the Options and enter MATTL66.

MATER'S COUNTDOWN CLEAN-UP MINI-GAME AND MATER'S SPEEDY CIRCUIT
Select Cheat Codes from the Options and enter TRGTEXC.

FAST START
Select Cheat Codes from the Options and enter IMSPEED.

INFINITE BOOST
Select Cheat Codes from the Options and enter VROOOOM.

ART
Select Cheat Codes from the Options and enter CONC3PT.

VIDEOS
Select Cheat Codes from the Options and enter WATCHIT.

CHICKEN LITTLE

INVINCIBILITY
Select Cheat Codes from the Extras menu and enter Baseball, Baseball, Baseball, Shirt.

BIG FEET
Select Cheat Codes from the Extras menu and enter Hat, Glove, Glove, Hat.

BIG HAIR
Select Cheat Codes from the Extras menu and enter Baseball, Bat, Bat, Baseball.

BIG HEAD
Select Cheat Codes from the Extras menu and enter Hat, Helmet, Helmet, Hat.

PAPER PANTS
Select Cheat Codes from the Extras menu and enter Bat, Bat, Hat, Hat.

SUNGLASSES
Select Cheat Codes from the Extras menu and enter Glove, Glove, Helmet, Helmet.

UNDERWEAR
Select Cheat Codes from the Extras menu and enter Hat, Hat, Shirt, Shirt.

DANCE DANCE REVOLUTION ULTRAMIX 3

ALL SONGS
Select Credits from the Options screen and play the Credits mini-game, then press the opposite of what the game indicates. (For example, press Up when it says Down and so on. Or, if it says Left + Right, press Up + Down.) You'll hear applause when the code is entered correctly.

THE DA VINCI CODE

GOD MODE
Select Codes from the Options screen and enter VITRUVIAN MAN.

EXTRA HEALTH
Select Codes from the Options screen and enter SACRED FEMININE.

MISSION SELECT
Select Codes from the Options screen and enter CLOS LUCE 1519.

ONE-HIT FIST KILL
Select Codes from the Options screen and enter PHILLIPS EXETER.

ONE-HIT WEAPON KILL
Select Codes from the Options screen and enter ROYAL HOLLOWAY

ALL VISUAL DATABASE
Select Codes from the Options screen and enter APOCRYPHA

ALL VISUAL DATABASE AND CONCEPT ART
Select Codes from the Options screen and enter ET IN ARCADIA EGO.

DESTROY ALL HUMANS! 2

SALAD DAYS WITH POX & CRYPTO MOVIE
Pause the game and select Archives. Hold Left Thumbstick and press Ⓐ Ⓧ Ⓨ Ⓑ Ⓧ Ⓑ Ⓨ Ⓐ Ⓐ.

DIGIMON RUMBLE ARENA 2

ONE-HIT KILLS
At the Title screen, press Right, Up, Left, Down, Ⓐ, Left Trigger + Right Trigger.

EVOLVE ENERGY ITEM
At the Title screen, press Ⓨ, Right, Down, Ⓑ, Left Trigger, Ⓐ, Right Trigger, Ⓐ, Ⓨ.

EVOLVE METER ALWAYS FULL
At the Title screen, press Ⓧ, Right, Ⓐ, Ⓨ, Left, Ⓑ, Left Trigger + Right Trigger.

EA SPORTS ARENA FOOTBALL

BIG BALL
While at the line of scrimmage, press Left Trigger + Ⓨ, Up, Up.

SMALL BALL
While at the line of scrimmage, press Left Trigger + Ⓨ, Down, Down.

NORMAL SIZE BALL
While at the line of scrimmage, press Left Trigger + Ⓨ, Up, Down.

MAX STATS IN QUICK PLAY
Load a profile with the name IronMen. This will maximize all players' stats in Quick Play.

ERAGON

FURY MODE
Pause the game, hold Left Trigger + Right Trigger and press ✕, ✕, Ⓑ, Ⓑ.

FLATOUT 2

ALL CARS AND 1,000,000 CREDITS
Select Enter Code from Extras and enter GIEVEPIX

1,000,000 CREDITS
Select Enter Code from the Extras and enter GIVECASH.

PIMPSTER CAR
Select Enter Code from Extras and enter RUTTO.

FLATMOBILE CAR
Select Enter Code from Extras and enter WOTKINS.

MOB CAR
Select Enter Code from the Extras and enter BIGTRUCK.

SCHOOL BUS
Select Enter Code from Extras and enter GIEVCARPLZ.

ROCKET CAR
Select Enter Code from Extras and enter KALJAKOPPA.

TRUCK
Select Enter Code from the Extras and enter ELPUEBLO.

FORZA MOTORSPORT

START CAREER WITH 900,000,000 CREDITS
Start a new profile with the name tEAm4za.

ALL CARS
Start a new profile with the name nOsLiW.

ICE AGE 2: THE MELTDOWN

INFINITE PEBBLES
Pause the game and press Down, Down, Left, Up, Up, Right, Up, Down.

INFINITE ENERGY
Pause the game and press Down, Left, Right, Down, Down, Right, Left, Down.

INFINITE HEALTH
Pause the game and press Up, Right, Down, Up, Left, Down, Right, Left.

JUICED

ARCADE/CUSTOM MODE UNLOCKED
Select Cheats from the Extras menu and enter PINT.

L.A. RUSH

$5,000
During a game, press Up, Down, Left, Right, **B**, Left, **A**, Up.

UNLIMITED N20
During a game, press Up, Down, Left, Right, **X**, Up, Down, **B**, Up.

ALL CARS IN GARAGE PIMPED
During a game, press Up, Down, Left, Right, **B**, **X**, **A**, **Y**, Up, Down, Left, Right.

DISABLE POLICE
During a game, press Up, Down, Left, Right, **A**, **X**, Right, **Y**, Left.

FAST TRAFFIC
During a game, press Up, Down, Left, Right, **X**, Right, **B**, Left.

NO CATCH UP
Use C-VHARD as a profile name.

SLOWER OPPONENTS
Use C-EASY as a profile name.

LEGO STAR WARS II: THE ORIGINAL TRILOGY

BEACH TROOPER
At Mos Eisley Canteena, select Enter Code and enter UCK868. You still need to select Characters and purchase this character for 20,000 studs.

BEN KENOBI (GHOST)
At Mos Eisley Canteena, select Enter Code and enter BEN917. You still need to select Characters and purchase this character for 1,100,000 studs.

BESPIN GUARD
At Mos Eisley Canteena, select Enter Code and enter VHY832. You still need to select Characters and purchase this character for 15,000 studs.

BIB FORTUNA
At Mos Eisley Canteena, select Enter Code and enter WTY721. You still need to select Characters and purchase this character for 16,000 studs.

BOBA FETT

At Mos Eisley Canteena, select Enter Code and enter HLP221. You still need to select Characters and purchase this character for 175,000 studs.

DEATH STAR TROOPER

At Mos Eisley Canteena, select Enter Code and enter BNC332. You still need to select Characters and purchase this character for 19,000 studs.

EWOK

At Mos Eisley Canteena, select Enter Code and enter TTT289. You still need to select Characters and purchase this character for 34,000 studs.

GAMORREAN GUARD

At Mos Eisley Canteena, select Enter Code and enter YZF999. You still need to select Characters and purchase this character for 40,000 studs.

GONK DROID

At Mos Eisley Canteena, select Enter Code and enter NFX582. You still need to select Characters and purchase this character for 1,550 studs.

GRAND MOFF TARKIN

At Mos Eisley Canteena, select Enter Code and enter SMG219. You still need to select Characters and purchase this character for 38,000 studs.

GREEDO

At Mos Eisley Canteena, select Enter Code and enter NAH118. You still need to select Characters and purchase this character for 60,000 studs.

HAN SOLO (HOOD)

At Mos Eisley Canteena, select Enter Code and enter YWM840. You still need to select Characters and purchase this character for 20,000 studs.

IG-88

At Mos Eisley Canteena, select Enter Code and enter NXL973. You still need to select Characters and purchase this character for 30,000 studs.

IMPERIAL GUARD

At Mos Eisley Canteena, select Enter Code and enter MMM111. You still need to select Characters and purchase this character for 45,000 studs.

IMPERIAL OFFICER

At Mos Eisley Canteena, select Enter Code and enter BBV889. You still need to select Characters and purchase this character for 28,000 studs.

IMPERIAL SHUTTLE PILOT

At Mos Eisley Canteena, select Enter Code and enter VAP664. You still need to select Characters and purchase this character for 29,000 studs.

IMPERIAL SPY

At Mos Eisley Canteena, select Enter Code and enter CVT125. You still need to select Characters and purchase this character for 13,500 studs.

JAWA

At Mos Eisley Canteena, select Enter Code and enter JAW499. You still need to select Characters and purchase this character for 24,000 studs.

LOBOT

At Mos Eisley Canteena, select Enter Code and enter UUB319. You still need to select Characters and purchase this character for 11,000 studs.

PALACE GUARD

At Mos Eisley Canteena, select Enter Code and enter SGE549. You still need to select Characters and purchase this character for 14,000 studs.

REBEL PILOT

At Mos Eisley Canteena, select Enter Code and enter CYG336. You still need to select Characters and purchase this character for 15,000 studs.

REBEL TROOPER (HOTH)

At Mos Eisley Canteena, select Enter Code and enter EKU849. You still need to select Characters and purchase this character for 16,000 studs.

SANDTROOPER
At Mos Eisley Canteena, select Enter Code and enter YDV451. You still need to select Characters and purchase this character for 14,000 studs.

SKIFF GUARD
At Mos Eisley Canteena, select Enter Code and enter GBU888. You still need to select Characters and purchase this character for 12,000 studs.

SNOWTROOPER
At Mos Eisley Canteena, select Enter Code and enter NYU989. You still need to select Characters and purchase this character for 16,000 studs.

STROMTROOPER
At Mos Eisley Canteena, select Enter Code and enter PTR345. You still need to select Characters and purchase this character for 10,000 studs.

THE EMPEROR
At Mos Eisley Canteena, select Enter Code and enter HHY382. You still need to select Characters and purchase this character for 275,000 studs.

TIE FIGHTER
At Mos Eisley Canteena, select Enter Code and enter HDY739. You still need to select Characters and purchase this character for 60,000 studs.

TIE FIGHTER PILOT
At Mos Eisley Canteena, select Enter Code and enter NNZ316. You still need to select Characters and purchase this character for 21,000 studs.

TIE INTERCEPTOR
At Mos Eisley Canteena, select Enter Code and enter QYA828. You still need to select Characters and purchase this character for 40,000 studs.

TUSKEN RAIDER
At Mos Eisley Canteena, select Enter Code and enter PEJ821. You still need to select Characters and purchase this character for 23,000 studs.

UGNAUGHT
At Mos Eisley Canteena, select Enter Code and enter UGN694. You still need to select Characters and purchase this character for 36,000 studs.

MADDEN NFL 07

MADDEN CARDS
Select Madden Cards from My Madden, then select Madden Codes and enter the following:

CARD	PASSWORD	CARD	PASSWORD
#199 Gold Lame Duck Cheat	5LAWOO	#236 1982 Redskins Gold	WL8BRI
#200 Gold Mistake Free Cheat	XL7SP1	#237 1983 Raiders Gold	HOEW71
#210 Gold QB on Target Cheat	WROAOR	#238 1984 Dolphins Gold	M1AM1E
#220 Super Bowl XLI Gold	RLA9R7	#239 1985 Bears Gold	QOET08
#221 Super Bowl XLII Gold	WRLUF8	#240 1986 Giants Gold	ZI8S2L
#222 Super Bowl XLIII Gold	NIEV4A	#241 1988 49ers Gold	SP2A8H
#223 Super Bowl XLIV Gold	M5AB7L	#242 1990 Eagles Gold	2L4TRO
#224 Aloha Stadium Gold	YI8P8U	#243 1991 Lions Gold	J1ETRI
#225 1958 Colts Gold	B57QLU	#244 1992 Cowboys Gold	W9UVI9
#226 1966 Packers Gold	1PL1FL	#245 1993 Bills Gold	DLA3I7
#227 1968 Jets Gold	MIE6WO	#246 1994 49ers Gold	DR7EST
#228 1970 Browns Gold	CL2TOE	#247 1996 Packers Gold	F8LUST
#229 1972 Dolphins Gold	NOEB7U	#248 1998 Broncos Gold	FIES95
#230 1974 Steelers Gold	YOOFLA	#249 1999 Rams Gold	S90USW
#231 1976 Raiders Gold	MOA11I	#250 Bears Pump Up the Crowd	B1OUPH
#232 1977 Broncos Gold	C8UM7U	#251 Bengals Cheerleader	DRL2SW
#233 1978 Dolphins Gold	VIU007	#252 Bills Cheerleader	1PLUYO
#234 1980 Raiders Gold	NLAPH3	#253 Broncos Cheerleader	3ROUJO
#235 1981 Chargers Gold	COAGI4	#254 Browns Pump Up the Crowd	T1UTOA

CARD	PASSWORD
#255 Buccaneers Cheerleader	S9EWRI
#256 Cardinals Cheerleader	57IEPI
#257 Chargers Cheerleader	F7UHL8
#258 Chiefs Cheerleader	PRI5SL
#259 Colts Cheerleader	1R5AMI
#260 Cowboys Cheerleader	Z2ACHL
#261 Dolphins Cheerleader	C5AHLE
#262 Eagles Cheerleader	PO7DRO
#263 Falcons Cheerleader	37USPO

CARD	PASSWORD
#264 49ers Cheerleader	KLOCRL
#265 Giants Pump Up the Crowd	C4USPI
#266 Jaguars Cheerleader	MIEH7E
#267 Jets Pump Up the Crowd	COLUXI
#268 Lions Pump Up the Crowd	3LABLU
#269 Packers Pump Up the Crowd	4HO7VO
#270 Panthers Cheerleader	F2IASP
#282 All AFC Team Gold	PRO9PH
#283 All NFC Team Gold	RLATH7

MAJOR LEAGUE BASEBALL 2K7

MICKEY MANTLE ON THE FREE AGENTS LIST
Select Enter Cheat Code from the My 2K7 menu and enter themick.

ALL CHEATS
Select Enter Cheat Code from the My 2K7 menu and enter Black Sox.

ALL EXTRAS
Select Enter Cheat Code from the My 2K7 menu and enter Game On.

UNLOCK EVERYTHING
Select Enter Cheat Code from the My 2K7 menu and enter Derek Jeter. This does not unlock the Topps cheats.

MIGHTY MICK CHEAT
Select Enter Cheat Code from the My 2K7 menu and enter mightymick.

TRIPLE CROWN CHEAT
Select Enter Cheat Code from the My 2K7 menu and enter triplecrown.

PINCH HIT MICK CHEAT
Select Enter Cheat Code from the My 2K7 menu and enter phmantle.

BIG BLAST CHEAT
Select Enter Cheat Code from the My 2K7 menu Rand enter m4murder.

MARVEL ULTIMATE ALLIANCE

UNLOCK ALL SKINS
At the Team menu, press Up, Down, Left, Right, Left, Right, Start.

UNLOCKS ALL HERO POWERS
At the Team menu, press Left, Right, Up, Down, Up, Down, Start.

ALL HEROES TO LEVEL 99
At the Team menu, press Up, Left, Up, Left, Down, Right, Down, Right, Start.

UNLOCK ALL HEROES
At the Team menu, press Up, Up, Down, Down, Left, Left, Left, Start.

XBOX®

UNLOCK DAREDEVIL
At the Team menu, press Left, Left, Right, Right, Up, Down, Up, Down, Start.

UNLOCK SILVER SURFER
At the Team menu, press Down, Left, Left, Up, Right, Up, Down, Left, Start.

GOD MODE
During gameplay, press Up, Down, Up, Down, Up, Left, Down, Right, Start.

TOUCH OF DEATH
During gameplay, press Left, Right, Down, Down, Right, Left, Start.

SUPER SPEED
During gameplay, press Up, Left, Up, Right, Down, Right, Start.

FILL MOMENTUM
During gameplay, press Left, Right, Right, Left, Up, Down, Down, Up, Start.

UNLOCK ALL COMICS
At the Review menu, press Left, Right, Right, Left, Up, Up, Right, Start.

UNLOCK ALL CONCEPT ART
At the Review menu, press Down, Down, Down, Right, Right, Left, Down, Start.

UNLOCK ALL CINEMATICS
At the Review menu, press Up, Left, Left, Up, Right, Right, Up, Start.

UNLOCK ALL LOAD SCREENS
At the Review menu, press Up, Down, Right, Left, Up, Up Down, Start.

UNLOCK ALL COURSES
At the Comic Missions menu, press Up, Right, Left, Down, Up, Right, Left, Down, Start.

NASCAR 07

$10,000,000
In Fight to the Top mode, enter your name as GiveMe More.

10,000,000 FANS
In Fight to the Top mode, enter your name as AllBow ToMe.

PRESTIGE LEVEL 10 WITH 2,000,000 POINTS
In Fight to the Top mode, enter your name as Outta MyWay.

100% TEAM PRESTIGE
In Fight to the Top mode, enter your name as MoMoney BlingBling.

ALL CHASE PLATES
In Fight to the Top mode, enter your name as ItsAll ForMe.

OLD SPICE TRACKS AND CARS.
In Fight to the Top mode, enter your name as KeepCool SmellGreat.

WALMART TRACK AND CARS
In Fight to the Top mode, enter your name as Walmart EveryDay.

NBA 2K7

MAX DURABILITY
Select Codes from the Features menu and enter ironman.

UNLIMITED STAMINA
Select Codes from the Features menu and enter norest.

+10 DEFENSIVE AWARENESS
Select Codes from the Features menu and enter getstops.

+10 OFFENSIVE AWARENESS
Select Codes from the Features menu and enter inthezone.

TOPPS 2K SPORTS ALL-STARS
Select Codes from the Features menu and enter topps2ksports.

ABA BALL
Select Codes from the Features menu and enter payrespect.

NBA BALLERS: PHENOM

VERSUS SCREEN CHEATS
You can enter the following codes at the Vs screen. The X button corresponds to the first number in the code, the Y is the second number, and the B button corresponds to the last number. Press the D-pad in any direction to enter the code.

EFFECT	CODE	EFFECT	CODE
Tournament Mode	0 1 1	Unlimited Juice	7 6 3
Big Head	1 3 4	House meter half full at start	3 6 7
Baby Ballers	4 2 3	Super block ability	1-2-4
Kid Ballers	4 3 3	Show Shot Percentage	0 1 2
2D Ballers	3 5 4	Alternate Gear	1 2 3
Speedy Players	2 1 3		

NBA LIVE 07

ADIDAS ARTILLERY II BLACK & THE RBK ANSWER 9 VIDEO
Select NBA Codes from My NBA Live and enter 99B6356HAN.

ADIDAS ARTILLERY II
Select NBA Codes and enter NTGNFUE87H.

ADIDAS BTB LOW AND THE MESSAGE FROM ALLEN IVERSON VIDEO
Select NBA Codes and enter 7FB3KS9JQ0.

ADIDAS C-BILLUPS
Select NBA Codes and enter BV6877HB9N.

ADIDAS C-BILLUPS BLACK
Select NBA Codes and enter 85NVLDMWS5.

ADIDAS CAMPUS LT
Select NBA Codes and enter CLT2983NC8.

ADIDAS CRAZY 8
Select NBA Codes and enter CC98KKL814.

ADIDAS EQUIPMENT BBALL
Select NBA Codes and enter 220IUJKMDR.

ADIDAS GARNETT BOUNCE
Select NBA Codes and enter HYIOUHCAAN.

ADIDAS GARNETT BOUNCE BLACK
Select NBA Codes and enter KDZ2MQL17W.

ADIDAS GIL-ZERO
Select NBA Codes and enter 23DN1PPOG4.

ADIDAS GIL-ZERO BLACK
Select NBA Codes and enter QQQ3JCUYQ7.

ADIDAS GIL-ZERO MID
Select NBA Codes and enter 1GSJC8JWRL.

ADIDAS GIL-ZERO MID BLACK
Select NBA Codes and enter 369V6RVU3G.

ADIDAS STEALTH
Select NBA Codes and enter FE454DFJCC.

ADIDAS T-MAC 6
Select NBA Codes and enter MCJK843NNC.

ADIDAS T-MAC 6 WHITE
Select NBA Codes and enter 84GF7EJG8V.

AIR JORDAN V
Select NBA Codes and enter PNBBX1EVT5.

AIR JORDAN V
Select NBA Codes and enter VIR13PC451.

AIR JORDAN V
Select NBA Codes and enter IB7G8NN91Z.

JORDAN MELO M3
Select NBA Codes and enter JUL38TC485.

CHARLOTTE BOBCATS 2006-2007 ALTERNATE JERSEY
Select NBA Codes and enter WEDX671H7S.

UTAH JAZZ 2006-2007 ALTERNATE JERSEY
Select NBA Codes and enter VCBI89FK83.

NEW JERSEY NETS 2006-2007 ALTERNATE JERSEY
Select NBA Codes and enter D4SAA98U5H.

WASHINGTON WIZARDS 2006-2007 ALTERNATE JERSEY
Select NBA Codes and enter QV93NLKXQC.

EASTERN ALL-STARS 2006-2007 ROAD JERSEY
Select NBA Codes and enter WOCNW4KL7L.

EASTERN ALL-STARS 2006-2007 HOME JERSEY
Select NBA Codes and enter 5654ND43N6.

WESTERN ALL-STARS 2006-2007 ROAD JERSEY
Select NBA Codes and enter XX93BVL20U.

WESTERN ALL-STARS 2006-2007 HOME JERSEY
Select NBA Codes and enter 993NSKL199.

NCAA FOOTBALL 07

#16 BAYLOR
Select Pennant Collection from My NCAA. Press Select and enter Sic Em.

#16 NIKE SPEED TD
Select Pennant Collection from My NCAA. Press Select and enter Light Speed.

#63 ILLINOIS
Select Pennant Collection from My NCAA. Press Select and enter Oskee Wow.

#160 TEXAS TECH
Select Pennant Collection from My NCAA. Press Select and enter Fight.

#200 FIRST AND FIFTEEN
Select Pennant Collection from My NCAA. Press Select and enter Thanks.

#201 BLINK
Select Pennant Collection from My NCAA. Press Select and enter For.

#202 BOING
Select Pennant Collection from My NCAA. Press Select and enter Registering.

#204 BUTTER FINGERS
Select Pennant Collection from My NCAA. Press Select and enter With EA.

#205 CROSSED THE LINE
Select Pennant Collection from My NCAA. Press Select and enter Tiburon.

#206 CUFFED
Select Pennant Collection from My NCAA. Press Select and enter EA Sports.

#207 EXTRA CREDIT
Select Pennant Collection from My NCAA. Press Select and enter Touchdown.

#208 HELIUM
Select Pennant Collection from My NCAA. Press Select and enter In The Zone.

#209 HURRICANE
Select Pennant Collection from My NCAA. Press Select and enter Turnover.

#210 INSTANT FREPLAY
Select Pennant Collection from My NCAA. Press Select and enter Impact.

#211 JUMBALAYA
Select Pennant Collection from My NCAA. Press Select and enter Heisman.

#212 MOLASSES
Select Pennant Collection from My NCAA .Press Select and enter Game Time.

#213 NIKE FREE
Select Pennant Collection from My NCAA. Press Select and enter Break Free.

#214 NIKE MAGNIGRIP
Select Pennant Collection from My NCAA. Press Select and enter Hand Picked.

#215 NIKE PRO
Select Pennant Collection from My NCA Press Select and enter No Sweat.

#219 QB DUD
Select Pennant Collection from My NCAA. Press Select and enter Elite 11.

#221 STEEL TOE
Select Pennant Collection from My NCAA. Press Select and enter Gridiron.

#222 STIFFED
Select Pennant Collection from My NCAA. Press Select and enter NCAA.

#223 SUPER DIVE
Select Pennant Collection from My NCAA. Press Select and enter Upset.

#224 TAKE YOUR TIME
Select Pennant Collection from My NCAA. Press Select and enter Football.

#225 THREAD & NEEDLE
Select Pennant Collection from My NCAA. Press Select and enter 06.

#226 TOUGH AS NAILS
Select Pennant Collection from My NCAA. Press Select and enter Offense.

#227 TRIP
Select Pennant Collection from My NCAA. Press Select and enter Defense.

#228 WHAT A HIT
Select Pennant Collection from My NCAA. Press Select and enter Blitz.

#229 KICKER HEX
Select Pennant Collection from My NCAA. Press Select and enter Sideline.

#273 2004 ALL-AMERICANS
Select Pennant Collection from My NCAA. Press Select and enter Fumble.

#274 ALL-ALABAMA
Select Pennant Collection from My NCAA. Press Select and enter Roll Tide.

#276 ALL-ARKANSAS
Select Pennant Collection from My NCAA. Press Select and enter Woopigsooie.

#277 ALL-AUBURN
Select Pennant Collection from My NCAA. Press Select and enter War Eagle.

#278 ALL-CLEMSON
Select Pennant Collection from My NCAA. Press Select and enter Death Valley.

#279 ALL-COLORADO
Select Pennant Collection from My NCAA. Press Select and enter Glory.

#280 ALL-FLORIDA
Select Pennant Collection from My NCAA. Press Select and enter Great To Be.

#281 ALL-FSU
Select Pennant Collection from My NCAA. Press Select and enter Uprising.

#282 ALL-GEORGIA
Select Pennant Collection from My NCAA. Press Select and enter Hunker Down.

#283 ALL-IOWA
Select Pennant Collection from My NCAA. Press Select and enter On Iowa.

#284 ALL-KANSAS STATE
Select Pennant Collection from My NCAA. Press Select and enter Victory.

#285 ALL-LSU
Select Pennant Collection from My NCAA. Press Select and enter Geaux Tigers.

#286 ALL-MIAMI
Select Pennant Collection from My NCAA. Press Select and enter Raising Cane.

#287 ALL-MICHIGAN
Select Pennant Collection from My NCAA. Press Select and enter Go Blue.

#288 ALL-MISSISSIPPI STATE
Select Pennant Collection from My NCAA. Press Select and enter Hail State.

#289 ALL-NEBRASKA
Select Pennant Collection from My NCAA. Press Select and enter Go Big Red.

#290 ALL-NORTH CAROLINA
Select Pennant Collection from My NCAA. Press Select and enter Rah Rah.

#291 ALL-NOTRE DAME
Select Pennant Collection from My NCAA. Press Select and enter Golden Domer.

#292 ALL-OHIO STATE
Select Pennant Collection from My NCAA. Press Select and enter Killer Nuts.

#293 ALL-OKLAHOMA
Select Pennant Collection from My NCAA. Press Select and enter Boomer.

#294 ALL-OKLAHOMA STATE
Select Pennant Collection from My NCAA. Press Select and enter Go Pokes.

#295 ALL-OREGON
Select Pennant Collection from My NCAA. Press Select and enter Quack Attack.

#296 ALL-PENN STATE
Select Pennant Collection from My NCAA. Press Select and enter We Are.

#297 ALL-PITTSBURGH
Select Pennant Collection from My NCAA. Press Select and enter Lets Go Pitt.

#298 ALL-PURDUE
Select Pennant Collection from My NCAA. Press Select and enter Boiler Up.

#299 ALL-SYRACUSE
Select Pennant Collection from My NCAA. Press Select and enter Orange Crush.

#300 ALL-TENNESSEE
Select Pennant Collection from My NCAA. Press Select and enter Big Orange.

#301 ALL-TEXAS
Select Pennant Collection from MyNCAA. Press Select and enter Hook Em.

#302 ALL-TEXAS A&M
Select Pennant Collection from My NCAA. Press Select and enter Gig Em.

#303 ALL-UCLA
Select Pennant Collection from My NCAA. Press Select and enter MIGHTY.

#304 ALL-USC
Select Pennant Collection from My NCAA. Press Select and enter Fight On.

#305 ALL-VIRGINIA
Select Pennant Collection from My NCAA. Press Select and enter Wahoos.

#306 ALL-VIRGINIA TECH
Select Pennant Collection from My NCAA. Press Select and enter Tech Triumph.

#307 ALL-WASHINGTON
Select Pennant Collection from My NCAA. Press Select and enter Bow Down.

#308 ALL-WISCONSIN
Select Pennant Collection from My NCAA. Press Select and enter U Rah Rah.

#311 ARK MASCOT
Select Pennant Collection from MyNCAA. Press Select and enter Bear Down.

#329 GT MASCOT
Select Pennant Collection from My NCAA. Press Select and enter RamblinWreck.

#333 ISU MASCOT
Select Pennant Collection from My NCAA. Press Select and enter Red And Gold.

#335 KU MASCOT
Select Pennant Collection from My NCAA. Press Select and enter Rock Chalk.

#341 MINN MASCOT
Select Pennant Collection from My NCAA. Press Select and enter Rah Rah Rah.

#344 MIZZOU MASCOT
Select Pennant Collection from My NCAA. Press Select and enter Mizzou Rah.

#346 MSU MASCOT
Select Pennant Collection from My NCAA. Press Select and enter Go Green.

#349 NCSU MASCOT
Select Pennant Collection from My NCAA. Press Select and enter Go Pack.

#352 NU MASCOT
Select Pennant Collection from My NCAA. Press Select and enter Go Cats.

#360 S CAR MASCOT
Select Pennant Collection from My NCAA. Press Select and enter Go Carolina.

#371 UK MASCOT
Select Pennant Collection from My NCAA. Press Select and enter On On UK.

#382 WAKE FOREST
Select Pennant Collection from My NCAA. Press Select and enter Go Deacs Go.

#385 WSU MASCOT
Select Pennant Collection from My NCAA. Press Select and enter All Hail.

#386 WVU MASCOT
Select Pennant Collection from My NCAA. Press Select and enter Hail WV.

NEED FOR SPEED CARBON

CASTROL CASH
At the Main menu, press Down, Up, Left, Down, Right, Up, ✖, Ⓑ. This will give you 10,000 extra cash.

INFINITE CREW CHARGE
At the Main menu, press Down, Up, Up, Right, Left, Left, Right, ✖.

INFINITE NITROUS
At the Main menu, press Left, Up, Left, Down, Left, Down, Right, ✖.

INFINITE SPEEDBREAKER
At the Main menu, press Down, Right, Right, Left, Right, Up, Down, ✖.

NEED FOR SPEED CARBON LOGO VINYLS
At the Main menu, press Right, Up, Down, Up, Down, Left, Right, ✖.

NEED FOR SPEED CARBON SPECIAL LOGO VINYLS
At the Main menu, press Up, Up, Down, Down, Down, Down, Up, ✖.

NFL HEAD COACH

CLOWN
Name your coach Red Nose.

JOHN MADDEN
Name your coach John Madden.

SANTA CLAUS
Name your coach Merry Christmas.

SUPER BOWL ALWAYS AT HOMETOWN
Name your coach Hometown Hero.

OUTRUN 2006: COAST 2 COAST

100% COMPLETE/UNLOCK EVERYTHING
Edit your license and change the name to ENTIRETY Select Done, then back out of all menus.

1000000 OUTRUN MILES
Edit your license and change the name to MILESANDMILES. Select Done, then back out of all menus.

OVER THE HEDGE

COMPLETE LEVELS
Pause the game, hold Left Trigger + Right Trigger and press **Y**, **B**, **Y**, **B**, **B**, **X**.

ALL MINIGAMES
Pause the game, hold Left Trigger + Right Trigger and press **Y**, **B**, **Y**, **Y**, **X**, **X**.

ALL MOVES
Pause the game, hold Left Trigger + Right Trigger and press **Y**, **B**, **Y**, **X**, **X**, **B**.

EXTRA DAMAGE
Pause the game, hold Left Trigger + Right Trigger and press **Y**, **B**, **Y**, **B**, **Y**, **X**.

MORE HP FROM FOOD
Pause the game, hold Left Trigger + Right Trigger and press **Y**, **B**, **Y**, **B**, **X**, **Y**.

ALWAYS POWER PROJECTILE
Pause the game, hold Left Trigger + Right Trigger and press **Y**, **B**, **Y**, **B**, **X**, **B**.

BONUS COMIC 14
Pause the game, hold Left Trigger + Right Trigger and press **Y**, **B**, **X**, **X**, **B**, **Y**.

BONUS COMIC 15
Pause the game, hold Left Trigger + Right Trigger and press **Y**, **Y**, **X**, **B**, **X**, **B**.

PETER JACKSON'S KING KONG: THE OFFICIAL GAME OF THE MOVIE

At the Main menu, hold Left Trigger + Right Trigger and press Down, **X**, Up, **Y**, Down, Down, Up, Up. Release Left Trigger + Right Trigger to get the Cheat option on the menu. The Cheat option is also available on the pause menu.

GOD MODE
Select Cheat and enter 8wonder

ALL CHAPTERS
Select Cheat and enter KKst0ry.

AMMO 999
Select Cheat and enter KK 999 mun.

MACHINE GUN
Select Cheat and enter KKcapone.

REVOLVER
Select Cheat and enter KKtigun.

SNIPER RIFLE
Select Cheat and enter KKsn1per.

INFINITE SPEARS
Select Cheat and enter lance 1nf.

EXTRAS
Select Cheat and enter KKmuseum.

ONE-HIT KILLS
Select Cheat and enter GrosBras.

RALLISPORT CHALLENGE 2

CARS AND TRACKS SET 1
Select Credits from the Options screen and press Down, Left, Down, Right, Up, Up.

CARS AND TRACKS SET 2
Select Credits from the Options screen and press Left, Left, Down, Down, Right, Right.

CARS AND TRACKS SET 3
Select Credits from the Options screen and press Down, Down, Left, Left, Up, Down.

CARS AND TRACKS SET 4
Select Credits from the Options and press Right, Down, Right, Down, Left, Up.

CARS AND TRACKS SET 5
Select Credits from the Options screen and press Left, Left, Right, Right, Down, Left.

CARS AND TRACKS SET 6
Select Credits from the Options screen and press Right, Up, Up, Up, Down, Left.

CARS AND TRACKS SET 7
Select Credits from the Options screen and press Left, Left, Left, Up, Up, Right.

CARS AND TRACKS SET 8
Select Credits from the Options screen and press Right, Up, Left, Up, Down, Right.

CARS AND TRACKS SET 9
Select Credits from the Options screen and press Down, Up, Down, Left, Left, Down.

CARS AND TRACKS SET 10
Select Credits from the Options screen and press Up, Up, Down, Down, Left, Right.

SHATTERED UNION

SKIP CURRENT WEEK IN CAMPAIGN MODE
At the US Map, press Start for the Options. Then select Cheat Menu and press ✕, Ⓨ, ✕, Ⓑ, Ⓐ.

WIN CIVIL WAR IN CAMPAIGN MODE
At the US Map, press Start for the Options. Then select Cheat Menu and press ✕, Ⓑ, Ⓐ, Ⓑ, Ⓨ.

$100,000
At the US Map, press Start for the Options. Then select Cheat Menu and press ✕, ✕, Ⓐ, Ⓐ, Ⓨ.

ARCADIA PLAINS
At the US Map, press Start for the Options. Then select Cheat Menu and press Ⓑ, ✕, ✕, ✕, Ⓐ.

ARIZONA TERRITORY
At the US Map, press Start for the Options. Then select Cheat Menu and press Ⓑ, ✕, ✕, Ⓐ, ✕.

CAROLINAS
At the US Map, press Start for the Options. Then select Cheat Menu and press Ⓑ, ✕, Ⓨ, ✕, Ⓐ.

CENTRAL CASCADES
At the US Map, press Start for the Options. Then select Cheat Menu and press Ⓑ, ✕, ✕, ✕, Ⓨ.

CENTRAL HEARTLAND
At the US Map, press Start for the Options. Then select Cheat Menu and press Ⓑ, ✕, ✕, Ⓑ, Ⓨ.

CUMBERLANDS
At the US Map, press Start for the Options. Then select Cheat Menu and press Ⓑ, ✕, Ⓨ, ✕, Ⓨ.

DAKOTAS
At the US Map, press Start for the Options. Then select Cheat Menu and press Ⓑ, ✕, ✕, Ⓑ, ✕.

EASTERN SHENANDOAH
At the US Map, press Start for the Options. Then select Cheat Menu and press **B, X, Y, Y, B**.

FLORIDA
At the US Map, press Start for the Options. Then select Cheat Menu and press **B, X, Y, X, B**.

GREAT BASIN
At the US Map, press Start for the Options. Then select Cheat Menu and press **B, X, X, Y, A**.

GREAT LAKES
At the US Map, press Start for the Options. Then select Cheat Menu and press **B, X, X, B, A**.

GREAT PLAINS
At the US Map, press Start for the Options. Then select Cheat Menu and press **B, X, X, B, B**.

MISSISSIPPI DELTA
At the US Map, press Start for the Options. Then select Cheat Menu and press **B, X, Y, X, X**.

NEW MEXICO
At the US Map, press Start for the Options. Then select Cheat Menu and press **B, X, X, Y, B**.

NEW YORK
At the US Map, press Start for the Options. Then select Cheat Menu and press **B, X, Y, Y, Y**.

NORTHERN CALIFORNIA
At the US Map, press Start for the Options. Then select Cheat Menu and press **B, X, X, Y, X**.

NORTHERN CASCADES
At the US Map, press Start for the Options. Then select Cheat Menu and press **B, X, X, X, B**.

NORTHERN NEW ENGLAND
At the US Map, press Start for the Options. Then select Cheat Menu and press **B, X, Y, Y, A**.

NORTHERN TEXAS
At the US Map, press Start for the Options. Then select Cheat Menu and press **B, X, X, A, A**.

OHIO VALLEY
At the US Map, press Start for the Options. Then select Cheat Menu and press **B, X, Y, Y, X**.

OKLAHOMA GRASSLANDS
At the US Map, press Start for the Options. Then select Cheat Menu and press **B, X, X, A, Y**.

SOUTHEASTERN CASCADES
At the US Map, press Start for the Options. Then select Cheat Menu and press **B, X, X, X, X**.

SOUTHERN CALIFORNIA
At the US Map, press Start for the Options. Then select Cheat Menu and press **B, X, X, Y, Y**.

SOUTHERN TEXAS
At the US Map, press Start for the Options. Then select Cheat Menu and press **B, X, X, A, B**.

SID MEIER'S PIRATES!

FOOD NEVER DWINDLES
Name your character Sweet Tooth.

INVINCIBLE SHIP
Name your character Bloody Bones Baz.

JEFF BRIGGS AS ABBOTT
Name your character Firaxis.

SNAPPY DRESSER
Name your character Bonus Frag.

BEST SHIP AND FULL CREW
Name your character D.Gackey

YOUR FLEET IS TWICE AS FAST
Name your character Sprinkler.

HIGHEST MORALE
Name your character B. Caudizzle.

DUELING INVINCIBILITY
Name your character Dragon Ma.

SID MEIER AS MYSTERIOUS STRANGER
Name your character Max Remington.

THE SIMS 2

During gameplay, press Left Trigger, Right Trigger, Up on D-pad, Ⓐ, Black. Now you can enter the following cheats:

ALL LOCATIONS
Press Ⓑ, White, Left, Ⓑ, Up, Ⓑ.

ALL CLOTHES
Press Ⓧ, Black, Down, Right, Ⓧ.

ALL OBJECTS
Press White, Ⓑ, Down, Left, Up.

ALL RECIPES
Press Black, Ⓧ, Up, Down, Right, Ⓐ.

MAX ALL MOTIVES
Press Up, Ⓑ, Up, Right, White.

§10,000
Press Right Trigger, Left Trigger, Black, Right, Left.

CHANGES SIM'S SKILL
Press Ⓨ, Ⓑ, Ⓧ, Black, D-pad Left.

JUMP AHEAD SIX HOURS
Press Ⓑ, Ⓧ, Left Trigger, Up, Down.

REMOVE MESSAGES
Press Right, Up, Right, Down, Right, Up, Down, Right.

STAR WARS: BATTLEFRONT II

INFINITE AMMO
Pause the game and press Up, Down, Left, Down, Down, Left, Down, Down, Left, Down, Down, Down, Left, Right.

INVINCIBILITY
Pause the game and press Up, Up, Up, Left, Down, Down, Down, Left, Up, Up, Up, Left, Right.

NO HUD
Pause the game and press Up, Up, Up, Up, Left, Up, Up, Down, Left, Down, Up, Up, Left, Right. Re-enter the code to enable HUD again.

ALTERNATE SOLDIERS
Pause the game and press Down, Down, Down, Up, Up, Left, Down, Down, Down, Down, Left, Up, Up, Up, Left.

ALTERNATE SOUNDS
Pause the game and press Up, Up, Left, Up, Down, Up, Up, Left, Down, Down, Down, Left, Up, Down, Down, Left, Right.

FUNNY MESSAGES WHEN REBELS DEFEATED
Pause the game and press Up, Down, Left, Down, Left, Right.

STAR WARS KNIGHTS OF THE OLD REPUBLIC II: THE SITH LORDS

CHANGE VOICES
Add a controller to the fourth port and press Black or White to raise and lower character voices.

SUPERMAN RETURNS: THE VIDEOGAME

INFINITE STAMINA
Pause the game, select Options and press Up, Up, Down, Down, Left, Right, Left, Right, Ⓨ, Ⓧ.

INFINITE CITY HEALTH
Pause the game, select Options and press Ⓨ, Right, Ⓨ, Right, Up, Left, Right, Ⓨ.

ALL MOVES
Pause the game, select Options and press Left, Ⓨ, Right, Ⓧ, Down, Ⓨ, Up, Down, Ⓧ, Ⓨ, Ⓧ.

ALL COSTUMES, TROPHIES AND THEATER ITEMS
Pause the game, select Options and press Left, Up, Right, Down, Ⓨ, Ⓧ, Ⓨ, Up, Right, Ⓧ.

TAK: THE GREAT JUJU CHALLENGE

BONUS SOUND EFFECTS

In Juju's Potions, select Universal Card and enter the following numbers for Bugs, Crystals and Fruits: 20, 17, 5.

BONUS SOUND EFFECTS 2

In Juju's Potions, select Universal Card and enter the following numbers for Bugs, Crystals and Fruits: 50, 84, 92.

BONUS MUSIC TRACK 1

In Juju's Potions, select Universal Card and enter the following numbers for Bugs, Crystals and Fruits: 67, 8, 20.

BONUS MUSIC TRACK 2

In Juju's Potions, select Universal Card and enter the following numbers for Bugs, Crystals and Fruits: 6, 18, 3.

MAGIC PARTICLES

In Juju's Potions, select Universal Card and enter the following numbers for Bugs, Crystals and Fruits: 24, 40, 11.

MORE MAGIC PARTICLES

In Juju's Potions, select Universal Card and enter the following numbers for Bugs, Crystals and Fruits: 48, 57, 57.

VIEW JUJU CONCEPT ART

In Juju's Potions, select Universal Card and enter the following numbers for Bugs, Crystals and Fruits: Art 33, 22, 28.

VIEW VEHICLE ART

In Juju's Potions, select Universal Card and enter the following numbers for Bugs, Crystals and Fruits: 11, 55, 44.

VIEW WORLD ART

In Juju's Potions, select Universal Card and enter the following numbers for Bugs, Crystals and Fruits: 83, 49, 34.

TEENAGE MUTANT NINJA TURTLES 3: MUTANT NIGHTMARE

INVINCIBILITY

Select Passwords from the Options menu and enter MDLDSSLR.

HEALTH POWER-UPS TURN INTO SUSHI

Select Passwords from the Options menu and enter SLLMRSLD.

NO HEALTH POWER-UPS

Select Passwords from the Options menu and enter DMLDMRLD.

ONE-HIT DEFEATS TURTLE

Select Passwords from the Options menu and enter LDMSLRDD.

MAX OUGI

Select Passwords from the Options menu and enter RRDMLSDL.

UNLIMTED SHURIKEN

Select Passwords from the Options menu and enter LMDRRMSR.

NO SHURIKEN

Select Passwords from the Options menu and enter LLMSRDMS.

DOUBLE ENEMY ATTACK

Select Passwords from the Options menu and enter MSRLSMML.

DOUBLE ENEMY DEFENSE

Select Passwords from the Options menu and enter SLRMLSSM.

THRILLVILLE

$50,000
During a game, press Ⓧ, Ⓑ, Ⓨ, Ⓧ, Ⓑ, Ⓨ, Ⓐ. Repeat this code as much as desired.

ALL PARKS
During a game, press Ⓧ, Ⓑ, Ⓨ, Ⓧ, Ⓑ, Ⓨ, Ⓧ.

ALL RIDES
During a game, press Ⓧ, Ⓑ, Ⓨ, Ⓧ, Ⓑ, Ⓨ, Ⓨ. Some rides still need to be researched.

COMPLETE MISSIONS
During a game, press Ⓧ, Ⓑ, Ⓨ, Ⓧ, Ⓑ, Ⓨ, Ⓑ. Then, at the Missions menu, highlight a mission and press Ⓧ to complete that mission. Some missions have Bronze, Silver, and Gold objectives. For these missions the first press of Ⓧ earns the Bronze, the second earns the Silver, and the third earns the Gold.

TOMB RAIDER: LEGEND

The following codes must be unlocked in the game before using them.

BULLETPROOF
During gameplay, hold Left Trigger and press Ⓐ. Right Trigger, Ⓨ Right Trigger, Ⓧ, Black.

DRAIN ENEMY HEALTH
During gameplay, hold Left Trigger and press Ⓧ, Ⓑ, Ⓐ, Black, Right Trigger, Ⓨ.

INFINITE ASSAULT RIFLE AMMO
During gameplay, hold Black and press Ⓐ, Ⓑ, Ⓐ, Left Trigger, Ⓧ, Ⓨ.

INFINITE GRENADE LAUNCHER AMMO
During gameplay, hold Black and press Left Trigger, Ⓨ, Right Trigger, Ⓑ, Left Trigger, Ⓧ.

INFINITE SHOTGUN AMMO
During gameplay, hold Black and press Right Trigger, Ⓑ, Ⓧ, Left Trigger, Ⓧ, Ⓐ.

INFINITE SMG AMMO
During gameplay, hold Black and press Ⓑ, Ⓨ, Left Trigger, Right Trigger, Ⓐ, Ⓑ.

EXCALIBUR
During gameplay, hold Black and press Ⓨ, Ⓐ, Ⓑ, Right Trigger, Ⓨ, Left Trigger.

SOUL REAVER
During gameplay, hold Black and press Ⓐ, Right Trigger, Ⓑ, Right Trigger, Left Trigger, Ⓧ.

NO TEXTURE MODE
During gameplay, hold Left Trigger and press Black, Ⓐ, Ⓑ, Ⓐ, Ⓨ, Right Trigger.

TIGER WOODS PGA TOUR 07

NIKE ITEMS
Select the Password option and enter JUSTDOIT.

TIM BURTON'S THE NIGHTMARE BEFORE CHRISTMAS: OOGIE'S REVENGE

PUMPKIN KING AND SANTA JACK COSTUMES
During gameplay, press Down, Up, Right, Left, Left Thumbstick, Right Thumbstick.

TONY HAWK'S PROJECT 8

SPONSOR ITEMS
As you progress through Career mode and move up the rankings, you gain sponsors and each comes with its own Create-a-skater item.

RANK REQUIRED	CAS ITEM UNLOCKED
Rank 040	Adio Kenny V2 Shoes
Rank 050	Quiksilver_Hoody_3
Rank 060	Birdhouse Tony Hawk Deck
Rank 080	Vans No Skool Gothic Shoes
Rank 100	Volcom Scallero Jacket
Rank 110	eS Square One Shoes
Rank 120	Almost Watch What You Say Deck
Rank 140	DVS Adage Shoe
Rank 150	Element Illuminate Deck
Rank 160	Etnies Sheckler White Lavender Shoes
Complete Skateshop Goal	Stereo Soundwave Deck

SKATERS
All of the skaters, except for Tony Hawk, must be unlocked by completing challenges in the Career Mode. They are useable in Free Skate and 2 Player modes.

SKATER	HOW THEY ARE UNLOCKED
Tony Hawk	Always Unlocked
Lyn-z Adams Hawkins	Complete Pro Challenge
Bob Burquist	Complete Pro Challenge
Dustin Dollin	Complete Pro Challenge
Nyjah Huston	Complete Pro Challenge
Bam Margera	Complete Pro Challenge
Rodney Mullen	Complete Pro Challenge
Paul Rodriguez	Complete Pro Challenge
Ryan Sheckler	Complete Pro Challenge
Daewon Song	Complete Pro Challenge
Mike Vallely	Complete Pro Challenge
Stevie Williams	Complete Pro Challenge
Travis Barker	Complete Pro Challenge
Kevin Staab	Complete Pro Challenge
Zombie	Complete Pro Challenge
Christaian Hosoi	Animal Chin Challenge
Jason Lee	Complete Final Tony Hawk Goal
Photographer	Unlock Shops
Security Guard	Unlock School
Bum	Unlock Car Factory
Beaver Mascot	Unlock High School
Real Estate Agent	Unlock Downtown
Filmer	Unlock High School
Skate Jam Kid	Rank #4
Dad	Rank #1
Colonel	All Gaps
Nerd	Complete School Spirit Goal

CHEAT CODES

Select Cheat Codes from the Options and enter the following codes. In game you can access some codes from the Options menu.

CHEAT CODE	RESULTS
plus44	Unlocks Travis Barker
hohohosoi	Unlocks Christian Hosoi
notmono	Unlocks Jason Lee
mixitup	Unlocks Kevin Staab
strangefellows	Unlocks Dad & Skater Jam Kid
themedia	Unlocks Photog Girl & Filmer
militarymen	Unlocks Colonel & Security Guard
jammypack	Unlocks Always Special
balancegalore	Unlocks Perfect Rail
frontandback	Unlocks Perect Manual
shellshock	Unlocks Unlimited Focus
shescaresme	Unlocks Big Realtor
birdhouse	Unlocks Inkblot deck
allthebest	Full Stats
needaride	All Decks unlocked and free, except for inkblot deck and gamestop deck
yougotitall	All specials unlocked and in player's special list and set as owned in skate shop
enterandwin	Unlocks Bum
wearelosers	Unlocks Nerd
manineedadate	Unlocks Mascot
suckstobedead	Unlocks Zombie
sellsellsell	Unlocks Skinny real estate agent
newshound	Unlocks Anchor man
badverybad	Unlocks Twin

ULTIMATE SPIDER-MAN

ALL CHARACTERS
Pause the game and select Controller Setup from the Options screen. Press Right, Down, Right, Down, Left, Up, Left, Right.

ALL COVERS
Pause the game and select Controller Setup from the Options screen. Press Left, Left, Right, Left, Up, Left, Left, Down.

ALL CONCEPT ART
Pause the game and select Controller Setup from the Options screen. Press Down, Down, Down, Up, Down, Up, Left, Left.

ALL LANDMARKS
Pause the game and select Controller Setup from the Options screen. Press Up, Right, Down, Left, Down, Up, Right, Left.

WORLD RACING 2

The following codes are case sensitive. You can enter them as many times as you want while creating a profile.

100 SPEEDBUCKS
Create a new profile with the name EC.

1,000 SPEEDBUCKS
Create a new profile with the name Visa.

10,000 SPEEDBUCKS
Create a new profile with the name MASTERCARD.

100,000 SPEEDBUCKS
Create a new profile with the name AmEx.

X-MEN: THE OFFICIAL GAME

DANGER ROOM ICEMAN
At the Cerebro Files menu, press Right, Right, Left, Left, Down, Up, Down, Up, Start.

DANGER ROOM NIGHTCRAWLER
At the Cerebro Files menu, press Up, Up, Down, Down, Left, Right, Left, Right, Start.

DANGER ROOM WOLVERINE
At the Cerebro Files menu, press Down, Down, Up, Up, Right, Left, Right, Left, Start.

YU-GI-OH! THE DAWN OF DESTINY

COSMO QUEEN CARD IN DECK
Enter your name as KONAMI.

TRI-HORN DRAGON CARD IN DECK
Enter your name as HEARTOFCARDS.

ZERA THE MANT CARD IN DECK
Enter your name as XBOX.

XBOX 360™

EVERYONE

CARS

FROGGER

LEGO STAR WARS II: THE ORIGINAL TRILOGY

CARS

MAJOR LEAGUE BASEBALL 2K7

NASCAR 08

NBA 2K7

NBA 2K8

NBA LIVE 07

NBA STREET HOMECOURT

NCAA FOOTBALL 07

NEED FOR SPEED CARBON

NHL 08

RATATOUILLE

ROCKSTAR GAMES PRESENTS TABLE TENNIS

SUPER PUZZLE FIGHTER II TURBO HD REMIX

TIGER WOODS PGA TOUR 07

TIGER WOODS PGA TOUR 08

VIRTUA TENNIS 3

VIVA PINATA

EVERYONE 10+

CRASH OF THE TITANS

NEED FOR SPEED CARBON

SHREK THE THIRD

SPIDER-MAN: FRIEND OR FOE

SUPER CONTRA

SURF'S UP

THRILLVILLE: OFF THE RAILS

TMNT

TEEN

AMPED 3

BATTLESTATIONS: MIDWAY

BLAZING ANGELS: SQUADRONS OF WWII

BLAZING ANGELS 2: SECRET MISSIONS OF WWII

CASTLEVANIA: SYMPHONY OF THE NIGHT

ERAGON

FATAL FURY SPECIAL

FIGHT NIGHT ROUND 3

FLATOUT: ULTIMATE CARNAGE

FULL AUTO

GUITAR HERO II

GUITAR HERO III: LEGENDS OF ROCK

JUICED 2: HOT IMPORT NIGHTS

LOST PLANET: EXTREME CONDITION

MARVEL ULTIMATE ALLIANCE

MONSTER MADNESS: BATTLE FOR SUBURBIA

PETER JACKSON'S KING KONG: THE OFFICIAL GAME OF THE MOVIE

SKATE

STUNTMAN IGNITION

SUPERMAN RETURNS: THE VIDEOGAME

TOMB RAIDER: LEGEND

TOM CLANCY'S GHOST RECON ADVANCED WARFIGHTER

TONY HAWK'S PROJECT 8

TRANSFORMERS: THE GAME

XBOX® 360

Table of Contents

AMPED 3

ALL SLEDS

Select Cheat Codes from the Options screen and press Right Trigger, ⊗, Left Trigger, Down, Right, Left Bumper, Left Trigger, Right Trigger, ⓨ, ⊗.

ALL GEAR

Select Cheat Codes from the Options and press ⓨ, Down, Up, Left, Right, Left Bumper, Right, Right Trigger, Right Trigger, Right Bumper.

ALL TRICKS

Select Cheat Codes from the Options screen and press Left Bumper, Right Trigger, ⓨ, Up, Down, ⊗, Left Trigger, Left, Right Bumper, Right Trigger.

ALL LEVELS

Select Cheat Codes from the Options screen and press ⊗, ⓨ, Up, Left, Left Bumper, Left Bumper, Right Trigger, ⊗, ⓨ, Left Trigger.

ALL CONFIGS

Select Cheat Codes from the Options screen and press Down, ⊗, Right, Left Bumper, Right, Right Bumper, ⊗, Right Trigger, Left Trigger, ⓨ.

SUPER SPINS

Select Cheat Codes from the Options screen and press ⊗(x4), ⓨ(x3), ⊗.

AWESOME METER ALWAYS FULL

Select Cheat Codes from the Options screen and press Up, Right Trigger, ⊗, ⓨ Left Bumper, ⊗, Down, Left Bumper, Right Trigger, Right Bumper.

ALL AWESOMENESS

Select Cheat Codes from the Options screen and press Right Bumper, Right Bumper, Down, Left, Up, Right Trigger, ⊗, Right Bumper, ⊗, ⊗.

ALL BUILD LICENSES

Select Cheat Codes from the Options screen and press Left, Right Trigger, Left Bumper, Right Trigger, ⊗, ⊗, ⓨ, Down, Up, ⊗.

ALL BUILD OBJECTS

Select Cheat Codes from the Options screen and press Left Trigger, Right Trigger, Up, Up, Right Bumper, Left, Right, ⊗, ⓨ, Left Bumper.

ALL CHALLENGES

Select Cheat Codes from the Options screen and press Right, Left Bumper, Left Trigger, ⊗, Left, Right Bumper, Right Trigger, ⓨ, Left Trigger, ⊗.

LOUD SPEAKERS

Select Cheat Codes from the Options screen and press ⓨ. Right Trigger, Right Trigger, Left Bumper, Down, Down, Left, Left, Right, Left Bumper.

LOW GRAVITY BOARDERS

Select Cheat Codes from the Options screen and press Right Trigger, Down, Down, Up, ⓧ, Left Bumper, ⓨ, Right Trigger, ⓨ, Down.

NO AI

Select Cheat Codes from the Options screen and press ⓧ, ⓧ, Left Bumper, Down, Right, Right, Up, ⓨ, ⓨ, Left Trigger.

ALL MUSIC

Select Cheat Codes from the Options screen and press Up, Left, Right Trigger, Right Bumper, Right Trigger, Up, Down, Left, ⓨ, Left Trigger.

BATTLESTATIONS: MIDWAY

ALL CAMPAIGN AND CHALLENGE MISSIONS

At the mission select, hold Right Bumper + Left Bumper + Right Trigger + Left Trigger and press ⓧ.

BLAZING ANGELS: SQUADRONS OF WWII

ALL MISSIONS, MEDALS, & PLANES

At the Main menu hold Left Trigger + Right Trigger and press ⓧ, Left Bumper, Right Bumper, ⓨ, ⓨ Right Bumper, Left Bumper, ⓧ.

GOD MODE

Pause the game, hold Left Trigger and press ⓧ, ⓨ, ⓨ, ⓧ Release Left Trigger, hold Right Trigger and press ⓨ, ⓧ, ⓧ, ⓨ. Re-enter the code to disable it.

INCREASED DAMAGE

Pause the game, hold Left Trigger and press Left Bumper, Left Bumper, Right Bumper. Release Left Trigger, hold Right Trigger and press Right Bumper, Right Bumper, Left Bumper. Re-enter the code to disable it.

BLAZING ANGELS 2: SECRET MISSIONS OF WWII

Achievements are disabled when using these codes.

ALL MISSIONS AND PLANES UNLOCKED
At the Main menu, hold Left Trigger + Right Trigger, and press ❌, Left Bumper, Right Bumper, 🅨, 🅨, Right Bumper, Left Bumper, ❌.

GOD MODE
Pause the game, hold Left Trigger, and press ❌, 🅨, 🅨, ❌. Release Left Trigger, hold Right Trigger and press 🅨, ❌, ❌, 🅨. Re-enter the code to disable it.

INCREASED DAMAGE WITH ALL WEAPONS
Pause the game, hold Left Trigger, and press Left Bumper, Left Bumper, Right Bumper. Release Left Trigger, hold Right Trigger, and press Right Bumper, Right Bumper, Left Bumper. Re-enter the code to disable it.

CARS

UNLOCK EVERYTHING
Select Cheat Codes from the Options and enter IF900HP.

ALL CHARACTERS
Select Cheat Codes from the Options and enter YAYCARS.

ALL CHARACTER SKINS
Select Cheat Codes from the Options and enter R4MONE.

ALL MINI-GAMES AND COURSES
Select Cheat Codes from the Options and enter MATTL66.

FAST START
Select Cheat Codes from the Options and enter IMSPEED.

INFINITE BOOST
Select Cheat Codes from the Options and enter VROOOOM.

ART
Select Cheat Codes from the Options and enter CONC3PT.

VIDEOS
Select Cheat Codes from the Options and enter WATCHIT.

CASTLEVANIA: SYMPHONY OF THE NIGHT

Before using the following codes, complete the game with 170%.

PLAY AS RICHTER BELMONT
Enter RICHTER as your name.

ALUCARD WITH AXELORD ARMOR
Enter AXEARMOR as your name.

ALUCARD WITH 99 LUCK AND OTHER STATS ARE LOW
Enter X-X!V"Q as your name.

CRASH OF THE TITANS

BIG HEAD CRASH
Pause the game, hold the Right Trigger, and press ❌, ❌, 🅨, 🅐.

SHADOW CRASH
Pause the game, hold the Right Trigger, and press 🅨, ❌, 🅨, 🅐.

ERAGON

UNLIMITED FURY MODE
Pause the game, hold Left Bumper + Left Trigger + Right Bumper + Right Trigger and press ✗, ✗, Ⓑ, Ⓑ.

FATAL FURY SPECIAL

CHEAT MENU
During a game, hold Start and push Ⓐ + ✗ + Ⓨ.

FIGHT NIGHT ROUND 3

ALL VENUES
Create a champ with a first name of NEWVIEW.

FLATOUT: ULTIMATE CARNAGE

MOB CAR IN SINGLE EVENTS
Select Enter Code from Extras and enter BIGTRUCK.

PIMPSTER IN SINGLE EVENTS
Select Enter Code from Extras and enter RUTTO.

ROCKET IN SINGLE EVENTS
Select Enter Code from Extras and enter KALJAKOPPA.

FROGGER

BIG FROGGER

At the one/two player screen, press Up, Up, Down, Down, Left, Right, Left, Right, **B**, **A**.

FULL AUTO

ALL TRACKS, VEHICLES, & WEAPONS

Create a new profile with the name magicman.

GUITAR HERO II

ALL SONGS

At the Main menu, press Blue, Yellow, Orange, Red, Yellow, Orange, Blue, Yellow, Blue, Yellow, Blue, Yellow, Blue, Yellow, Blue, Yellow.

HYPER SPEED

At the Main menu, press Blue, Orange, Yellow, Orange, Blue, Orange, Yellow, Yellow.

PERFORMANCE MODE

At the Main menu, press Blue, Blue, Yellow, Blue, Blue, Orange, Blue, Blue.

AIR GUITAR

At the Main menu, press Yellow, Blue, Yellow, Orange, Yellow, Blue.

EYEBALL HEAD CROWD

At the Main menu, press Yellow, Orange, Blue, Blue, Blue, Orange, Yellow.

MONKEY HEAD CROWD

At the Main menu, press Orange, Yellow, Blue, Blue, Yellow, Orange, Blue, Blue.

FLAME HEAD

At the Main menu, press Orange, Yellow, Yellow, Orange, Yellow, Yellow, Orange, Yellow, Yellow, Blue, Yellow, Yellow, Blue, Yellow, Yellow.

GUITAR HERO III: LEGENDS OF ROCK

To enter the following cheats, strum the guitar with the given buttons held. For example, if it says Yellow + Orange, hold Yellow and Orange as you strum. Air Guitar, Precision Mode and Performance Mode can be toggled on and off from the Cheats menu. You can also change between five different levels of Hyperspeed at this menu.

ALL SONGS

Select Cheats from the Options. Choose Enter Cheat and enter Yellow + Orange, Red + Blue, Red + Orange, Green + Blue, Red + Yellow, Yellow + Orange, Red + Yellow, Red + Blue, Green + Yellow, Green + Yellow, Yellow + Blue, Yellow + Blue, Yellow + Orange, Yellow + Orange, Yellow + Blue, Yellow, Red, Red + Yellow, Red, Yellow, Orange.

AIR GUITAR

Select Cheats from the Options. Choose Enter Cheat and enter Blue + Yellow, Green + Yellow, Green + Yellow, Red + Blue, Red + Blue, Red + Yellow, Red + Yellow, Blue + Yellow, Green + Yellow, Green + Yellow, Red + Blue, Red + Blue, Red + Yellow, Red + Yellow, Green + Yellow, Green + Yellow, Red + Yellow, Red + Yellow.

PRECISION MODE

Select Cheats from the Options. Choose Enter Cheat and enter Green + Red, Green + Red, Green + Red, Red + Yellow, Red + Yellow, Red + Blue, Red + Blue, Yellow + Blue, Yellow + Orange, Yellow + Orange, Green + Red, Green + Red, Green + Red, Red + Yellow, Red + Yellow, Red + Blue, Red + Blue, Yellow + Blue, Yellow + Orange, Yellow + Orange.

HYPERSPEED

Select Cheats from the Options. Choose Enter Cheat and enter Orange, Blue, Orange, Yellow, Orange, Blue, Orange, Yellow.

PERFORMANCE MODE

Select Cheats from the Options. Choose Enter Cheat and enter Red + Yellow, Red + Blue, Red + Orange, Red + Blue, Red + Yellow, Green + Blue, Red + Yellow, Red + Blue.

JUICED 2: HOT IMPORT NIGHTS

FRITO-LAY INFINITY G35 CAR

Select Cheats and Codes from the DNA Lab menu and enter MNCH.

HIDDEN CHALLENGE AND A BMW Z4

Select Cheats and Codes from the DNA Lab menu and enter GVDL. Defeat the challenge to earn the BMW Z4.

LEGO STAR WARS II: THE ORIGINAL TRILOGY

BEACH TROOPER

At Mos Eisley Canteena, select Enter Code and enter UCK868. You still need to select Characters and purchase this character for 20,000 studs.

BEN KENOBI (GHOST)

At Mos Eisley Canteena, select Enter Code and enter BEN917. You still need to select Characters and purchase this character for 1,100,000 studs.

BESPIN GUARD

At Mos Eisley Canteena, select Enter Code and enter VHY832. You still need to select Characters and purchase this character for 15,000 studs.

BIB FORTUNA

At Mos Eisley Canteena, select Enter Code and enter WTY721. You still need to select Characters and purchase this character for 16,000 studs.

BOBA FETT

At Mos Eisley Canteena, select Enter Code and enter HLP221. You still need to select Characters and purchase this character for 175,000 studs.

DEATH STAR TROOPER

At Mos Eisley Canteena, select Enter Code and enter BNC332. You still need to select Characters and purchase this character for 19,000 studs.

EWOK

At Mos Eisley Canteena, select Enter Code and enter TTT289. You still need to select Characters and purchase this character for 34,000 studs.

GAMORREAN GUARD

At Mos Eisley Canteena, select Enter Code and enter YZF999. You still need to select Characters and purchase this character for 40,000 studs.

GONK DROID

At Mos Eisley Canteena, select Enter Code and enter NFX582. You still need to select Characters and purchase this character for 1,550 studs.

GRAND MOFF TARKIN

At Mos Eisley Canteena, select Enter Code and enter SMG219. You still need to select Characters and purchase this character for 38,000 studs.

GREEDO

At Mos Eisley Canteena, select Enter Code and enter NAH118. You still need to select Characters and purchase this character for 60,000 studs.

HAN SOLO (HOOD)

At Mos Eisley Canteena, select Enter Code and enter YWM840. You still need to select Characters and purchase this character for 20,000 studs.

IG-88

At Mos Eisley Canteena, select Enter Code and enter NXL973. You still need to select Characters and purchase this character for 30,000 studs.

IMPERIAL GUARD

At Mos Eisley Canteena, select Enter Code and enter MMM111. You still need to select Characters and purchase this character for 45,000 studs.

IMPERIAL OFFICER

At Mos Eisley Canteena, select Enter Code and enter BBV889. You still need to select Characters and purchase this character for 28,000 studs.

IMPERIAL SHUTTLE PILOT

At Mos Eisley Canteena, select Enter Code and enter VAP664. You still need to select Characters and purchase this character for 29,000 studs.

IMPERIAL SPY

At Mos Eisley Canteena, select Enter Code and enter CVT125. You still need to select Characters and purchase this character for 13,500 studs.

JAWA

At Mos Eisley Canteena, select Enter Code and enter JAW499. You still need to select Characters and purchase this character for 24,000 studs.

LOBOT

At Mos Eisley Canteena, select Enter Code and enter UUB319. You still need to select Characters and purchase this character for 11,000 studs.

PALACE GUARD

At Mos Eisley Canteena, select Enter Code and enter SGE549. You still need to select Characters and purchase this character for 14,000 studs.

REBEL PILOT

At Mos Eisley Canteena, select Enter Code and enter CYG336. You still need to select Characters and purchase this character for 15,000 studs.

REBEL TROOPER (HOTH)

At Mos Eisley Canteena, select Enter Code and enter EKU849. You still need to select Characters and purchase this character for 16,000 studs.

SANDTROOPER

At Mos Eisley Canteena, select Enter Code and enter YDV451. You still need to select Characters and purchase this character for 14,000 studs.

SKIFF GUARD

At Mos Eisley Canteena, select Enter Code and enter GBU888. You still need to select Characters and purchase this character for 12,000 studs.

SNOWTROOPER

At Mos Eisley Canteena, select Enter Code and enter NYU989. You still need to select Characters and purchase this character for 16,000 studs.

STROMTROOPER

At Mos Eisley Canteena, select Enter Code and enter PTR345. You still need to select Characters and purchase this character for 10,000 studs.

THE EMPEROR

At Mos Eisley Canteena, select Enter Code and enter HHY382. You still need to select Characters and purchase this character for 275,000 studs.

TIE FIGHTER

At Mos Eisley Canteena, select Enter Code and enter HDY739. You still need to select Characters and purchase this character for 60,000 studs.

TIE FIGHTER PILOT

At Mos Eisley Canteena, select Enter Code and enter NNZ316. You still need to select Characters and purchase this character for 21,000 studs.

TIE INTERCEPTOR

At Mos Eisley Canteena, select Enter Code and enter QYA828. You still need to select Characters and purchase this character for 40,000 studs.

TUSKEN RAIDER

At Mos Eisley Canteena, select Enter Code and enter PEJ821. You still need to select Characters and purchase this character for 23,000 studs.

UGNAUGHT

At Mos Eisley Canteena, select Enter Code and enter UGN694. You still need to select Characters and purchase this character for 36,000 studs.

LOST PLANET: EXTREME CONDITION

The following codes are for Single Player Mode on Easy Difficulty only.

500 THERMAL ENERGY

Pause the game and press Up, Up, Down, Down, Left, Right, Left, Right, ❌, ❤, Right Bumper + Left Bumper.

INFINITE AMMUNITION

Pause the game and press Right Trigger, Right Bumper, ❤, ❌, Right, Down, Left, Left Bumper, Left Trigger, Right Trigger, Right Bumper, ❤, ❌, Right, Down, Left, Left Bumper, Left Trigger, Right Trigger, Left Trigger, Left Bumper, Right Bumper, ❤, Left, Down, ❌, Right Bumper + Left Bumper.

INFINITE HEALTH

Pause the game and press Down (x3), Up, ❤,Up, ❤, Up, ❤, Up(x3), Down, ❌, Down, ❌, Down, ❌, Left, ❤, Right, ❌, –Left, ❤, Right, ❌, Right Bumper + Left Bumper.

CHANGE CAMERA ANGLE IN CUT SCENES

During a cut scene, press ❷, ❹, ❌, ❤, ❷, ❹, ❌, ❤, ❷, ❹, ❌, ❤.

MAJOR LEAGUE BASEBALL 2K6

UNLOCK EVERYTHING
Select Enter Cheat Code from the My 2K6 menu and enter Derek Jeter.

TOPPS 2K STARS
Select Enter Cheat Code from the My 2K6 menu and enter Dream Team.

SUPER WALL CLIMB
Select Enter Cheat Code from the My 2K6 menu and enter Last Chance. Enable the cheats by selecting My Cheats or selecting Cheat Codes from the in-game Options screen.

SUPER PITCHES
Select Enter Cheat Code from the My 2K6 menu and enter Unhittable. Enable the cheats by selecting My Cheats or selecting Cheat Codes from the in-game Options screen.

ROCKET ARMS
Select Enter Cheat Code from the My 2K6 menu and enter Gotcha. Enable the cheats by selecting My Cheats or selecting Cheat Codes from the in-game Options screen.

BOUNCY BALL
Select Enter Cheat Code from the My 2K6 menu and enter Crazy Hops. Enable the cheats by selecting My Cheats or selecting Cheat Codes from the in-game Options.

MAJOR LEAGUE BASEBALL 2K7

MICKEY MANTLE ON THE FREE AGENTS LIST
Select Enter Cheat Code from the My 2K7 menu and enter themick.

ALL CHEATS
Select Enter Cheat Code from the My 2K7 menu and enter Black Sox.

ALL EXTRAS
Select Enter Cheat Code from the My 2K7 menu and enter Game On.

UNLOCK EVERYTHING

Select Enter Cheat Code from the My 2K7 menu and enter Derek Jeter. This does not unlock the Topps cheats.

MIGHTY MICK CHEAT

Select Enter Cheat Code from the My 2K7 menu and enter mightymick.

TRIPLE CROWN CHEAT

Select Enter Cheat Code from the My 2K7 menu and enter triplecrown.

PINCH HIT MICK CHEAT

Select Enter Cheat Code from the My 2K7 menu and enter phmantle.

BIG BLAST CHEAT

Select Enter Cheat Code from the My 2K7 menu Rand enter m4murder.

MARVEL ULTIMATE ALLIANCE

UNLOCK ALL SKINS

At the Team menu, press Up, Down, Left, Right, Left, Right, Start.

UNLOCKS ALL HERO POWERS

At the Team menu, press Left, Right, Up, Down, Up, Down, Start.

ALL HEROES TO LEVEL 99

At the Team menu, press Up, Left, Up, Left, Down, Right, Down, Right, Start.

UNLOCK ALL HEROES

At the Team menu, press Up, Up, Down, Down, Left, Left, Left, Start.

UNLOCK DAREDEVIL

At the Team menu, press Left, Left, Right, Right, Up, Down, Up, Down, Start.

UNLOCK SILVER SURFER

At the Team menu, press Down, Left, Left, Up, Right, Up, Down, Left, Start.

GOD MODE

During gameplay, press Up, Down, Up, Down, Up, Left, Down, Right, Start.

TOUCH OF DEATH

During gameplay, press Left, Right, Down, Down, Right, Left, Start.

SUPER SPEED

During gameplay, press Up, Left, Up, Right, Down, Right, Start.

FILL MOMENTUM

During gameplay, press Left, Right, Right, Left, Up, Down, Down, Up, Start.

UNLOCK ALL COMICS

At the Review menu, press Left, Right, Right, Left, Up, Up, Right, Start.

UNLOCK ALL CONCEPT ART

At the Review menu, press Down, Down, Down, Right, Right, Left, Down, Start.

UNLOCK ALL CINEMATICS

At the Review menu, press Up, Left, Left, Up, Right, Right, Up, Start.

UNLOCK ALL LOAD SCREENS

At the Review menu, press Up, Down, Right, Left, Up, Up Down, Start.

UNLOCK ALL COURSES

At the Comic Missions menu, press Up, Right, Left, Down, Up, Right, Left, Down, Start.

MONSTER MADNESS: BATTLE FOR SUBURBIA

Pause the game and press Up, Up, Down, Down, Left, Right, Left, Right, **B**, **A**. This brings up a screen where you can enter the following cheats. With the use of some cheats profile saving, level progression, and Xbox Live Achievements are disabled until you return to the Main menu.

EFFECT	CHEAT
Animal Sounds	patrickdugan
Disable Tracking Cameras	ihatefunkycameras
Faster Music	upthejoltcola
First Person	morgythemole

EFFECT	CHEAT
Infinite Secondary Items	stevebrooks
Objects Move Away from Player	southpeak
Remove Film Grain	reverb

NASCAR 08

ALL CHASE MODE CARS
Select Cheat Codes from the Options menu and enter checkered flag.

EA SPORTS CAR
Select Cheat Codes from the Options menu and enter ea sports car.

FANTASY DRIVERS
Select Cheat Codes from the Options menu and enter race the pack.

WALMART CAR AND TRACK
Select Cheat Codes from the Options menu and enter walmart everyday.

NBA 2K7

MAX DURABILITY
Select Codes from the Features menu and enter ironman.

UNLIMITED STAMINA
Select Codes from the Features menu and enter norest.

+10 DEFFENSIVE AWARENESS
Select Codes from the Features menu and enter getstops.

+10 OFFENSIVE AWARENESS
Select Codes from the Features menu and enter inthezone.

TOPPS 2K SPORTS ALL-STARS
Select Codes from the Features menu and enter topps2ksports.

ABA BALL
Select Codes from the Features menu and enter payrespect.

NBA 2K8

2KSPORTS TEAM
Select Codes from the Features menu and enter 2ksports.

VISUAL CONCEPTS TEAM
Select Codes from the Features menu and enter Vcteam.

ABA BALL
Select Codes from the Features menu and enter Payrespect.

NBA LIVE 07

ADIDAS ARTILLERY II BLACK AND THE RBK ANSWER 9 VIDEO
Select NBA Codes from My NBA Live and enter 99B6356HAN.

ADIDAS ARTILLERY II
Select NBA Codes and enter NTGNFUE87H.

ADIDAS BTB LOW AND THE MESSAGE FROM ALLEN IVERSON VIDEO
Select NBA Codes and enter 7FB3KS9JQO.

ADIDAS C-BILLUPS
Select NBA Codes and enter BV6877HB9N.

ADIDAS C-BILLUPS BLACK
Select NBA Codes and enter 85NVLDMWS5.

ADIDAS CAMPUS LT
Select NBA Codes and enter CLT2983NC8.

ADIDAS CRAZY 8
Select NBA Codes and enter CC98KKL814.

ADIDAS EQUIPMENT BBALL
Select NBA Codes and enter 22OIUJKMDR.

ADIDAS GARNETT BOUNCE
Select NBA Codes and enter HYIOUHCAAN.

ADIDAS GARNETT BOUNCE BLACK
Select NBA Codes and enter KDZ2MQL17W.

ADIDAS GIL-ZERO
Select NBA Codes and enter 23DN1PPOG4.

ADIDAS GIL-ZERO BLACK
Select NBA Codes and enter QQQ3JCUYQ7.

ADIDAS GIL-ZERO MID
Select NBA Codes and enter 1GSJC8JWRL.

ADIDAS GIL-ZERO MID BLACK
Select NBA Codes and enter 369V6RVU3G.

ADIDAS STEALTH
Select NBA Codes and enter FE454DFJCC.

ADIDAS T-MAC 6
Select NBA Codes and enter MCJK843NNC.

ADIDAS T-MAC 6 WHITE
Select NBA Codes and enter 84GF7EJG8V.

CHARLOTTE BOBCATS 2006-2007 ALTERNATE JERSEY
Select NBA Codes and enter WEDX671H7S.

UTAH JAZZ 2006-2007 ALTERNATE JERSEY
Select NBA Codes and enter VCBI89FK83.

NEW JERSEY NETS 2006-2007 ALTERNATE JERSEY
Select NBA Codes and enter D4SAA98U5H.

WASHINGTON WIZARDS 2006-2007 ALTERNATE JERSEY
Select NBA Codes and enter QV93NLKXQC.

EASTERN ALL-STARS 2006-2007 AWAY JERSEY
Select NBA Codes and enter WOCNW4KL7L.

EASTERN ALL-STARS 2006-2007 HOME JERSEY
Select NBA Codes and enter 5654ND43N6.

WESTERN ALL-STARS 2006-2007 AWAY JERSEY
Select NBA Codes and enter XX93BVL20U.

WESTERN ALL-STARS 2006-2007 HOME JERSEY
Select NBA Codes and enter 993NSKL199.

NBA STREET HOMECOURT

ALL TEAMS
At the Main menu, hold Right Bumper + Left Bumper
and press Left, Right, Left, Right.

ALL COURTS
At the Main menu, hold Right Bumper + Left Bumper and
press Up, Right, Down, Left.

BLACK/RED BALL
At the Main menu, hold Right Bumper + Left Bumper and press Up, Down, Left, Right.

NCAA FOOTBALL 07

#16 BAYLOR
Select Pennant Collection from My NCAA. Press Select and enter Sic Em.

#16 NIKE SPEED TD
Select Pennant Collection from My NCAA. Press Select and enter Light Speed.

#63 ILLINOIS
Select Pennant Collection from My NCAA. Press Select and enter Oskee Wow.

#160 TEXAS TECH
Select Pennant Collection from My NCAA. Press Select and enter Fight.

#200 FIRST AND FIFTEEN
Select Pennant Collection from My NCAA. Press Select and enter Thanks.

#201 BLINK
Select Pennant Collection from My NCAA. Press Select and enter For.

#202 BOING
Select Pennant Collection from My NCAA. Press Select and enter Registering.

#204 BUTTER FINGERS
Select Pennant Collection from My NCAA. Press Select and enter With EA.

#205 CROSSED THE LINE
Select Pennant Collection from My NCAA. Press Select and enter Tiburon.

#206 CUFFED
Select Pennant Collection from My NCAA. Press Select and enter EA Sports.

#207 EXTRA CREDIT
Select Pennant Collection from My NCAA. Press Select and enter Touchdown.

#208 HELIUM
Select Pennant Collection from My NCAA. Press Select and enter In The Zone.

#209 HURRICANE
Select Pennant Collection from My NCAA. Press Select and enter Turnover.

#210 INSTANT FREPLAY
Select Pennant Collection from My NCAA. Press Select and enter Impact.

#211 JUMBALAYA
Select Pennant Collection from My NCAA. Press Select and enter Heisman.

#212 MOLASSES
Select Pennant Collection from My NCAA. Press Select and enter Game Time.

#213 NIKE FREE
Select Pennant Collection from My NCAA. Press Select and enter Break Free.

#214 NIKE MAGNIGRIP
Select Pennant Collection from My NCAA. Press Select and enter Hand Picked.

#215 NIKE PRO
Select Pennant Collection from My NCAA. Press Select and enter No Sweat.

#219 QB DUD
Select Pennant Collection from My NCAA. Press Select and enter Elite 11.

#221 STEEL TOE
Select Pennant Collection from My NCAA. Press Select and enter Gridiron.

#222 STIFFED
Select Pennant Collection from My NCAA. Press Select and enter NCAA.

#223 SUPER DIVE
Select Pennant Collection from My NCAA. Press Select and enter Upset.

#224 TAKE YOUR TIME
Select Pennant Collection from My NCAA. Press Select and enter Football.

#225 THREAD & NEEDLE
Select Pennant Collection from My NCAA. Press Select and enter 06.

#226 TOUGH AS NAILS
Select Pennant Collection from My NCAA. Press Select and enter Offense.

#227 TRIP
Select Pennant Collection from My NCAA. Press Select and enter Defense.

#228 WHAT A HIT
Select Pennant Collection from My NCAA. Press Select and enter Blitz.

#229 KICKER HEX
Select Pennant Collection from My NCAA. Press Select and enter Sideline.

#273 2004 ALL-AMERICANS
Select Pennant Collection from My NCAA. Press Select and enter Fumble.

#274 ALL-ALABAMA
Select Pennant Collection from My NCAA. Press Select and enter Roll Tide.

#276 ALL-ARKANSAS
Select Pennant Collection from My NCAA. Press Select and enter Woopigsooie.

#277 ALL-AUBURN
Select Pennant Collection from My NCAA. Press Select and enter War Eagle.

#278 ALL-CLEMSON
Select Pennant Collection from My NCAA. Press Select and enter Death Valley.

#279 ALL-COLORADO
Select Pennant Collection from My NCAA. Press Select and enter Glory.

#280 ALL-FLORIDA
Select Pennant Collection from My NCAA. Press Select and enter Great To Be.

#281 ALL-FSU
Select Pennant Collection from My NCAA. Press Select and enter Uprising.

#282 ALL-GEORGIA
Select Pennant Collection from My NCAA. Press Select and enter Hunker Down.

#283 ALL-IOWA
Select Pennant Collection from My NCAA. Press Select and enter On Iowa.

#284 ALL-KANSAS STATE
Select Pennant Collection from My NCAA. Press Select and enter Victory.

#285 ALL-LSU
Select Pennant Collection from My NCAA. Press Select and enter Geaux Tigers.

#286 ALL-MIAMI
Select Pennant Collection from My NCAA. Press Select and enter Raising Cane.

#287 ALL-MICHIGAN
Select Pennant Collection from My NCAA. Press Select and enter Go Blue.

#288 ALL-MISSISSIPPI STATE
Select Pennant Collection from My NCAA. Press Select and enter Hail State.

#289 ALL-NEBRASKA
Select Pennant Collection from My NCAA. Press Select and enter Go Big Red.

#290 ALL-NORTH CAROLINA
Select Pennant Collection from My NCAA. Press Select and enter Rah Rah.

#291 ALL-NOTRE DAME
Select Pennant Collection from My NCAA. Press Select and enter Golden Domer.

#292 ALL-OHIO STATE
Select Pennant Collection from My NCAA. Press Select and enter Killer Nuts.

#293 ALL-OKLAHOMA
Select Pennant Collection from My NCAA. Press Select and enter Boomer.

#294 ALL-OKLAHOMA STATE
Select Pennant Collection from My NCAA. Press Select and enter Go Pokes.

#295 ALL-OREGON
Select Pennant Collection from My NCAA. Press Select and enter Quack Attack.

#296 ALL-PENN STATE
Select Pennant Collection from My NCAA. Press Select and enter We Are.

#297 ALL-PITTSBURGH
Select Pennant Collection from My NCAA. Press Select and enter Lets Go Pitt.

#298 ALL-PURDUE
Select Pennant Collection from My NCAA. Press Select and enter Boiler Up.

#299 ALL-SYRACUSE
Select Pennant Collection from My NCAA. Press Select and enter Orange Crush.

#300 ALL-TENNESSEE
Select Pennant Collection from My NCAA. Press Select and enter Big Orange.

#301 ALL-TEXAS
Select Pennant Collection from My NCAA. Press Select and enter Hook Em.

#302 ALL-TEXAS A&M
Select Pennant Collection from My NCAA. Press Select and enter Gig Em.

#303 ALL-UCLA
Select Pennant Collection from My NCAA. Press Select and enter MIGHTY.

#304 ALL-USC
Select Pennant Collection from My NCAA. Press Select and enter Fight On.

#305 ALL-VIRGINIA
Select Pennant Collection from My NCAA. Press Select and enter Wahoos.

#306 ALL-VIRGINIA TECH
Select Pennant Collection from My NCAA. Press Select and enter Tech Triumph.

#307 ALL-WASHINGTON
Select Pennant Collection from My NCAA. Press Select and enter Bow Down.

#308 ALL-WISCONSIN
Select Pennant Collection from My NCAA. Press Select and enter U Rah Rah.

#311 ARK MASCOT
Select Pennant Collection from My NCAA. Press Select and enter Bear Down.

#329 GT MASCOT
Select Pennant Collection from My NCAA. Press Select and enter RamblinWreck.

#333 ISU MASCOT
Select Pennant Collection from My NCAA. Press Select and enter Red And Gold.

#335 KU MASCOT
Select Pennant Collection from My NCAA. Press Select and enter Rock Chalk.

#341 MINN MASCOT
Select Pennant Collection from My NCAA. Press Select and enter Rah Rah Rah.

#344 MIZZOU MASCOT
Select Pennant Collection from My NCAA. Press Select and enter Mizzou Rah.

#346 MSU MASCOT
Select Pennant Collection from My NCAA. Press Select and enter Go Green.

#349 NCSU MASCOT
Select Pennant Collection from My NCAA. Press Select and enter Go Pack.

#352 NU MASCOT
Select Pennant Collection from My NCAA. Press Select and enter Go Cats.

#360 S CAR MASCOT
Select Pennant Collection from My NCAA. Press Select and enter Go Carolina.

#371 UK MASCOT
Select Pennant Collection from My NCAA. Press Select and enter On On UK.

#382 WAKE FOREST
Select Pennant Collection from My NCAA. Press Select and enter Go Deacs Go.

#385 WSU MASCOT
Select Pennant Collection from My NCAA. Press Select and enter All Hail.

#386 WVU MASCOT
Select Pennant Collection from My NCAA. Press Select and enter Hail WV.

NEED FOR SPEED CARBON

CASTROL CASH
At the Main menu, press Down, Up, Left, Down, Right, Up, ❌, ⓑ. This will give you 10,000 extra cash.

INFINITE CREW CHARGE
At the Main menu, press Down, Up, Up, Right, Left, Left, Right, ❌.

INFINITE NITROUS
At the Main menu, press Left, Up, Left, Down, Left, Down, Right, ❌.

INFINITE SPEEDBREAKER
At the Main menu, press Down, Right, Right, Left, Right, Up, Down, ❌.

NEED FOR SPEED CARBON LOGO VINYLS
At the Main menu, press Right, Up, Down, Up, Down, Left, Right, ❌.

NEED FOR SPEED CARBON SPECIAL LOGO VINYLS
At the Main menu, press Up, Up, Down, Down, Down, Down, Up, ❌.

NHL 08

ALL RBK EDGE JERSEYS
At the RBK Edge Code option, enter h3oyxpwksf8ibcgt.

PETER JACKSON'S KING KONG: THE OFFICIAL GAME OF THE MOVIE

At the Main menu hold Left Bumper + Right Bumper + Left Trigger + Right Trigger and press Down, Up, ⓨ, ❌, Down, Down, ⓨ, ⓨ. Release the buttons to access the Cheat option. The Cheat option will also be available on the pause menu. You cannot record your scores using cheat codes.

GOD MODE
Select Cheat and enter 8wonder.

ALL CHAPTERS
Select Cheat and enter KKst0ry.

AMMO 999
Select Cheat and enter KK 999 mun.

MACHINE GUN
Select Cheat and enter KKcapone.

REVOLVER
Select Cheat and enter KKtigun.

SNIPER RIFLE
Select Cheat and enter KKsn1per.

INFINITE SPEARS
Select Cheat and enter lance 1nf.

ONE-HIT KILLS
Select Cheat and enter GrosBras.

EXTRAS
Select Cheat and enter KKmuseum.

RATATOUILLE

UNLIMITED RUNNING
At the Cheat Code screen, enter SPEEDY.

ALL MULTIPLAYER AND SINGLE PLAYER MINI GAMES
At the Cheat Code screen, enter MATTELME.

ROCKSTAR GAMES PRESENTS TABLE TENNIS

Use of the following codes will disable achievements.

SWEATY CHARACTER VIEWER
After loading the map and before accepting the match, press Right Trigger, Up, Down, Left Trigger, Left, Right, **Y**, **X**, **X**, **Y**.

SMALL CROWD AUDIO
After loading the map and before accepting the match, press Down, Down, Down, Left Bumper, Left Trigger, Left Bumper, Left Trigger.

BIG BALL
After loading the map and before accepting the match, press Left, Right, Left, Right, Up, Up, Up, **X**.

COLORBLIND SPINDICATOR (ONLY IN NEWER PATCH)
After loading the map and before accepting the match, press Up, Down, **X**, **X**, **Y**, **Y**.

SILHOUETTE MODE
After loading the map and before accepting the match, press Up, Down, **Y**, **Y**, Left Bumper, Left Trigger, Right Trigger, Right Bumper.

BIG PADDLES CHEAT (ONLY IN NEWER PATCH)
After loading the map and before accepting the match, press Up, Left, Up, Right, Up, Down, Up, Up, **X**, **X**.

UNLOCK ALL
After loading the map and before accepting the match, press Up, Right, Down, Left, Left Bumper, Right, Up, Left, Down, Right Bumper.

VINTAGE AUDIO
After loading the map and before accepting the match, press Up, Up, Down, Down, Left, Right, Left, Right, Left Bumper, Right Bumper.

BIG CROWD AUDIO
After loading the map and before accepting the match, press Up, Up, Up, Right Bumper, Right Trigger, Right Bumper, Right Trigger.

OFFLINE GAMERTAGS
After loading the map and before accepting the match, press ❌, 🅨, ❌, 🅨, ❌, 🅨, Left Trigger, Right Trigger, Down, Down, Down.

SHREK THE THIRD

10,000 GOLD COINS
At the gift shop, press Up, Up, Down, Up, Right, Left.

SKATE

BEST BUY CLOTHES
At the Main menu, press Up, Down, Left, Right, ❌, Right Bumper, 🅨, Left Bumper.

SPIDER-MAN: FRIEND OR FOE

NEW GREEN GOBLIN AS A SIDEKICK
While standing in the Helicarrier between levels, press Left, Down, Right, Right, Down, Left.

SANDMAN AS A SIDEKICK
While standing in the Helicarrier between levels, press Right, Right, Right, Up, Down, Left.

VENOM AS A SIDEKICK
While standing in the Helicarrier between levels, press Left, Left, Right, Up, Down, Down.

5000 TECH TOKENS
While standing in the Helicarrier between levels, press Up, Up, Down, Down, Left, Right.

STUNTMAN IGNITION

3 PROPS IN STUNT CREATOR MODE
Select Cheats from Extras and enter COOLPROP.

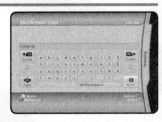

ALL ITEMS UNLOCKED FOR CONSTRUCTION MODE
Select Cheats from Extras and enter NOBLEMAN.

MVX SPARTAN

Select Cheats from Extras and enter fastride.

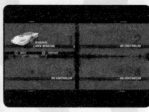

ALL CHEATS

Select Cheats from Extras and enter Wearefrozen.
This unlocks the following cheats: Slo-mo Cool, Thrill
Cam, Vision Switcher, Nitro Addiction, Freaky Fast, and
Ice Wheels.

ALL CHEATS

Select Cheats from Extras and enter Kungfoopete.

ICE WHEELS CHEAT

Select Cheats from Extras and enter IceAge.

NITRO ADDICTION CHEAT

Select Cheats from Extras and enter TheDuke.

VISION SWITCHER CHEAT

Select Cheats from Extras and enter GFXMODES.

SUPER CONTRA

UNLIMITED LIVES AND SUPER MACHINEGUN

At the Main menu, select Arcade Game, and then press Up, Up, Down, Down, Left, Right, Left, Right, **B**, **A**.
Achievements and the Leaderboard are disabled with this code.

SUPERMAN RETURNS: THE VIDEOGAME

GOD MODE

Pause the game, select Options and press Up, Up, Down, Down, Left, Right, Left, Right, **Y**, **X**.

INFINITE CITY HEALTH

Pause the game, select Options and press **Y**, Right, **Y**, Right, Up, Left, Right, **Y**.

ALL POWER-UPS

Pause the game, select Options and press Left, **Y**, Right, **X**, Down, **Y**, Up, Down, **X**, **Y**, **X**.

ALL UNLOCKABLES

Pause the game, select Options and press Left, Up, Right, Down, **Y**, **X**, **Y** Up, Right, **X**.

FREE ROAM AS BIZARRO

Pause the game, select Options and press Up, Right, Down, Right, Up, Left, Down, Right, Up.

SUPER PUZZLE FIGHTER II TURBO HD REMIX

PLAY AS AKUMA
At the Character Select screen, highlight Hsien-Ko and press Down.

PLAY AS DAN
At the Character Select screen, highlight Donovan and press Down.

PLAY AS DEVILOT
At the Character Select screen, highlight Morrigan and press Down.

PLAY AS ANITA
At the Character Select screen, hold Left Bumper + Right Bumper and choose Donovan.

PLAY AS HSIEN-KO'S TALISMAN
At the Character Select screen, hold Left Bumper + Right Bumper and choose Hsien-Ko.

PLAY AS MORRIGAN AS A BAT
At the Character Select screen, hold Left Bumper + Right Bumper and choose Morrigan.

SURF'S UP

ALL CHAMPIONSHIP LOCATIONS
Select Cheat Codes from the Extras menu and enter FREEVISIT.

ALL LEAF SLIDE STAGES
Select Cheat Codes from the Extras menu and enter GOINGDOWN.

ALL MULTIPLAYER LEVELS
Select Cheat Codes from the Extras menu and enter MULTIPASS.

ALL BOARDS
Select Cheat Codes from the Extras menu and enter MYPRECIOUS.

ASTRAL BOARD
Select Cheat Codes from the Extras menu and enter ASTRAL.

MONSOON BOARD
Select Cheat Codes from the Extras menu and enter MONSOON.

TINE SHOCKWAVE BOARD
Select Cheat Codes from the Extras menu and enter TINYSHOCKWAVE.

ALL CHARACTER CUSTOMIZATIONS
Select Cheat Codes from the Extras menu and enter TOPFASHION.

PLAY AS ARNOLD
Select Cheat Codes from the Extras menu and enter TINYBUTSTRONG.

PLAY AS ELLIOT
Select Cheat Codes from the Extras menu and enter SURPRISEGUEST.

PLAY AS GEEK
Select Cheat Codes from the Extras menu and enter SLOWANDSTEADY.

PLAY AS TANK EVANS
Select Cheat Codes from the Extras menu and enter IMTHEBEST.

PLAY AS TATSUHI KOBAYASHI
Select Cheat Codes from the Extras menu and enter KOBAYASHI.

PLAY AS ZEKE TOPANGA
Select Cheat Codes from the Extras menu and enter THELEGEND.

ALL VIDEOS AND SPEN GALLERY
Select Cheat Codes from the Extras menu and enter WATCHAMOVIE.

ART GALLERY
Select Cheat Codes from the Extras menu and enter NICEPLACE.

THRILLVILLE: OFF THE RAILS

$50,000
While in a park, press ✗, Ⓑ, Ⓨ, ✗, Ⓑ, Ⓨ, Ⓐ.

500 THRILL POINTS
While in a park, press Ⓑ, ✗, Ⓨ, Ⓑ, ✗, Ⓨ, ✗.

ALL PARKS
While in a park, press ✗, Ⓑ, Ⓨ, ✗, Ⓑ, Ⓨ, ✗.

ALL RIDES IN CURRENT PARK
While in a park, press ✗, Ⓑ, Ⓨ, ✗, Ⓑ, Ⓨ, Ⓨ.

MISSION UNLOCK
While in a park, press ✗, Ⓑ, Ⓨ, ✗, Ⓑ, Ⓨ, Ⓑ.

ALL MINI-GAMES IN PARTY PLAY
While in a park, press ✗, Ⓑ, Ⓨ, ✗, Ⓑ, Ⓨ, Right.

TIGER WOODS PGA TOUR 07

BIG HEAD MODE FOR CROWDS
Select Password and enter tengallonhat.

TIGER WOODS PGA TOUR 08

ALL COURSES
Select Password from EA Sports Extras and enter greensfees.

ALL GOLFERS
Select Password from EA Sports Extras and enter allstars.

WAYNE ROONEY
Select Password from EA Sports Extras
and enter playfifa08.

INFINITE MONEY
Select Password from EA Sports Extras and enter cream.

TMNT

CHALLENGE MAP 2

At the Main menu, hold the Left Bumper and press Ⓐ, Ⓐ, Ⓑ, Ⓐ.

DON'S BIG HEAD GOODIE

At the Main menu, hold the Left Bumper and press Ⓑ, Ⓨ, Ⓐ, Ⓧ.

TOMB RAIDER: LEGEND

The following codes must be unlocked in the game before using them.

BULLETPROOF

During a game, hold Left Trigger and press Ⓐ, Right Trigger, Ⓨ, Right Trigger, Ⓧ, Left Bumper.

DRAIN ENEMY HEALTH

During a game, hold Left Trigger and press Ⓧ, Ⓑ, Ⓐ, Left Bumper, Right Trigger, Ⓨ.

INFINITE ASSAULT RIFLE AMMO

During a game, hold Left Bumper and press Ⓐ, Ⓑ, Ⓐ, Left Trigger, Ⓧ, Ⓨ.

INFINITE GRENADE LAUNCHER AMMO

During a game, hold Left Bumper and press Left Trigger, Ⓨ, Right Trigger, Ⓑ, Left Trigger, Ⓧ

INFINITE SHOTGUN AMMO

During a game, hold Left Bumper and press Right Trigger, Ⓑ, Ⓧ, Left Trigger, Ⓧ, Ⓐ.

INFINITE SMG AMMO

During a game, hold Left Bumper and press Ⓑ, Ⓨ, Left Trigger, Right Trigger, Ⓐ, Ⓑ.

EXCALIBUR

During a game, hold Left Bumper and press Ⓨ, Ⓐ, Ⓑ, Right Trigger, Ⓨ, Left Trigger.

SOUL REAVER

During a game, hold Left Bumper and press Ⓐ, Right Trigger, Ⓑ, Right Trigger, Left Trigger, Ⓧ.

ONE-SHOT KILL

During a game, hold Left Trigger and press Ⓨ, Ⓐ, Ⓨ, Ⓧ, Left Bumper, Ⓑ.

TEXTURELESS MODE

During a game, hold Left Trigger and press Left Bumper, Ⓐ, Ⓑ, Ⓐ, Ⓨ, Right Trigger.

TOM CLANCY'S GHOST RECON ADVANCED WARFIGHTER

ALL MISSIONS
At the Mission Select screen, hold Back + Left Trigger + Right Trigger and press ✪, Right Bumper, ✪, Right Bumper, ✪.

FULL HEALTH
Pause the game, hold Back + Left Trigger + Right Trigger and press Left Bumper, Left Bumper, Right Bumper, ✪, Right Bumper, ✪.

INVINCIBLE
Pause the game, hold Back + Left Trigger + Right Trigger and press ✪, ✪, ✪, Right Bumper, ✪, Left Bumper.

TEAM INVINCIBLE
Pause the game, hold Back + Left Trigger + Right Trigger and press ✪, ✪, ✪, Right Bumper, ✪, Left Bumper.

UNLIMITED AMMO
Pause the game, hold Back + Left Trigger + Right Trigger and press Right Bumper, Right Bumper, Left Bumper, ✪, Left Bumper, ✪.

TONY HAWK'S PROJECT 8

SPONSOR ITEMS
As you progress through Career mode and move up the rankings, you gain sponsors and each comes with its own Create-a-skater item.

RANK REQUIRED	CAS ITEM UNLOCKED
Rank 040	Adio Kenny V2 Shoes
Rank 050	Quiksilver_Hoody_3
Rank 060	Birdhouse Tony Hawk Deck
Rank 080	Vans No Skool Gothic Shoes
Rank 100	Volcom Scallero Jacket
Rank 110	eS Square One Shoes
Rank 120	Almost Watch What You Say Deck
Rank 140	DVS Adage Shoe
Rank 150	Element Illuminate Deck
Rank 160	Etnies Sheckler White Lavender Shoes
Complete Skateshop Goal	Stereo Soundwave Deck

SKATERS
All of the skaters, except for Tony Hawk, must be unlocked by completing challenges in the Career Mode. They are useable in Free Skate and 2 Player modes.

SKATER	HOW THEY ARE UNLOCKED
Tony Hawk	Always Unlocked
Lyn-z Adams Hawkins	Complete Pro Challenge
Bob Burquist	Complete Pro Challenge

SKATER	HOW THEY ARE UNLOCKED
Dustin Dollin	Complete Pro Challenge
Nyjah Huston	Complete Pro Challenge
Bam Margera	Complete Pro Challenge
Rodney Mullen	Complete Pro Challenge
Paul Rodriguez	Complete Pro Challenge
Ryan Sheckler	Complete Pro Challenge
Daewon Song	Complete Pro Challenge
Mike Vallely	Complete Pro Challenge
Stevie Willams	Complete Pro Challenge
Travis Barker	Complete Pro Challenge
Kevin Staab	Complete Pro Challenge
Zombie	Complete Pro Challenge
Christaian Hosoi	Rank #1
Jason Lee	Complete Final Tony Hawk Goal
Photographer	Unlock Shops
Security Guard	Unlock School
Bum	Unlock Car Factory
Beaver Mascot	Unlock High School
Real Estate Agent	Unlock Downtown
Filmer	Unlock High School
Skate Jam Kid	Rank #4
Dad	Rank #1
Colonel	All Gaps
Nerd	Complete School Spirit Goal

CHEAT CODES

Select Cheat Codes from the Options and enter the following codes. In game you can access some codes from the Options menu.

CHEAT CODE	RESULTS
plus44	Unlocks Travis Barker
hohohosoi	Unlocks Christian Hosoi
notmono	Unlocks Jason Lee
mixitup	Unlocks Kevin Staab
strangefellows	Unlocks Dad & Skater Jam Kid
themedia	Unlocks Photog Girl & Filmer
militarymen	Unlocks Colonel & Security Guard
jammypack	Unlocks Always Special
balancegalore	Unlocks Perfect Rail
frontandback	Unlocks Perect Manual
shellshock	Unlocks Unlimited Focus
shescaresme	Unlocks Big Realtor
birdhouse	Unlocks Inkblot deck
allthebest	Full Stats
needaride	All Decks unlocked and free, except for inkblot deck and gamestop deck
yougotitall	All specials unlocked and in player's special list and set as owned in skate shop
wearelosers	Unlocks Nerd and a Bum
manineedadate	Unlocks Beaver Mascot
suckstobedead	Unlocks Officer Dick
HATEDANDPROUD	Unlocks the Vans unlockable item

TONY HAWK'S PROVING GROUND

Select Cheat Codes from the Options and enter the following cheats. Some codes need to be enabled by selecting Cheats from the Options during a game.

UNLOCK	CHEAT
Unlocks Boneman	CRAZYBONEMAN
Unlocks Bosco	MOREMILK
Unlocks Cam	NOTACAMERA
Unlocks Cooper	THECOOP
Unlocks Eddie X	SKETCHY
Unlocks El Patinador	PILEDRIVER
Unlocks Eric	FLYAWAY
Unlocks Mad Dog	RABBIES
Unlocks MCA	INTERGALACTIC
Unlocks Mel	NOTADUDE
Unlocks Rube	LOOKSSMELLY
Unlocks Spence	DAPPER
Unlocks Shayne	MOVERS
Unlocks TV Producer	SHAKER
Unlock FDR	THEPREZPARK
Unlock Lansdowne	THELOCALPARK
Unlock Air & Space Museum	THEINDOORPARK
Unlocks all Fun Items	OVERTHETOP
Unlocks all CAS items	GIVEMESTUFF
Unlocks all Decks	LETSGOSKATE
Unlock all Game Movies	WATCHTHIS
Unlock all Lounge Bling Items	SWEETSTUFF
Unlock all Lounge Themes	LAIDBACKLOUNGE
Unlock all Rigger Pieces	IMGONNABUILD
Unlock all Video Editor Effects	TRIPPY
Unlock all Video Editor Overlays	PUTEMONTOP
All specials unlocked and in player's special list	LOTSOFTRICKS
Full Stats	BEEFEDUP
Give player +50 skill points	NEEDSHELP

The following cheats lock you out of the Leaderboards:

UNLOCK	CHEAT
Unlocks Perfect Manual	STILLAINTFALLIN
Unlocks Perfect Rail	AINTFALLIN
Unlock Super Check	BOOYAH
Unlocks Unlimited Focus	MYOPIC
Unlock Unlimited Slash Grind	SUPERSLASHIN
Unlocks 100% branch completion in NTT	FOREVERNAILED
No Bails	ANDAINTFALLIN

You can not use the Video Editor with the following cheats:

UNLOCK	CHEAT
Invisible Man	THEMISSING
Mini Skater	TINYTATER
No Board	MAGICMAN

TRANSFORMERS: THE GAME

The following cheats disable saving and achievements:

INFINITE HEALTH
At the Main menu, press Left, Left, Up, Left, Right, Down, Right.

INFINITE AMMO
At the Main menu, press Up, Down, Left, Right, Up, Up, Down.

NO MILITARY OR POLICE
At the Main menu, press Right, Left, Right, Left, Right, Left, Right.

ALL MISSIONS
At the Main menu, press Down, Up, Left, Right, Right, Right, Up, Down.

BONUS CYBERTRON MISSIONS
At the Main menu, press Right, Up, Up, Down, Right, Left, Left.

GENERATION 1 SKIN: JAZZ
At the Main menu, press Left, Up, Down, Down, Left, Up, Right.

GENERATION 1 SKIN: MEGATRON
At the Main menu, press Down, Left, Left, Down, Right, Right, Up.

GENERATION 1 SKIN: OPTIMUS PRIME
At the Main menu, press Down, Right, Left, Up, Down, Down, Left.

GENERATION 1 SKIN: ROBOVISION OPTIMUS PRIME
At the Main menu, press Down, Down, Up, Up, Right, Right, Right.

GENERATION 1 SKIN: STARSCREAM
At the Main menu, press Right, Down, Left, Left, Down, Up, Up.

VIRTUA TENNIS 3

KING & DUKE
At the Main menu, press Up, Up, Down, Down, Left, Right, Left, **LB**, **RB**.

ALL GEAR
At the Main menu, press Left, Right, Ⓑ, Left, Right, Ⓑ, Up, Down.

ALL COURTS
At the Main menu, press Up, Up, Down, Down, Left, Right, Left, Right.

WIN ONE MATCH TO WIN TOURNAMENT
At the Main menu, press Ⓑ, Left, Ⓑ, Right, Ⓑ, Up, Ⓑ, Down.

VIVA PINATA

NEW ITEMS IN PET STORE
Select New Garden and enter chewnicorn as the name.

NEW ITEMS IN PET STORE
Select New Garden and enter bullseye as the name.

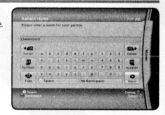

NEW ITEMS IN PET STORE
Select New Garden and enter goobaa as the name.

NEW ITEMS IN PET STORE
Select New Garden and enter kittyfloss as the name.

ONLINE GAMING FOR KIDS: A PARENT'S GUIDE

There are plenty of great games for kids on the web, but which ones are best for your child, and how can you ensure they don't visit a site that's inappropriate? Well, we've compiled a list of the most impressive and trusted gaming spots for kids, then categorized them by age. Visit these sites and determine which ones your family likes most. Once you've determined your favorites, you can then make accessing them safe and easy for your child in just three easy steps:

Safe Online Gaming for Kids is as Easy as 1-2-3

Here's how you can create an **Internet Games Page**—a clickable document that allows your child to safely and easily visit your family's favorite online gaming sites for kids:

1.   Open a new document in Word.

2.   Type in the urls (web site addresses) listed in this section that best suit your child's age and interests. After each url, press ENTER to automatically create a Hyperlink. The address will then appear in blue, underlined text. That means you can now immediately go directly to that web site. Just simultaneously press CTRL and click on the blue text. See our note below for an even slicker way of doing this.

3.   When your list of Hyperlinks is complete, save the file as "[Your Child's Name]'s Games" on your computer's desktop.

User Friendly Links

If you think your child might find it difficult to visit his or her favorite gaming sites by selecting from a list of long and sometimes unwieldy internet addresses, then customize the lists on your Internet Games Page by renaming them with something more easily recognizable. It's easy... simply type the name you wish to use (LEGO, for example) and highlight the word with your mouse. Next, right-click on the highlighted word and select Hyperlink from the window that pops up. Another window appears with your cursor blinking in the empty Address field. Type in the proper url here (in the case of LEGO, you would type "http://play.lego.com/en-US/games/default.aspx" into this field), then click OK. The word you highlighted on your Internet Games Page is now a Hyperlink. Using our example, that means your child can simply click on (left-click + CTRL) the word "LEGO" to visit the LEGO games site!

You can even dress up this document with colorful backgrounds and clip art to make it even more personal and appealing. You now have a resource that provides a quick and easy path for your child to access safe and entertaining gaming sites that you have seen and trust.

BEST ONLINE GAMING SITES FOR KIDS

Ages 6-7

Children in this age group may not be as computer savvy and certainly won't have as strong reading skills as older kids, so you may need to get your child started until he or she is comfortable navigating these sites and properly understands the rules to the games.

Slime Slinger Online Game
http://www.scholastic.com/goosebumps/slimeslinger/game.asp
A fun game based on the popular Goosebumps series of books.

Highlights Kids Hidden Pictures
http://www.highlightskids.com/GamesandGiggles/HiddenPics/
HIddenPixFlashObjects/h8hpiArchive.asp
More than just games, these puzzle-oriented offerings really work kids' brains.

CBeebies at BBC
http://www.bbc.co.uk/cbeebies/fun/
Lots of cute games for younger kids.

Yahooligans Games
http://kids.yahoo.com/games
Loads of fun for all ages here with a wide variety of games—puzzles, arcade, sports, and more!

Pauly's Playhouse Online Games
http://www.paulysplayhouse.com/paulys_playhouse/game_page/game.html
Wow! This site has loads of games! All pretty simple and most will have your child smiling from ear to ear.

Nick.com Games Online
http://www.nick.com/games/
Lots of good stuff here, all associated with Nick programming your child likely already enjoys.

Lego Club Games
http://play.lego.com/en-US/games/default.aspx
Great interactive fun that provides exciting scenarios that simulate playing with LEGO toys.

Barbie.com Games Online
http://barbie.everythinggirl.com/activities/fun_games/
Let's face it, most girls like Barbie as much as just about anything. The games your daughter plays on this site will not disappoint her.

EDUCATIONAL FUN!

Chicken Stacker

http://pbskids.org/lions/games/stacker.html

You can never go wrong with PBS when it comes to kids, and Between the Lions is one of many great programs. This game based on the show helps kids build their word power.

Play Kids Games.com

http://www.playkidsgames.com/

Everything from simple math to word and memory games. Plenty here for the next age group, too.

Ages 8-9

Scholastic Games

http://www.scholastic.com/kids/games.htm

Solve mysteries, answer trivia, collect rare items, and more! The fun here is all based on popular books with this age group.

Monkeybar TV

http://www.hasbro.com/monkeybartv/default.cfm?page=Entertainment/
OnlineGames/GameHome

This site is operated by Hasbro, so the characters and toys associated with the games are all classics known and loved by kids and adults—including Transformers, Littlest Pet Shop, Monopoly, GI Joe, Star Wars, and others!

Cartoon Network Games Online

http://www.cartoonnetwork.com/games/index.html

Kids can't read and be active all the time, and cartoons nicely fill that need to laugh and take it easy. This is the place for hilarious games from hilarious toons.

I Spy Games Online

http://www.scholastic.com/ispy/play/

Another Scholastic gem that allows kids to use their powers of observation online!

Disney Channel Games Online

http://tv.disney.go.com/disneychannel/games/index.html

Have you ever met a fourth grader who isn't into Disney? Hannah Montana, Kim Possible, Zack & Cody... what's not to like? This site has plenty of familiar faces and fun stuff.

Kidnetics Active Online Games

http://www.kidnetic.com/

Fitness focused games and projects for kids.